Elite Sport and Sport-for-Al

Sport is often perceived as being divided into two separate domains: mass participation and elite. In many countries, policy and funding in these two fields are managed by separate agencies, and investment is often seen as a choice between the two. *Elite Sport and Sport-for-All* explores the points of connection and sources of tension between elite and mass-participation sport. The book's multi-disciplinary and international line-up of contributors seeks to define, examine and develop solutions to this problematic relationship.

Drawing on research and case studies from around the world – with examples from Denmark, Canada, South Africa and Israel – the book examines key contemporary issues including:

- does effective talent identification require depth of participation?
- do elite performances inspire greater participation?
- the role of the Paralympic movement in mass participation and elite sport
- and the economic aspects of their co-existence.

The first study of its kind, *Elite Sport and Sport-for-All* addresses a central dichotomy in sport policy and, as such, is important reading for all students, researchers, policy-makers or administrators working in sport development and policy.

Richard Bailey is Senior Researcher at the International Council of Sport Science and Physical Education, and is a well-known writer, researcher and public speaker on the intersection of physical activity, sport and human development.

The late Professor Margaret Talbot OBE was President of the International Council of Sport Science and Physical Education, and a leading authority on physical education and sport.

Perspectives

The Multidisciplinary Series of Physical Education and Sport Science

By publishing Perspectives, ICSSPE aims to facilitate the application of sport science results to practical areas of sport by integrating the various sport science branches. In each volume of Perspectives, expert contributions from different disciplines address a specific physical education or sport science theme, which has been identified by a group of leading international experts.

ICSSPE Editorial Board Members

Also available in this series:
Published by ICSSPE - www.icsspe.org

School Sport and Competition
Edited by Steve Bailey

Physical Activity and Ageing
Edited by Steve Bailey

The Business of Sport
Edited by Dalene Kluka and Guido Schilling

Sport and Information Technology
Edited by Gretchen Ghent, Darlene Kluka

Health Enhancing Physical Activity
Edited by Pekka Oja and Jan Borms

Aspects of Sport Governance
Edited by Darlene Kluka, William Stier Jr. and Guido Schilling

Sport for Persons with a Disability
Edited by Colin Higgs and Yves Vanlandewijck

Talent Identification and Development
The Search for Sporting Excellence
Edited by Richard Fisher and Richard Bailey

Published by Routledge - www.routledge.com/sport

Children, Obesity and Exercise
Edited by Andrew Hills, Neil King and Nuala Byrne

Lifelong Engagement in Sport and Physical Activity
Participation and Performance Across the Lifespan
Edited by Nicholas Holt and Margaret Talbot

Elite Sport and Sport-for-All
Bridging the Two Cultures?
Edited by Richard Bailey and Margaret Talbot

Elite Sport and Sport-for-All

Bridging the Two Cultures?

Edited by
Richard Bailey and Margaret Talbot

Routledge
Taylor & Francis Group

LONDON AND NEW YORK

First published 2015
by Routledge

2 Park Square, Milton Park, Abingdon, Oxon OX14 4RN
711 Third Avenue, New York, NY 10017, USA

*Routledge is an imprint of the Taylor & Francis Group,
an informa business*

First issued in paperback 2017

British Library Cataloguing-in-Publication Data
A catalogue record for this book is available from the British Library

Library of Congress Cataloging in Publication Data
Library of Congress Cataloging-in-Publication Data
Elite sport and sport-for-all : bridging the two cultures? / edited by Richard Bailey and Margaret
Talbot.
pages cm -- (Perspectives: The Multidisciplinary Series of Physical Education and Sport Science)
Includes bibliographical references and index.
ISBN 978-1-138-82190-3 (Hardback) -- ISBN 978-1-315-74305-9 (eBook) 1. Sports--Sociological
aspects. 2. Sports--Cross-cultural studies. 3. Elite (Social sciences)--Cross-cultural studies. 4. Sports
administration. 5. Athletic ability. I. Bailey, Richard, 1966- II. Talbot, Margaret.
GV706.5.E584 2015
306.4'83--dc23
2015002741

ISBN: 978-1-138-82190-3 (hbk)
ISBN: 978-1-138-70754-2 (pbk)

Typeset in Bembo by
Servis Filmsetting Ltd, Stockport, Cheshire

This book is dedicated to those who strive to promote sport, education and equality, building on the vision of Professor Margaret Talbot.

Contents

Notes on editors and contributors

Editors

The late Margaret Talbot was President of the International Council of Sport Science and Physical Education (ICSSPE) and Principal of Margaret Talbot Consulting. Throughout a long a distinguished career, Margaret has been Chief Executive of the Association for Physical Education (United Kingdom), Chief Executive of the Central Council of Physical Recreation, the umbrella organisation for UK non-governmental sport organisations, and Carnegie Research Professor and Head of Sport at Leeds Metropolitan University.

Margaret was a life-long researcher, advocate and activist for equity in sport and physical education and continually fought to defend and promote the statutory entitlement to physical education as the cornerstone of its status and development.

Margaret Talbot was appointed Officer of the Order of the British Empire (OBE) for services to physical education and sport in 1993 and was the 'expert' on the IOC Culture and Olympic Education Commission.

Richard Bailey is a former university professor, and now works as a writer, researcher and public speaker on the intersection of physical activity, sport and human development. He is Senior Researcher for the International Council of Physical Education and Sport Science, the worldwide umbrella organisation for sport, and also a research consultant for organisations such as Nike, UNESCO, the World Health Organisation, the International Olympic Committee, the English Premier League, the Professional Golfers Association and sportscoachUK. Richard was the director of the English Talent Development Strategy for Schools, the first systematic review of Gifted and Talented Education, the IOC review of the benefits of sports for school systems, the UNESCO review of the social and economic outcomes of physical activity, and was lead author of the Human Capital Model of physical activity outcomes. He has written 20 books, and more than 200 academic articles.

Contributors

Koen Breedveld is Professor of Sport Sociology and Sport Policy at Radboud University and Managing Director of the Mulier Institute. Professor Breedveld has been engaged in sports research for over 16 years. His interest is in analysing behaviours and beliefs as regards sports and relating these to broader social and cultural trends and developments.

Christoph Breuer is a Professor for Sport Management at the Department of Sport Economics and Sport Management, German Sport University Cologne. He was awarded a PhD and a Habilitation from the German Sport University Cologne. Since 2014 he is the Pro Vice Chancellor (Resources) of this university. His main research interests are the development of non-profit sports clubs, the effectiveness of sponsorships in sport and determinants of sport participation. He has a track record of generating research grant money from a variety of stakeholders, including public institutions, sport organisations and commercial businesses. He is on the Editorial Board of several journals, including *European Sport Management Quarterly* and *Sport Management Review* and serves as an ad hoc referee for a variety of journals.

Cora Burnett is a Professor at the University of Johannesburg in the Department of Sport and Movement Studies. She holds two doctorates – one in the field of physical education and one in anthropology. She established herself in the sociology of sport as Vice-President of the International Association of the Sociology of Sport and in 2014 co-authored a book with Jay Coakley which is currently a main prescribed text in South African universities. In the past decade she led several national and international studies for SRSA (Sport and Recreation South Africa), the Australian Sport Commission, European Union supported GIZ/YDF (Youth Developoment through Football) programme and CSI (corporate social investment) work across Africa. She is currently engage with research for the Commonwealth Games Federation and IOC.

Stiliani 'Ani' Chroni has a background in sport sciences and sport psychology. She has been in academia for two decades, teaching and conducting research. She has two main research lines: one explores the psychological safety/well-being of sport participants; the second focuses on athletes' and coaches' on-the-field experiences that influence persistence and performance. She is a certified Sport Psychology Consultant both in Greece and the USA. Since 2004 she has worked on gender and equity issues (research and advocacy) with an emphasis on female athletes' sexual harassment. She coordinated the University of Thessaly's 'Gender and Equity Issues' EU-funded programme; developed material on gender equity for the Greek school programme; organised the First International Forum on 'Youth Sport with a Gender Perspective' in Greece; and served as an expert on the 2012 EU programme 'Sexualized Violence in Sport'. Currently, she serves as the

President for WomenSport International, a research-based advocacy organization that holds a special consultative status for the UN.

Dave Collins is Professor of Coaching and Performance at the University of Central Lancashire, UK. To date, he has published over 200 peer review publications and 40 books/chapters. Research interests include performer–coach development, cognitive expertise and the promotion of peak performance. As a performance psychologist, he has worked with over 60 World or Olympic medallists plus professional teams and performers. Dave is a Director of the Rugby Coaches Association, iZone Driver Performance, Fellow of the Society of Martial Arts, ZSL and BASES, Associate Fellow of the British Psychological Society and an ex-Royal Marine.

Peter Donnelly is a Professor of Kinesiology and Physical Education and Director of the Centre for Sport Policy Studies at the University of Toronto. His research focuses on issues of equity and access in sports. He has led and contributed to a number of studies documenting the ways in which the reality of sports fails to live up to its moral claims and the rhetoric of sports leaders; and through collaborative advocacy he has worked to correct the injustices and inadequacies he has documented. He is co-author, with Jay Coakley, of the Canadian edition of *Sport in Society: Issues and Controversies*, and a former editor of the *International Review of Sport Sociology* and the *Sociology of Sport Journal*.

Paul Hover is Senior Researcher at the Mulier Institute and coordinator of the Netherlands Olympic Study Network. He has 13 years of research experience. Drawing on a range of disciplines, including sociology, economics and marketing, the last six years his work has focused on measuring, informing and improving sport events policies. Paul authored reports, book chapters and books about sports events and their role and meaning in society.

Mary A. Hums was the 2009 North American Society for Sport Management (NASSM) Earle F. Zeigler Lecturer, the 2014 NASSM Diversity Award Recipient, an Erasmus Mundus Visiting International Scholar at Katholieke Universiteit of Leuven, Belgium, and represented the United States at the International Olympic Academy in Olympia, Greece. Hums worked the Paralympic Games in Atlanta, Salt Lake City, Athens and Vancouver. Hums co-authored Article 30.5 of the UN Convention on the Rights of Persons with Disabilities and is a Research Fellow at the Institute for Human Centered Design. As the author/editor of five books and 100+ articles and book chapters, her research focuses on sport for people with disabilities and also sport and human rights. She earned her PhD from Ohio State University, an MBA and MA from the University of Iowa, and a BBA from the University of Notre Dame.

Bruce Kidd is a Professor of Kinesiology and Physical Education, University of Toronto, and Vice-President and Principal, University of Toronto

Scarborough. He has written extensively on the history and politics of sport, with a focus on athletes' rights, equity and sport for development and peace, and has frequently served as an advisor to sports bodies and governments in Canada and internationally. He is currently the Chair of the Selection Committee for Canada's Sports Hall of Fame and Past Chair of the Commonwealth Advisory Body on Sport. His most recent book, *Critical Support for Sport* (2014), is a collection of articles and interventions written over 40 years of scholarship and activism.

Trygve Laub Asserhøj holds a Master in Sociology from the University of Copenhagen (2010). Since the beginning of 2011 Trygve Laub Asserhøj has worked as an analyst with the Danish Institute for Sports Studies. His work is focused mainly on quantitative analysis of trends in participation, volunteering and youth dropout and retention in sports. He is the author of a number of books, reports and articles, of which some are available in English, and he has presented his research at international conference meetings and workshops including the European Association for Sport Management and the European Association for Sociology of Sport.

Douglas W. McLaughlin is an Associate Professor in the Department of Kinesiology at California State University Northridge. He is a past Secretary-Treasurer of the International Association for the Philosophy of Sport. He has published in sport philosophy and Olympic studies.

Uri Schaefer is the Director of the Israeli Sport Authority, Acting President of ICSSPE and Past President of ICCE. He graduated from Wingate College for Physical Education and Sport and holds BA and MA degrees from Tel Aviv University, School of Education. He received his PhD from the Hungary University of Physical Education in Budapest. His dissertation received the Sport Science Award of the International Council of Sport Science and Physical Education (ICSSPE), on behalf of the IOC President. In 1997 he initiated and was among the founders of the International Council for Coaching Excellence (ICCE). Dr Schaefer held office as the CEO of the Wingate Institute (1997–2008), Israel's National Sport Center. As of 2008 he has served as Director of the Israeli Sport Authority in the Ministry of Culture and Sport. Dr Schaefer is a member of the ICSSPE President's Committee. He has published many articles and papers in his field of expertise.

Rasmus K. Storm holds a position as Senior Academic Researcher at the Danish Institute for Sports Studies. He has managed several research projects on Danish elite sport, edited and co-edited four books on sport, and has published in a variety of international sport science and sport management journals – such as *European Sport Management Quarterly*, *International Journal of Sport Management and Marketing*, and *Soccer & Society*. He is regularly interviewed in the Danish media; moreover, he gives a large number of public lectures and writes regularly in Danish newspapers.

Cesar R. Torres is a Professor in the Department of Kinesiology, Sport Studies and Physical Education at the College at Brockport, State University of New York. He is a Fellow of the National Academy of Kinesiology and a past President of the International Association for the Philosophy of Sport. Torres is the editor of *The Bloomsbury Companion to the Philosophy of Sport* (Bloomsbury, 2014). He has published extensively in sport philosophy and sport history, both in English and Spanish.

Pamela Wicker is a Senior Lecturer at the Department of Sport Economics and Sport Management, German Sport University Cologne, where she obtained her PhD in 2009. In 2011 and 2012 she was employed at Griffith University, Australia, and is still associated with this university as an Associate Professor (Adjunct). In 2014 she obtained her Habilitation at the German Sport University Cologne. Her main research interests are financing and resource management in non-profit sports clubs, economics of sport consumer behaviour, labour market economics and valuation of intangible effects and public goods in sport. She is the Social Media Editor of *Sport Management Review* and serves on the Editorial Boards of the *International Journal of Sport Finance*, *Sport Management Review*, *Managing Leisure*, and *Journal of Sport & Tourism*.

Eli A. Wolff directs the Inclusive Sports Initiative at the Institute for Human Centered Design and is also the co-director of the Royce Fellowship for Sport and Society at Brown University. Eli is a graduate of Brown University and is currently pursuing his PhD through the German Sport University of Cologne. Eli was a member of the United States Paralympic Soccer Team in the 1996 and 2004 Paralympic Games.

Foreword

The inspiration for this edited book was a conversation between myself and my co-editor, the late Professor Margaret Talbot. We were discussing the famous lecture given by the scientist and writer C.P. Snow entitled *The Two Cultures* (2001 [1959]). Snow argued that intellectual discussions in the West tended to be split into two separate and competing cultures – the sciences and the humanities – and that this was a major hindrance to solving the world's problems.

'It's like that in sport, isn't it?' one of us remarked. 'Except the two cultures of sport are elite sport and mass participation.'

While we might like to envisage 'sport' in terms of a continuum of engagement, in reality it is often the case that politicians, policy makers and analysts, researchers and academics, sports developers, educationists and coaches and the general public assume that sport falls into two relatively distinct domains: sport-for-all, and high-level performance. In fact, in many countries, policy and funding for these areas are dealt with by entirely separate agencies, and it is a common claim that there is an inevitable choice between investment for one or the other. Such decisions reinforce the sense that not only are the two cultures separate, but also that a political and economic gulf limits or even prevents conversation between them.

This division has been reflected in books and articles on sport: some focus on topics like talent development and elite performance; others discuss widening participation in sport and public health benefits of physical activity and sport. Very few talk about their interface.

We found the notion of 'two cultures' so useful a metaphor in capturing the conceptual and practical organisation of sport that it remained our working title for most of the preparation and planning stages of this book. Its aim is to examine the distinctive elements and relationships between the cultures, and to begin an articulation of possible points of connection and sources of tension. It also evaluates the claims made about the separation of the two cultures, such as:

- they serve different aims and audiences;
- they draw on different skills from players;

- within finite resources, investment in one inevitably means less for the other;
- that different types of coaches are needed to support the different athletes.

And it evaluates observations made about connections:

- federations' memberships include both grass-roots participants and international performers, sometimes within the same club;
- effective talent development requires sufficient depth of participation;
- elite performances might inspire greater participation.

As you will see, each chapter addresses the central aim in a different way. Some question the common presumption that, while they are distinctive domains, there still exists a synergistic relationship so that each feeds and supports the other. Other chapters offer cases studies of the potential relationship in different contexts.

Cesar Torres and Douglas McLaughlin begin the book with some philosophical ground-clearing. They argue that, rather than seeing the relationship as necessarily competitive, elite sport should support sport-for-all. Their position is based on a conception of sport as an 'intersubjective moral enterprise' in which the different facets of sport are reciprocal, with both offering avenues to more fulfilling lives. According to Torres and McLaughlin, there is a mutual relationship of dependency between sport-for-all and elite sport, and neither should be subservient to the other.

Next come a series of chapters examining the issue with evidence and experience. Drawing on data from the London 2012 Olympic Games and the 2013 European Youth Olympic Festival in Utrecht, the Netherlands, Koen Breedveld and Paul Hover offer a critical examination of the claims often made by politicians about the significance of elite sport events for national pride, cohesion, urban regeneration, sports participation or the economy. They show that little is known on how, if at all, society benefits from these sport events, but go on to suggest some expectations and strategies necessary if there are going to be benefits for the wider community.

Christoph Breuer and Pamela Wicker bring economic expertise to the issue of the relationship between elite performance and mass participation sports. They explore the 'trickle-down effect', where top-level events are claimed to inspire people to participate in sport themselves. They offer new analysis that evaluates the economic benefits that might accrue from such benefits, in terms of health improvements and creation of social capital. The chapter goes on to discuss the organizational dimension of clubs providing sporting opportunities for all and, on occasion, for the talented few.

The 'trickle-down effect' is also the focus of Rasmus Storm and Trygve Laub's chapter, although their concern is more narrowly focused on its effects within the context of Danish sport. Storm and Laub offer a valuable review of the literature on this topic that clearly demonstrates that the topic is far more complex and value-laden than politicians and policy makers would often have us believe. They then bring the debate fully up-to-date by introducing new empirical data that directly tests the trickle-down effect in the real world.

Attention then shifts to North America, as Peter Donnelly and Bruce Kidd offer a critical analysis of the effects of the increasing separation of elite sport from mass participation in Canadian sports policy. This chapter traces the history of this widening divide from the 1976 Olympics in Montreal, subsequent advances in sport science, especially the improvements in talent identification that enable coaches to select promising athletes at ever younger ages, and neo-liberal cutbacks to public recreation and school sports. Donnelley and Kidd argue that public policy should give equal weight to the goals of 'excellence' and 'sport-for-all', and that a new effort needs to be made to re-democratise Canadian sport.

While most of the previous chapters questioned the logic and evidence of top-down benefits, Dave Collins' and my chapter does the opposite. We suggest that, despite evident differences between approaches to talent development, many share a set of common characteristics and presumptions, which we label the Standard Model of Talent Development. Our analysis questions the value of the almost universally accept 'pyramid' approach to talent development.

The next set of chapters offers insights into the relationship between elite sport and sport-for-all within specific contexts. Cora Burnett, for example, reports from South Africa. After setting the scene by describing how the political changes in her country have tracked in the world of sport, Burnett discusses the practical difficulties of bridging competing demands of high-profile sporting success and opportunities for the wider population. Her chapter discusses strategies to redress differences of resource-allocation, legislation, policies and programmes, and the difficulties of addressing the polarised and fragmented delivery of 'sport-for-all' programmes at school and community levels.

Mary Hums and Eli Wolff offer an important perspective on inclusion and disability. Their chapter examines the dimensions of elite, recreational and inclusive sport for development, particularly as they relate to the Paralympic Movement. It presents an overview of the participation and competition opportunities enjoyed by people with disabilities in sport, and the authors address the vital question of how to find a place where sport-for-all truly means *all*, including people with disabilities.

Much of the literature on the relationship between elite sport and mass participation is focused on relatively large countries, and it is useful to remember that this does not reflect the realities of international sport. Uri Schaefer contributes to the conversation by sharing information about the situation in a small country, Israel. He outlines the historical background to Israel's current sports system and follows the Israeli Sports Authority's process of establishing a strategy, executing it and working towards long-term results. Equality, legislation, ethics and regulation are among the list of issues which needed to be addressed in order to promote both competitive and non-competitive sport.

An issue that is normally overlooked in discussions of progression towards elite sport is that of sexual exploitation in women's sport. Stiliani 'Ani' Chroni offers an honest, sometimes shocking account of this vitally important topic, delving into the intricate choice and consequences faced by the female athlete upon experiencing sexual exploitation. She deconstructs the complex dynamics that characterise the coach–athlete relationship, and gives case studies of when this relationship has become exploitative. The need for alternatives among the infrastructures of grass-root and elite sport are highlighted as crucial for the retention and well-being of the female athlete.

Finally, Dave Collins and I return with a call for decision makers and stakeholders to ease the tension that has been traced throughout many of the chapters in this book. Our argument is based on the need for all involved to reconceptualise the goals of sport so that they need not be mutually exclusive, and under certain circumstances, all can be supported by the same initiative. We offer a perspective – the Three Worlds model – in which the different contexts of sports participation are inherently connected and mutually achievable through single, if carefully designed, comprehensive interventions. We go on to discuss some of the conditions necessary for the realisation of unification of these worlds, and an example of a possible practical approach is presented.

As has already been noted, this volume began as a collaborative enterprise with Margaret Talbot. Sadly, she was unable to see it to fruition as she passed away on Tuesday 2 December 2014, following a long illness.

It is appropriate to quote at length an extract from ICSSPE's announcement following Margaret's death, since it summarises some of her remarkable contributions to sport and education, and will give some notion of the sense of loss felt by so many people around the world:

> Margaret Talbot was a life-long advocate and activist for equity in sport and physical education, and fought continually to defend the statutory entitlement to quality physical education around the world. She was the author of numerous books, research reports and international policy documents, all of which expressed her strong sympathy for communities in need, for women, persons with disabilities and children.
>
> Margaret Talbot was elected as succeeding President of ICSSPE following Gudrun Doll-Tepper, and has led the Council from 2009 until now. Prior to this, she was Vice President for Education from 1999 until 2008. Gudrun Doll-Tepper commented:
>
> 'I was so grateful to Margaret for all the energy, ideas and commitment she put into the work of ICSSPE, and for making so many of our visions become reality. During the years of my presidency Margaret was a driving force to help changing the "Face of ICSSPE". I was so glad that she took over this extremely responsible and challenging position and was convinced she would lead the organisation with a clear strategy and with her

heart, and so it happened. She was a leader, a researcher, a teacher – and a good friend.'

Margaret Talbot had also been President of the International Association of Physical Education and Sport for Girls and Women from 1997 to 2005. In addition to her voluntary positions, she had been Chief Executive of the Central Council of Physical Recreation, and the Association for Physical Education, both based in the United Kingdom. She was also Chair of the Education Committee of the International Paralympic Committee.

Earlier in her outstanding career, Margaret Talbot had been Carnegie Research Professor at Leeds Metropolitan University, United Kingdom, where she was also the Head of Sport. Before that, she had worked at Trinity and All Saints College in Leeds. For her extraordinary services to physical education and sport, Margaret Talbot was appointed an Officer of the Order of the British Empire (OBE) in 1993.

Speaking on behalf of ICSSPE's President's Committee and Executive Board, Acting President Uri Schaefer said:

> Margaret will be deeply missed, among others for her visionary leadership and for her determination. She never stopped advocating for an ethically healthy sport and for providing opportunities for all members of society to be physically active and for children to grow and to learn in a healthy way by enjoying participation in physical education.

Reference

Snow, C.P. (2001) [1959]. *The Two Cultures*. Cambridge: Cambridge University Press.

1 More fulfilling lives through sport

An intersubjective justification for balancing elite sport and sport-for-all

Cesar R. Torres and Douglas W. McLaughlin

More than ten years ago, the Ninth World Sport-for-All Congress debated the relationship between sport-for-all and elite sport. The theme of the congress was telling: 'Sport-for-all and elite sport: rivals or partners?'. Although the congress concluded that 'The critical evidence suggested that sport-for-all and elite sport constitute two distinct domains with discrete aims and working procedures', the congress' call for action recommended that all stakeholders 'consider sport-for-all and elite sport as a single entity, since both can benefit from each other' and that they 'use elite sport as an encouragement for sport-for-all as sport-for-all is a basis for elite'. Even more, the congress also recommended 'sport-for-all to be supported by elite sport, as elite sport relies on the support of sport-for-all' (Ninth World Sport-for-all Congress, 2002, pp. 1–2).

At first glance, these recommendations appear reasonable. However, despite the congress' call to consider sport-for-all and elite sport as equal and as having the potential to mutually reinforce each other, sport-for-all seems to have been given a subservient role. For instance, sport-for-all merits support from elite sport because the former serves as a basis for the latter. Likewise, sport-for-all deserves the support of elite sport because the latter depends on the support of the former. The subservient role typically, albeit not necessarily intentionally, assigned to sport-for-all in its relationship to elite sport is not new. Pierre de Coubertin, the founder of the International Olympic Committee (IOC) in the late nineteenth century, believed in the primacy of elite sport over sport-for-all. He famously wrote that 'For one hundred to go in for physical education, fifty have to go in for sport. For fifty to go in for sport, twenty will have to specialize. For twenty to specialize, five will have to show themselves capable of astounding feats.' Coubertin was convinced that this was a 'basic truth', from which 'It is impossible to get away' (Coubertin, 1997, p. 236).

In Coubertin's vision, elite sport would radiate into sport-for-all and drive mass athletic participation. However, as much as he was concerned with sport-for-all, Coubertin believed that international and national Olympic authorities as well as international sport federations (ISFs) should concentrate on elite sport and the few athletes 'capable of astounding feats'. Sport-for-all was the purview of public authorities. Coubertin wrote that 'all sports ... placed as free of cost as possible at the disposal of *all* citizens – will be one of the duties of the modern municipal system' (Coubertin, 2000b, p. 556). In this view, international and national Olympic authorities as well as ISFs are responsible neither for the organisation nor the funding of sport-for-all. Although the *Olympic Charter* now stipulates that one of the roles of the National Olympic Committees is 'to encourage the development of high performance sport as well as sport-for-all' and that one of the roles of the ISFs is 'to ensure the development of their sports throughout the world', the organisational and funding structure advocated by Coubertin still predominates (International Olympic Committee, 2013, pp. 57, 54). Such structure at best distances and at worst disconnects sport-for-all from elite sport. The consequence is that elite sport does not invest much in the development of sport-for-all.

The goal of this chapter is to argue that elite sport should actively and earnestly support sport-for-all. Our argument will be based neither on utilitarian grounds (i.e. that sport-for-all might lead to better talent identification and selection or that it might serve to nurture the talent identified and selected) nor on strategic or prudential grounds (i.e. that sport-for-all should be supported because elite sport relies on it). Rather, ours will be a principled argument based on understanding sport as an intersubjective moral enterprise. We will first outline the tenets of an intersubjective moral approach to sport. This will in turn allow us to argue that their reciprocal relationship demands elite sport to provide substantive support sport-for-all. It should be noted that elite sport does not refer to an abstract concept, but rather to organised groups of individuals that have invested heavily and almost exclusively in the development of competitive opportunities for those at the highest level of performance. Our argument will indicate that it better suits all sportspeople to have a more balanced approach that focuses on sport-for-all as well as elite sport. We will conclude by showing that both elite sport and sport-for-all present avenues to live more fulfilling lives. Our analysis will also allow us to provide a better rationale to 'consider sport-for-all and elite sport as a single entity' and argue why neither variety of sport should be subservient to the other.

An intersubjective moral approach to sport

Sport is a complex social practice that provides a variety of opportunities for participation. While these opportunities differ in quality and character, they share distinctive features. The sustenance of these features requires institutions in order to provide governance and structure for those participating in sporting practices. While analyses of sport often start at the institutional level, it is necessary and beneficial to account for the nature of persons in order to better understand the institutions that facilitate participation in sport. Two fundamental attributes of persons are that they are both social and moral beings. The recognition of these attributes serves as the ground of an intersubjective moral approach to sport that allows us to elucidate the social nature of sporting practices and makes evident the moral obligations of sporting institutions.

Intersubjectivity accounts for how our experience is constituted in a network of social relations. As described by Russon, humans 'are fundamentally involved in an intersubjective project of mutual recognition or confirmation' (Russon, 2003, p. 51). Our subjectivity, our very sense of self, is forged in and through our relations with others. This means that our experiences are never fully our own because their very possibility and intelligibility depend upon our social interactions that are responsible for the 'formation of our identities' and reveal how 'the real substance of our lives is to be found in our dealings with other people' (Russon, 2003, p. 51). The interhuman sphere of communication serves as the basis of our development as humans and the ground from which we forge our sense of values and meaning. That is, it is in our intersubjective negotiation with others that we develop a self as well as a vision of how selves should treat each other.

Our embodiment is an important feature of our intersubjective experience and social relations. As embodied beings, 'all forms of experience are thus forms of bodily engagement with the world' (Russon, 2003, p. 51). This is important when reflecting on sport. Consider the mission of athletic footwear and apparel company Nike. It includes the phrase 'If you have a body, you are an athlete' (Nike, 2014). While holists can object to the language of the slogan because people do not *have* bodies but rather *are* their bodies and cynics along with sceptics can cringe at its crass commercialism, the slogan undoubtedly speaks to the primacy of embodiment. Not only is having a body a condition for being an athlete, but also the basis for engaging the sports world.

But our lived embodied selves reveal another striking feature of our intersubjective experience. Human experience is developmental in nature. Our sense of self is informed by the skills we possess and is never static. As we develop new skills, our sense of self and our bodily capabilities develop. Developing new competencies allows us to meet more difficult challenges and correspondingly change the characteristic of our intersubjective experiences. This provides an important corrective to Nike's slogan. If you have a body, you are *capable* of being an athlete. Obviously, developing these capabilities takes part in a social network of shared experiences and commitments. In this sense, our intersubjective world determines and grounds our sense of meaning and value. McIntyre (2012, pp. 84, 85) emphasises that '*Shared interests imply shared values*' and '*Shared values imply shared feelings or sentiments*'. But just as our shared interests, values and sentiments are the conditions 'for the credibility requisite to belonging to a community', our shared intercorporeal and developmental social experiences are the conditions for our interest, values and sentiments (McIntyre, 2012, p. 84). McIntyre (2012, p. 61) also highlights that communities function 'as a "we" that – together – has a common experience and understanding of how things are or ought to be'. It is through 'an association of persons who together, communally, constitute a domain of common interests and concerns' that we are able to live fulfilling lives (McIntyre, 2012, p. 73). This is most relevant in the sports world.

Sport philosophers have implicitly embedded the intersubjective nature of sport in their analysis of this social practice. For instance, Kretchmar (1975) refers to the communities of shared interests and concerns that emerge around sport practices as 'testing families'. Similarly, Simon (2010, p. 27) presents a moral account of sport as 'a mutually acceptable quest for excellence through challenge'. The characteristics of sport remarked by Simon and Kretchmar indicate that an intersubjective approach to this social practice provides insights into moral considerations both in sport participation and sport governance.

For example, several international organisations consider that the practice of sport is a human right. The *Olympic Charter* places sport at the centre of the Olympic project and indeed enumerates in one of its fundamental principles of Olympism that 'The practice of sport is a human right' (International Olympic Committee, 2013, p. 11). In the same vein, the United Nations also recognises sport as a fundamental right. It intends that 'The right of access to and participation in sport and play has long been recognised in a number of international conventions. In 1978, UNESCO described sport and physical education as a "fundamental right for all".' However, the United Nations laments that 'until today, the right to play and sport has too often been ignored or disrespected' (United Nations, n.d.). An intersubjective account of sport provides a solid justification for declaring sport a human right. It also provides insights into how a moral approach to sport should be implemented. What it means to defend and promote sport as a human right is made manifest while participating in a community of common interest. McIntyre's (2012, pp. 89–90) characterisation of communities includes the following features: 'the members of a community are "persons"', 'they are joined by empathic relations' and 'their activities are coordinated and driven by a communal will to achieve communal aims'. This implicates the role of empathy and responsibility that individual members of a community have toward their community. The integrity of sporting communities depends upon sportspeople to preserve and promote the integrity of their social practice. An intersubjective approach to sport grounds the moral approach to sport because it contextualises the grounds for empathy and responsibility.

Based on our intercorporeal experience, we have the potential to develop a 'way of living together in harmonious understanding' (Sheets-Johnstone, 2008, p. 294). We empathise with each other because we recognise ourselves in the other. Our intersubjectivity forges not only a basis for shared interests and values, but also the ability to identify injustice and unfairness. Knowing what it is like to benefit or suffer from a situation allows us to infer what it is like for others to benefit or suffer in the same or similar situations. This empathetic awareness comes with responsibility. The mutual recognition of other participants requires that we respond to their needs. It is not possible to merely opt out of our intersubjective experience. Neither is it possible to opt out of the ethical responsibility that intersubjectivity imposes upon us. Others are constitutive features of our own experience just as we are constitutive features of their experience.

Empathy and responsibility provide the basis for being sensitive to and responding to moral quandaries in sport. Yet, they do not guarantee easy resolutions to complex problems. An intersubjective moral approach to sport 'does not mean that our dealings with others are inherently smooth or happy; it means only that we inherently inhabit the interhuman sphere of communication and contact' (Russon, 2003, p. 56). People can interpret matters in different ways. Jim Parry (2006, p. 190) writes that the Olympic philosophy 'emphasizes the role of sport in global culture, international understanding, peaceful coexistence, and social and moral education'. While this takes seriously a commitment to a global community, Parry also points out that the Olympic Movement is composed of many cultures. Nations participating in the Olympic Movement have myriad interpretations on the meaning of sport and the meaning of Olympism. Reconciling these pluralistic and sometimes competing claims is an ambitious and challenging endeavour. Approaching ambitious and challenging endeavours with empathy allows for a developmental account of how sport functions in the lives of people. Although there may be no universal agreement, being empathetic to different perspectives and experiences helps to build understanding. As Weiss (2008, p. 13) contends, 'To claim that a context, horizon, or perspective is socially constructed does not mean that all individuals who share that context, horizon or perspective experience these latter in the same way'.

Recognising the interests and values of others allows for a more complete and balanced moral approach to sport. In turn, approaching sport governance with empathy and responsibility to the constituents of the sporting practice promotes rules and regulations that promote sport as a fundamental human right. An intersubjective moral approach to sport allows us to take seriously the social, developmental and moral character of sport. It provides a basis for interpreting and reconciling the perspectives and interests of impacted persons. Ambiguity may exist regarding some issues, but recognising that our moral approach is always in process not only requires continued work and thoughtful attention, but also brings about the possibility of mutual understanding. Taking responsibility to engage concerns and find resolutions that take into account the positions of others are crucial to promoting sport practices that approach our most cherished ideals of what sport can be.

Sport-for-all and elite sport: a reciprocal relationship

It is instructive to start this section by briefly exploring what sport-for-all and elite sport mean and entail. Historically, the distinction seems to have had a social class connotation. As early as the 1910s, Coubertin (2000a, p. 172) argued that after working 30 years for sport 'to make it the habitual pleasure of the lower middle class' and not just a sporadic practice of rich youth, it was 'necessary for this pleasure to enter the lives of the adolescent proletariat'. He summarised his proposal by claiming: 'All forms of sport for everyone' but realised its prematurity, admitting that 'that is no doubt a formula which is going to be criticized as madly utopian' (Coubertin 2000a, p. 173). Utopian or not, for some time sport-for-all continued to be contrasted to sport for the affluent. Progressively, though, the class connotation gave way to a different kind of opposition, one that refers to the aim of athletic participation. 'Today', as DaCosta and Miragaya (2002, p. 15) observe, 'Sport-for-All refers to any kind of sport practiced without the pressures of top sport'. That is, sport-for-all is typically understood as encompassing opportunities, both formal and informal, for all people to practise sport and engage in physical activity that are not focused on achieving the highest level of performance. At the core of sport-for-all resides not only the relatively old idea to expand opportunities for all people to practise sport and engage in physical activity, but also the promotion of health and social benefits. This is seen in the IOC's Sport-for-All Commission's 'dual rationale for the promotion of sport-for-all with an emphasis on sport as an intrinsic human right, and on sport as a vehicle for extrinsic health and social benefits' (Henry, 2011, p. 1).

Elite sport, by contrast, typically refers to competitive opportunities for those at the highest level of performance. It is characterised by what Coakley (2007) critically calls the 'performance ethic', which highlights skill development, dedication, competition, distinction and outcomes. On a less critical note, it could be contended, without ignoring the excesses and vices that affect it, that elite sport is concerned with the achievement of excellence and the virtues that such achievement demands. One way or another, by definition, elite sport is reserved for the small group of athletes that excel or have the potential to excel in sport. Explanations of why governments and the public alike find elite sport appealing, and in plenty of cases around the world invest great sums towards elite sport, are numerous and 'include international prestige and diplomatic recognition, ideological competition and a belief that international sporting success generates domestic political benefits' (Houlihan and Green, 2008, p. 2). It is also commonly argued that elite sport can produce beneficial social outcomes, such as a sense of community, integration and belonging. All of this is difficult to document and catalogue. However, even if the utility repeatedly invoked to support elite sport is materialised, it remains apparent that its focus and aspirations differ from those of sport-for-all.

It is important to remark that in spite of their particular focus and aspirations, sport-for-all and elite sport resemble each other in a fundamental way. To put it bluntly, sport inextricably binds them. Sport-for-all and elite sport are of the same genus. Whatever personal motivations they may have, participants in one and the other partake in alike practices. The structure of sport does not change if sport is practised by the masses or the athletic elite. A commonly accepted theory of sport maintains that such structure is defined by rules that establish a goal and limit the means available to accomplish such a goal in order to create a challenging problem meant primarily to test physical skills (see Suits, 1978; Meier, 1988). Paraphrasing Suits, it can be contended 'that sports are structured by the voluntary attempt to overcome unnecessary obstacles through the implementation of physical skills' (Torres, 2010, p. 30). For example, the centrality and allure of football and basketball resides in their testing of a highly specialised set of skills to control a ball with foot and hand, respectively. While the quality of execution and play would certainly differ in a recreational league than in a professional tournament, football and basketball players in these different settings are engaged in an equivalent quest to overcome the unnecessary obstacles that provide these sports with their unique identity.

Remarking that sport-for-all and elite sport are inextricably bound is quite relevant for an intersubjective moral approach to sport. They both form the interhuman sporting sphere. Rather than existing on separate planes, sport-for-all and elite sport coexist in a complex network of social interactions. Since our experience and identity are made possible and constituted in such complex networks of social relations, our sporting experience and identity are equally made possible and constituted in the interhuman sporting sphere. To put it differently, our sporting experience and identity are influenced, informed and negotiated in the complex network of relations in and between sport-for-all and elite sport. This process includes all different modes of sporting involvement: from playing to spectating, from coaching to refereeing, from organising to collecting, and beyond. We could even discriminate different modes of engagement within each of these modes of sporting involvement. For example, playing includes sandlot games as much as high school or club games. None of this means that sport-for-all and elite sport hold the same significance for all people, but rather that people are affected by and partake in different but interrelated ways in both sport-for-all and elite sport, as well as the different modes of involvement they afford. What this also means is that because our sporting experience and identity are always already intersubjective, our sporting values are forged in and reflect this actuality, which, to reiterate, include the complex network of relations in and between sport-for-all and elite sport.

Evidently, sport, likewise for the masses and for elite performers, is a 'we' affair. Participants in sport share a common interest in uniquely crafted artificial problems around which vibrant communities develop. This shared common interest implies concern for the particular set of skills meant to be tested by a particular sport as well as for its standards of excellence. Even more, testing families, as Kretchmar calls these communities of shared athletic interests, 'are wellsprings of care and social interaction that promote an appreciation of relevant similarities and differences' (McLaughlin and Torres, 2005, p. 42). It is in their similarities as much as in their differences that participants in sport-for-all and elite sport co-witness and bear testimony to an activity 'undertaken and valued fundamentally because of the challenges the rules create' (Simon *et al.*, 2015, p. 27). When sport is understood as a mutual enterprise presupposing a cooperative effort, participants in both sport-for-all and elite sport belong to closely related testing families that owe each other, at least, basic moral considerations of respect and fairness. In short, the mutuality inherent in sport indicates that it is valuable 'for both the intrinsic value of meeting interesting challenges and for what we can learn about ourselves and others through the attempt to meet the competitive tests' (Simon *et al.*, 2015, p. 47). Cooperation out of a common interest in the skills and excellences that define sport impels the formation of caring communities pregnant with possibilities for participants to develop a sense of self through belonging to a 'we' – a collective of developing selves.

As said, belonging to a community involves having common goals and interests as well as values. Yet, having a communal take, for example, on sport neither makes uniform nor trivialises its experience. A communal sporting experience is not an identical sporting experience. For example, a lunch-hour volleyball game, a scheduled junior high school softball season game and an Olympic field hockey game all seem to generate markedly different stories. As part of a long tradition, the lunch-hour volleyball game could be played with much intensity and emotion. Or it could be endured for 60 minutes without such characteristics. Being the last of the season and without much at stake, the players in the high school softball game could be attentive but not particularly taken by it. Or at the end of a dismal season they could give maximal effort to close on a high note. The Olympic field hockey game could be one in which nervousness takes over enthralling athleticism and flair. Or it could be an exhilarating game. Yet, whatever the particularities, idiosyncrasies, emphases, divergences, continuities and discontinuities of these and other possible stories around these games, they all emerge as people 'participate communally as members of a whole that binds them together' (Husserl, 1989; cited in McIntyre, 2012, p. 90). Recognising the togetherness of the sporting 'we', intersubjectivity accounts for, and appreciates, this narrative pluralism.

In turn, the narrative pluralism implicit in sporting communities suggests the necessity to recognise the multiple stories advanced by both sport-for-all and elite sport. It also suggests that the identity of sport is forged in and through the constant negotiation between these two forms of sport. While sport-for-all and elite sport are not reducible to one another, they overlap in multiple and intricate ways. This is forcefully seen in the way in which people move in and between the different modes of sporting involvement mentioned above. Here are a few possibilities. The current professional basketball star began her career in a basketball community programme. A mother's interest in expanding her son's Little League participation led her to become a sport organiser. The former high school rowing enthusiast is now an avid weekend canoeist. Yesterday's runners and golfers remain runners and golfers, participating in these activities as much as spectating them. The former high school champion wrestler enrolled in college to be a physical education teacher and a coach. The football referee is active in the sport's local referees association, and is also a collector of football memorabilia. The aspiring young ice hockey player admires and is enthused by the deeds of seasoned international players on Olympic rinks. The seasoned biker volunteers in a biking camp. These rich and complex overlapping permutations between sport-for-all and elite sport, in which a plurality of narratives unfold, manifest a relationship between the two that is much stronger and deeper than is often recognised. These relationships could be seen as a crucible in which sport, and its practitioners, achieves its, and their, character.

The recognition of the multiple stories advanced by both sport-for-all and elite sport reminds us that our social being is developmental. Indeed, the narrative pluralism implicit in sporting communities 'opens us to an inter-subjective horizon in which who we and our family members are is subject to redefinition' (Russon, 2003, p. 67). Sportspeople, then, need opportunities for sporting exploration, growth and affirmation. To put it differently, they need opportunities to narrate their stories and redefine who they are and what sport means. Both sport-for-all and elite sport offer such opportunities. As implied in the preceding paragraph's examples of the way in which people move in and between the different modes of sporting involvement, there is no set trajectory for the way sportspeople relate to and combine the opportunities for explora-tion, growth and affirmation offered by sport-for-all and elite sport. Skill 'relates to the developing character of intersubjectivity' (McLaughlin and Torres, 2011, p. 279) and is intimately connected with the sporting trajectories we carve for ourselves. Sport-for-all as much as elite sport has the potential to fully engage our bodily capacities. Thus, bringing up again our correction to Nike's slogan, we are all *capable* of being, or perhaps even better to say *becoming*, athletes. It follows that the lack of opportunities to engage in sport, for all and elite, means missing out the chance to access a horizon of profound human possibilities based on and amplifying our intercorporeal condition. In addition to creating such sporting opportunities, we should also be aware of opportunities that insuf-ficiently engage participants or prevent them from savouring the ensuing expe-riences. In this regard, consider, for example, the quality of the opportunities that many females around the world are still being offered to engage in sport. That is when they are indeed being offered any opportunity at all. All this allows us to appreciate better why the practice of sport is considered a human right.

We would like to close this section by stressing the relevance and implications that the moral dimension of intersubjectivity has for the reciprocal connection that exists between sport-for-all and elite sport. Levinas (2000) most famously advanced the moral connotation of intersubjectivity, proposing that the other makes a moral claim on us that we cannot ignore. Moreover, as we have argued elsewhere, 'The other is constitutive of our own subjectivity, which means both that subjectivity is always intersubjective and also always ethically consti-tuted' (McLaughlin and Torres, 2011, p. 275). So, according to Perpich (2008, p. 134), asking whether we have an obligation to value the other,

> mistakes the other for an object within the world, rather than seeing the relationship to the other as the condition of my having a world at all and being able to find value in it. If I value anything at all, then, I am already in a relationship with the other.

There is no opting out of our relationships with and responsibilities to the sportspeople with whom we share the playing fields. Disputing the ball with a rival in a wheelchair rugby game, swimming directly behind another competitor in an open-water event or tackling an opposing player in a football game not only inevitably puts us in touch with opponents, but also compels us to recognise, empathise with and be responsible for them. This mutual dependency, which is doubly constitutive and moral, extends beyond individual sportspeople and reaches into sport-for-all and elite sport. These two forms of sport are mutually dependent and make moral claims on each other. However, as seen in the introduction, despite the subservient role that sport-for-all is typically assigned vis-à-vis elite sport, the latter does not recognise a responsibility regarding the organisation or the funding of the former. This attitude denies the mutual relationship of dependency between sport-for-all and elite sport and the moral responsibility they have to each other. In light of this relationship, as well as its ensuing responsibilities, and since elite sport benefits from the flow of athletes that sport-for-all regularly provides, elite sport should actively and earnestly support sport-for-all. This seems to be all the more urgent because in their quest for athletic success on the world stage many national governments have increasingly funded elite sport without due consideration of sport-for-all. In short, the attention that elite sport attracts too often results in diverting resources away from sport-for-all. It goes without saying that elite sport is more visible and is financially more powerful than sport-for-all.

The active and substantial support elite sport owes sport-for-all can be manifested in myriad forms. These can include direct subsidies from national and international sport federations or professional sports organisations to sport-for-all institutions, massive sport programmes run by national and international sport federations or professional sports organisations, partnerships between elite sport and sport-for-all institutions, etc. There is no single recipe for such elite sport support, which may differ according to specific cultural, economic and social contexts. Nevertheless, what is clear is that regardless of the form it takes, such elite sport support should seek to honestly break the impoverishment and subservient role sport-for-all has had and is typically assigned. Elite sport support towards sport-for-all should not be seen as charity, but rather as the responsibility grown out of the intersubjective recognition that it is formed by sport-for-all and must, in some strong form, answer to it.

Conclusions

Sport in all its various forms can provide avenues for living more fulfilling lives. Suits (1978) persuasively argued that playing games is the central activity of the good life. But why would games in general and sport in particular lead to a more fulfilling life? Although a comprehensive list of reasons would be too much to enumerate here, some key features of the value of sport are instructive. Sport provides an opportunity to aspire and achieve astounding feats. While not everyone will attain an elite level of performance, everyone can develop new skills and abilities that in turn lead to new skills and abilities. Through this development, all participants can discover new horizons of performance. Even beginners and mediocre performers who keep at it can grow into deeper experiences. Tasks that once seemed improbable or impossible can become achievable and even routine. The deepened sense of self that is possible through involvement in sport is one of the prime values of sport itself. It is a strong justification for the claim that sport is a human right. For this reason, meaningful opportunities to participate in sport are something that should be available for everyone.

The excellence that is experienced from accomplishing astounding feats in sport is not merely absolute excellence. Whereas elite sport focuses on and celebrates absolute excellence, sport-for-all focuses on how all participants can experience excellence relative to their own skills and abilities as well as past performances. Not only does this make sport personally meaningful, but it also strengthens the sporting community and the relation among their members. Those who endure and struggle to improve their performance have a greater awareness of and appreciation for the more elite performers.

The recognition that all sport participants can experience more fulfilling lives through sport confirms the call to 'consider sport-for-all and elite sport as a single entity'. This does not mean that the varieties of sporting opportunities are reducible to one another. Rather, sporting communities are similar to diverse ecosystems in which the health of the component parts is intertwined and dependent on the overall well-being of the system. The full realisation of the goods of sport requires a holistic approach that incorporates and integrates elite sport and sport-for-all. Policy, fiduciary and normative claims substantiate calls for elite sport to actively and earnestly support sport-for-all, given their mutual dependency. A policy agenda that focuses exclusively on elite sport not only threatens the most vulnerable participants but also jeopardises the sporting community as a whole. Such practices lead to an inequality in the distribution of the goods among members of the entire system. In turn, this inequality has repercussions all throughout it. This is one of the most important reasons why those involved in elite sport still have a fiduciary responsibility for the entire structure of sport.

Elite sport has historically enjoyed a preferred status. It has higher visibility, more financial resources and more power within the governance of the sport. Nonetheless, to revel in that privilege at the expense of or indifference toward sport-for-all is to neglect the larger community that facilitates elite sport. Such an approach will have long-term negative repercussions for elite sport. Yet, the more fundamental concern goes beyond elite sport itself to the broader sporting community. Elite sport can strategically marshal its resources in order to enhance the values, excellences and goods that are intrinsic to that whole community. Considering this broader community ushers in normative concerns.

An intersubjective moral approach to sport makes evident the 'we-subjectivity' of testing families. The differences between elite sport and sport-for-all are more differences in degree than differences in kind. Whether associating more with elite sport or sport-for-all, participants can recognise their involvement with a larger sporting community that shares an interest in fostering the goods available through participation in it. As outlined above, members of a sporting community are compelled to have empathy and responsibility toward one another. While neither variety of sport should be subservient to the other, elite sport generates more resources that can be used to improve the sporting community as a whole. Efforts to improve the well-being of the entire community are not necessarily at the expense of elite sport. This is not a zero-sum equation in which resources directed toward sport-for-all are diverted from elite sport. When done prudently and responsibly, the improvements in the sporting community can achieve the same effect of a rising tide that lifts all boats. Not only do the members of the sporting community individually benefit, but the whole sporting community is also improved.

It is ultimately misleading to frame questions about sport-for-all and elite sport as if they were distinct entities. An intersubjective moral approach to sport takes seriously the ways in which elite sport and sport-for-all are part of a larger system that has intrinsic goods and values that require careful stewardship. If sport is a human right that allows participants to achieve more fulfilling lives, then it is important to ensure efforts are implemented to enhance the opportunities and experiences of all sport practitioners.

References

Coakley, J. (2007) *Sport in Society. Issues and Controversies*. 9th edn. New York: McGraw Hill.

Coubertin, P. (1997) *Olympic Memoirs*. Lausanne: International Olympic Committee.

Coubertin, P. (2000a) Olympic letter XI: The sporting spirit of students. In N. Müller (ed.) *Pierre de Coubertin 1863–1937. Olympism Selected Writings*. Lausanne: International Olympic Committee. pp. 172–173.

Coubertin, P. (2000b) Speech given at the opening of the Olympic Congresses at the city hall of Prague, May 29, 1925. In N Müller (ed.), *Pierre de Coubertin 1863–1937. Olympism Selected Writings*. Lausanne: International Olympic Committee. pp. 555–559.

DaCosta, L. and Miragaya, A. (2002) *Worldwide Experiences and Trends in Sport-for-All*. Oxford: Meyer and Meyer Sport.

Henry, I. (2011) European policy systems and sport-for-all as a policy objective. Paper written in the framework of the IOC's OSC Postgraduate Grant Selection Committee.

Houlihan, B. and Green, M. (2008) *Comparative Elite Sport Development. Systems, Structures and Public Policies*. Oxford: Elsevier.

International Olympic Committee. (2013) *Olympic Charter*. Lausanne: International Olympic Committee.

Kretchmar, R.S. (1975) From test to contest: An analysis of two kinds of counterpoint in sport. *Journal of the Philosophy of Sport*, 2: 23–30.

Levinas, E. (2000) *Ethics and Infinity*. Pittsburgh, PA: Duquesne University Press.

McIntyre, R. (2012) 'We-Subjectivity'. Husserl on community and communal constitution. In C. Fricke and D. Føllesdal (ed.), *From Intersubjectivity and Objectivity in Adam Smith and Edmund Husserl*. Frankfurt: Ontos Verlag. pp. 61–92.

McLaughlin, D.W. and Torres, C.R. (2011) Sweet tension and its phenomenological description. Sport, intersubjectivity and horizon. *Sport, Ethics and Philosophy*, 5 (3): 270–284.

McLaughlin, D.W. and Torres, C.R. (2005) Fit to be tied! The relevance of ties in teaching physical education. *Journal of Physical Education, Recreation and Dance*, 76 (9): 38–42.

Meier, K. (1988) Triad trickery: playing with sport and games. *Journal of the Philosophy of Sport*, 15: 11–30.

Nike (2014) About Nike, Inc. [online]. Available from: http://nikeinc.com/pages/about-nike-inc (accessed 1 July 2014).

Ninth World Sport-for-All Congress 'Sport-for-all and elite sport: rivals or partners?' (2002) *Declaration*. Arnhem, n.p. pp. 1–2.

Parry, P. (2006) Sport and Olympism. Universals and multiculturalism. *Journal of the Philosophy of Sport*, 33 (2): 188–204.

Perpich, D. (2008) *The Ethics of Emmanuel Levinas*. Stanford, CA: Stanford University Press.

Russon, J.E. (2003) *Human Experience: Philosophy, Neurosis, and the Elements of Everyday Life*. Albany, NY: State University of New York Press.

Sheets-Johnstone, M. (2008) *The Roots of Morality*. University Park, PA: Penn State University Press.

Simon, R.L. (2010) *Fair Play. The Ethics of Sport*. 3rd edn. Boulder, CO: Westview Press.

Simon, R.L., Torres, C.R. and Hager P.F. (2015) *Fair Play. The Ethics of Sport*. 4th edn. Boulder, CO: Westview Press.

Suits, B. (1978) *The Grasshopper: Games, Life and Utopia*. Toronto: University of Toronto Press.

Torres, C.R. (2010) The danger of selectively changing the rules in youth sport. The case of the strike zone. *Journal of Physical Education, Recreation and Dance*, 81 (5): 29–34.

United Nations (n.d.) Why sport? [online]. Available from: www.un.org/wcm/content/ site /sport/home/sport (accessed 1 July 2014).

Weiss, G. (2008) *Refiguring the Ordinary*. Bloomington, IN: Indiana University Press.

2 Elite sports: what is it good for?

The case of EYOF Utrecht 2013

Koen Breedveld and Paul Hover

Introduction

In the late 1970s, the International Olympic Committee (IOC) was facing a serious challenge: after two Olympic Games that were flawed with problems, Mexico 1968 and Munich 1972, it had become increasingly difficult to find new cities that would act as hosts for the Olympics. By that time, the dream of uniting the world through sports had given way to the more sinister picture of rebels and politicians using sports as their podium – and not shying away from rioting and violence to reach their purposes. That bleak picture did not alter much when it became clear that the Montreal Games of 1976 had burdened its citizens with a heavy tax-load, and when the start of the Afghan War elicited a world-wide boycott of the 1980 Moscow Games.

One can imagine, then, how relieved the IOC was when, in the 1970s, Los Angeles introduced itself as the sole candidate for hosting the 1984 Games. In the shortest period in the history of the Olympics and with the smallest budget ever, LA set out to organise the Games of the XXIII Olympiad. Neglecting for a moment the Russian counter boycott, the 1984 Games went down well. The LA Games will be remembered foremost because of the four gold medals of American sprinter and long jumper Carl Lewis – and for the performance of Lionel Richie (at the closing ceremony). Relying on existing sporting facilities, Los Angeles proved that it was possible to organise Games with substantial private investments and without large deficits. After that, it appeared that the Olympic Games were in an upward swing again. Seoul 1988 went along without much turmoil (ignoring for a moment that seven out of the eight male 100-metre sprinters were caught doping). Barcelona 1992 became a showcase on how to use sports for urban regeneration. Atlanta 1996 may have gone down in history as the 'shame games', but it also gave rise to the idea that the Games could add to the goals of business. And Sydney 2000 revamped the idea of using the Games for boosting national moral – delivering 58 medals of which 16 gold went to the home-team (in the medal table, Australia ended fourth after the USA, Russia and China – in 1976 the Aussies won only one silver and four bronze medals).

Such was the renewed view on the Olympics that in the twenty-first century, cities and governments found themselves fighting for a chance to host mega-events. Millions are being spent on bidding proposals, billions on building the necessary facilities – neglecting largely the very real possibility that these in time will turn into 'white elephants'. Nowadays, the decision that one has won the bidding-competition (an opportunity to spend large amounts of tax money) is celebrated as a true victory. However, ministers and mayors still need to legitimise their projects by pointing at the good for society that come out of such projects. Hence, claims are made of the significance of elite sporting events for serious matters such as national pride, cohesion, urban regeneration, sport-participation or better even, the economy. Usually, these claims are backed up by bold statements from gold-medallists, business tycoons and other VIPs, telling of their first-hand experiences with the strengths and importance of elite sports. A report by a consultancy firm will point at the number of foreigners that can be expected to visit the event, and the jobs and expenditures that will accrue from this. Once the event is over, statistics on visitor numbers and expenditures will be combined with pictures of cheering children and applauding adults, to convince democratic institutions that the investment in the event was indeed money well spent.

In fact, however, little is known on how, if at all, investments in grass-roots sports, sports participation or society benefit from elite sporting events (Bottenburg *et al.*, 2012; Richards and De Brito, 2013). The claims that are made are generally not being based on outcomes of independent systematic research (Coalter, 2007).

In this chapter we set out to bring together some of the evidence for the impact of elite sporting events on grass-roots sports (and society at large). For that, we rely on a review of the existing literature, especially of the London 2012 Games, and on our own research of the European Youth Olympic Festival (EYOF), in 2013, in Utrecht. The outline of the chapter is as follows: first, we will provide a brief overview of the existing literature on the effects of elite sport-events, and especially of the literature on the London 2012 Games. Next, we will report on our work on EYOF Utrecht 2013, drawing out the event, the research that was carried out as well as its outcomes. Our focus throughout the chapter will be on non-economic effects of sporting events. We will end this chapter with a brief statement of our main findings.

Elite sporting events: beyond economic effects

So far, the main research on the effects of sporting events has focused on the economic benefits. Juggling investments and expenditures, economists have come up with calculations for the costs and benefits of mega-events. Even though there is debate over the exact numbers, the current viewpoint seems to be that the event itself will 'pay for itself' – meaning that costs for logistics, security and organising committees balance revenues generated by sponsoring and by sales of tickets, media-rights and merchandise. The tricky part is investment in facilities – whether they be sporting stadiums, roads, public transport or housing. Generally, these costs run into the billions. Also, they supersede the scope of the project, both in time and money. The balance sheet of sporting events depends greatly upon the question of whether such investments are called for and if so, whether these need to be attributed to the event. Another tricky issue are 'crowding out effects', the fact that tourists stay away from cities that host events and locals stay away from the area because of the event (Preuss, 2011).

When it comes to other effects of sporting events, the picture becomes less clear. Not a lot of research is done into the question of how sporting events add to national pride, social cohesion or sport participation. Most often, references are made to the many people that visit the event or that follow the event through the media (newspapers, television, internet). However, the scope of the event in terms of visitors or followers via the media does not provide an indication to what extent (if at all) a sports event positively – or negatively – impacts on attitudes and behaviour. Scientists often warn for exaggerated expectations of what the organisation of a single sporting event can lead to (Coalter, 2007; Miah and García, 2012).

Compared to research into economic effects, social effects of sporting events are less frequently the subject of research for two reasons. First, event organisers and their public and private investors are predominantly economically oriented. This means that there is a need for a clear picture of income and costs of the event organisation, and regularly for a calculation of social effects of the event. The second reason, which is related to the first one, is that methods for measuring the social impact of sporting events are less well developed than their economic counterparts. Besides methodological difficulties, debates are raised about whether or not to quantify and monetise (and how) social effects. Once monetised, these effects can be integrated in a social cost–benefit analysis (Baarsma, 2000; Carson *et al.*, 2001; Vekeman *et al.*, 2013). On the other hand, opponents argue that social effects can only be put in qualitative terms. According to these critics, integrating monetised social effects is too much of an artificial calculation (Hausman, 2012).

Sporting events can lead to a sense of pride, community and happiness among residents or among the population of the country that shows sporting excellence (Kavetsos and Szymanski, 2010; Zimbalist, 2010; Heere *et al.*, 2013). For some countries, like Canada, the primary catalyst even was the domestic concern with national identity and the challenge posed by the growing influence of Québec separatism on national politics (Green and Houlihan, 2005). Regarding the research into effects of sporting events on national pride, a distinction between national *sporting* pride and national pride is relevant. For example, the outcomes of a study by Elling *et al.* (2014) demonstrated that internationally appealing Dutch sporting achievements during events do not directly lead to an increase in general feelings of national pride, although sporting achievements do seem to nurture these feelings through eruptions of national sporting pride (and well-being). This study also showed that in order to awaken feelings of national sporting pride it is not necessary to organise the event within the country's borders.

The 'fever of expectations' (Mean *et al.*, 2004) that frequently arises with the organisation of sporting events among policy makers recurrently refers to the manifestation of a demonstration effect. The demonstration effect, also referred to as a trickle-down effect, is a process by which people are inspired by elite sport, sportspeople or sports events to participate themselves (Weed 2009). The empirical evidence for the creation of this effect is limited and at best mixed (Bottenburg *et al.*, 2012; Frawley, 2013). A study by Weed (2009) suggests that the demonstration effect may lead to re-engaging lapsed participants, increased participation of frequency among participants and changing the type of sports practised (activity switching). This implicates that demonstration effects rarely occur among inactive people, possibly caused by an experienced competence gap.

Many of these findings are also applicable to the London 2012 Games. The realisation of social goals was at the heart of the organisation of the Olympic and Paralympic Games in London in 2012. As far as legacy was concerned, the 2012 Games focused on four areas: increasing grass-roots sports participation, exploiting opportunities for economic growth, promoting community engagement and social participation and making sure that the Olympic Park area met the requirements for post-event use (DCMS, 2010). The starting point for the realisation of these objectives was excellent. The organisation of the games ran well and there was plenty of national elite sport success (with British Olympians and Paralympians coming third in the medal ranking). Probably even more important was that there were many large investments in supplemental projects, like Places People Play. This was a £135 million initiative for investments in sports infrastructure, sport volunteers and sport stimulation campaigns. Compared to the total budget for the 2012 Olympics, which was £9,325 billion, of which a large part was meant for the revitalisation of East London (NAO, 2007), this is relatively small.

As with any other sporting mega-event, the measurement of the effects is surrounded by methodological challenges (see DCMS, 2011). Nevertheless, evaluations suggest positive developments in the period after the Games in the British capital. Two-thirds of British people reported in November 2012 that they were surprised about the degree to which the Games united the country (Ipsos MORI, 2012). According to Legacy Trust UK (2013), negative associations with the Games were practically absent among British youth in February 2013. Furthermore, the UK Government and the Mayor of London (2014) report nearly two years after the extinguishing of the Olympic Flame that many social ambitions have been realised. For example, the registration of 34,000 volunteers on the Team London website. Additionally, the Inspire project, launched four years before the Games, aimed to give the British population the chance to be 'part of the London 2012 Games'. The Inspire programme has awarded more than 2,700 extraordinary, non-commercial projects with an Inspire mark as an acknowledgement of their excellence and as a promotional tool to allow them to connect with the Games and reach out to new audiences. One in six people in the UK has been involved in an Inspire project. Thirty-nine per cent of the Inspire-project contact persons claimed their project would not have taken place if London had not been chosen to host the Games. They also declare that 69 per cent of projects have been able to get young people involved in sport for the first time (LOCOG, 2012).

On the other hand, not all expectations and social objectives were met. Probably the most prominent is the struggle to stimulate grass-roots sports participation nationwide. In order to leverage the momentum of the Games to increase grass-roots sports participation, the National Governing Bodies played a key role, which was questioned by academics (Centre for Social Justice, 2011; Hughes, 2013). Furthermore, sports clubs were sceptical about the 'Olympic opportunities'. According to the Sport and Recreation Alliance (2013), prior to the 2012 Olympic and Paralympic Games few clubs (14 per cent) saw the upcoming Games as representing an opportunity for them. Afterwards, 73 per cent of clubs suggested that the government was not doing enough to help community sport create a legacy of sport participation. Where has this led to, in terms of levels of sports participation? According to Sport England's Active People Survey, the level of sports participation (at least once per week) among adults nationwide was 35.5 per cent in 2013/2014, compared to 35.8 per cent in 2007/2008 (and 34.2 per cent in 2005/2006). Therefore, the Games do not seem to have had a positive impact on national sports participation (with the possible exception of the 2005/2006–2007/2008 period). As for London, sports participation seemed to increase a bit in the years before and after the Games (October 2010/2011 35.4 per cent, 2011/2012 36.5 per cent, 2012/2013 37.2 per cent), but after that decreased again (2013/2014 36.7 per cent). This does not seem to be a satisfactory Olympic grass-roots sports participation legacy. Looking at this 'return on investment', Jeremy Hunt, Secretary of State for Culture, Olympics, Media and Sport, admitted that 'There can be no plug and play sporting legacy from the games, ... the challenge is not simply to build sports facilities but to fill them' (DCMS, 2012). Still, the experience of leveraging opportunities of the Olympics to increase grass-roots sports participation has been a learning process for policy makers, sport marketers and other sports professionals, and has led to a growing body of knowledge and experience which is expected to contribute positively to British sports (marketing) in the future.

EYOF Utrecht 2013

The European Youth Olympic Festival was held 14–19 July 2013. It was the 23rd time that such an event (originally an idea from the former IOC president Jacques Rogge) was held. At the EYOF 2,271 13–18-year-old talented players from 49 European countries competed for 690 medals in nine branches of sport (track-and-field, swimming, cycling, gymnastics, judo, tennis, basketball, handball and volleyball). These young athletes were accompanied by 1,100 supervisors. One thousand officials and referees, and 2,150 volunteers, helped organise the matches and the event. The competition took place over seven different venues, four of which were close to each other and to the 'Olympic house' at the east side of the city of Utrecht; the other three were a bit further away (in the west and middle of the city). The opening ceremony (with King Willem of Orange and Jacques Rogge) was held at the football stadium of the local football club, also on the east side of the city. The closing ceremony was in the immediate surroundings of the stadium. In the heart of the city a meeting point was arranged.

Before and during the event, side-events were organised. The goal of the side-event was especially to use the power of the event to generate social revenue (beyond the scope of the event itself). The main side events were the following:

- Sporting days. In two weeks in early June, schools for primary education (ages 8–12) and secondary education (13–14) came to one of the venues for a day of sports and fun. Before hand, they had received information packages on EYOF and on Olympism, to be used in class.
- Urban Tour. This was a moving spectacle of 'street versions' of the nine EOYF sports. The spectacle was installed at 13 different locations, both in Utrecht and in other cities, always for one day, and was open for children to join in.
- Flame relay. From 11 July to 14 July the Olympic Flame was carried through the city and the province of Utrecht. Needless to say, the Flame was carried by some celebrities, but also schools and sports clubs were invited to join in.

The official name of the side events was 'Achmea High Five Challenge' (Achmea H5C – Achmea, the sponsor, is an insurance company). A name different from EYOF was chosen partly to please the main sponsor, and partly because it was believed that this would benefit the project.

The event itself was organised by the city of Utrecht, with outside help from a temporary-work agency. The competitions were organised by the nine sports federations that were involved. The side events were organised jointly by the city of Utrecht and the Achmea organisation, with help from a sports marketing organisation. A steering committee involving the city, the province, Achmea and NOC★NSF was installed so as to safeguard the course of the project. Total investment were estimated to be €10.3 million, of which €4.5 million was covered by the local, regional and national government, €3.0 million from private sponsors, €1.4 million from participants and another €1.4 million from NOC★NSF (the Dutch Olympic committee).

EYOF research

As part of the project, research was carried out to study the effects of EYOF. The research was commissioned to a team of researchers from the Mulier

Institute, Utrecht University and Hogeschool Utrecht (Breedveld *et al.*, 2014). The research consisted of the following:

- Questionnaires administered during and after the event to 927 participants, 12 chefs de mission, 273 volunteers, 100 sport clubs, 1,927 visitors, 410 inhabitants of Utrecht and 3,000 Dutchmen and -women. The methods used varied from face-to-face interviews, computer assisted personal interviewing (CAPI) and paper-and-pencil questionnaires (Mulier Institute).
- Longer, open interviews with 20 representatives of 12 organisations involved in the EYOF organisation (Utrecht University).
- Questionnaires filled out by 999 children that took part in the side events, 100 longer semi-open interviews with children and open interviews with a smaller number of involved teachers and supervisors (Hogeschool Utrecht).
- Document analysis and analysis of data provided by third parties (like media companies).
- Participatory observation during the event.

EYOF: results in general

With 26,000 visitors paying 60,000 visits to the EYOF, and 20,000 children taking part in the side events, the event reached a wide audience. The formal goal of the event, selling 14,000 tickets, was realised. EYOF generated 1,672 articles in the media about the event, of which 85 were radio or TV items. The website drew 250,000 unique visitors; the EYOF page on Facebook had 20,000 users; 3,200 people were following the event on Twitter. On the day of the opening, with the presence of the King of the Netherlands and IOC former president Jacques Rogge, the event was a trending topic on Twitter. It was estimated that the media coverage represented free publicity for the city and the event organisers with a value of €2.7 million. The actual economic impact for the city of Utrecht and its direct neighbouring cities was calculated at €4.8 million (expenditures by the organising committee, participants, officials, visitors and anybody else attending or taking part in the event).

EYOF: side events

As for the side events, 12,500 children from 100 different schools took part in the sporting days in June prior to the main event. Some 4,000 children participated in the Urban Tour, which had street adaptations to the nine EYOF sports. As a reference, there are 23,000 children aged 8–14 living in the city of Utrecht, 110,000 in the province of Utrecht and 1.4 million in the Netherlands.

With these numbers, the organisation reached the targets that had been set in advance. Overall, children were quite content to take part in any of the events

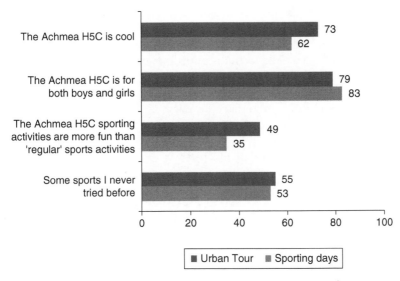

Figure 2.1 Viewpoint on sporting days and Urban Tour; percentage of participants that (totally) agreed to the following statements.
Source: Breedveld *et al.*, 2014.

(see Figure 2.1). Most children found the activities to be cool, and to be open and inviting both to boys and girls. Half of the children at the sporting days said the activities were more fun than 'regular' sports, one-third of the children thought this of the activities at the Urban Tour. Roughly half of the children said that at either of the events they had tried out sports they had not previously attempted. Children graded the sporting days as 8.7 (on a scale from 1 to 10, in which anything lower or equal to 5 is considered 'unsatisfactory') and the Urban Tour as 8.0 (not shown in Figure 2.1).

In general, children that were already active in sports rated these side events a bit more highly than children that were not active in sports (e.g. 77 per cent versus 68 per cent on the question of how cool children thought the Urban Tour activities were). More important perhaps was the finding that schools that had active programmes for sports and PE were more involved in the events than schools that were less into sports and PE. In that sense, the side events seem to capitalise on already existing interests of school head masters, rather than eliciting new interests.

Prior to the sporting days, information packages were put together on EYOF, on sports in general and on the Olympic Movement. The idea was that these packages would be used in class so that participation in the sporting days would be about more than just taking part in sports. It was found, however, that not many schools made use of the educational material. By the time schools had been integrated in the process (late spring), the school programme had already been established and there was no more room in the curricula to make use of the packages.

The Flame relay attracted 800 visitors according to the organisation. Given that a great number of celebrities participated in this side event and that the distance the Flame relay covered was 140 kilometres over four days, that is not an impressive number. The overall view is that organisations that could have played a role in stimulating children (and adults) to take part in this event, e.g. schools or clubs, were contacted too late, with too few interesting offers, leaving too little room for them to shape the event in such a way that participation would benefit them too, for them to make it attractive to them to take part in the relay.[1]

The sporting days and the Urban Tour were all organised by a commercial agency. Sport federations had been involved in setting up the activities, but local sport clubs had not been asked to become involved. Nor were schools or community services involved, or at least not very intensively. For the Urban Tour, the main advantage of working with professionals was that the same quality could be provided time and time again, at all 13 locations. The downfall was that sport clubs and their volunteers did not feel committed to the project. The top-down approach left them few opportunities to get actively involved and integrate the project in their programmes and activities. As a consequence, it is doubtful whether the side events, although they undoubtedly generated some initial interest in sporting activities among children, have resulted in lasting effects for sport participation.

EYOF: main event

The main event generally seems to have elicited positive effects, especially among participants, volunteers and visitors. Of the 2,271 participants, 62 per cent were very satisfied with the event and 25 per cent were slightly satisfied (Figure 2.2). Generally, the younger participants were slightly more satisfied than the older participants. Catering and transport (the organisation used local buses rather than taxis or coaches, and the system did not work well in the beginning) were among the issues that caused the most debate. Chefs de missions were sometimes a bit more critical, though 8 out of 10 were positive about the city itself.

As for the 2,150 volunteers ('Festival makers' in the event's jargon), the event apparently was a very rewarding experience. Only 5 per cent of the volunteers – most between 24 and 64, half women, half men, educated slightly above average and with an over-representation of active sportsmen and women – reported to not be proud of the event (Figure 2.2). Ninety-two per cent were proud of the activities they had contributed to and 91 per cent were proud of their own contribution. Twenty-nine per cent said that volunteering in the event had superseded their expectations, 53 per cent said that the event had lived up to their expectations and only 18 per cent were (slightly) disappointed. The volunteers, all wearing very recognisable purple EYOF T-shirts, applauded the atmosphere and their many contacts with the athletes. They apparently easily ignored the fact that flaws existed in the organisation,

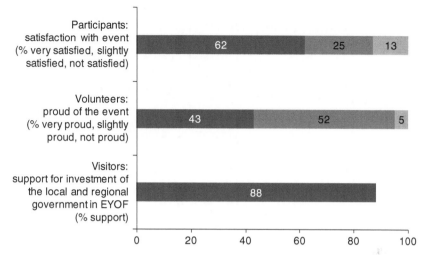

Figure 2.2 Viewpoint on EYOF 2013 among participants, visitors and volunteers (per cent).
Source: Breedveld *et al.*, 2014.

that drinks were sometimes not sufficiently available (it was unusually hot on the days of the EYOF) and that their chores were sometimes far beneath their professional standards (academics acting as bus-drivers, driving athletes and official around in old, battered buses).

Equally enthusiastic were the 26,000 visitors, 88 per cent of which stated that it was good that the city had invested in the EYOF event (Figure 2.2). Seventy-two per cent said that the event fitted the city, and equal numbers said the event was a promotion for the city. The event was graded 8.0 (scale 1–10). Ninety-seven per cent said they would recommend the event to their friends. Eighty-four per cent believed the event contributed to promotion of sport in the region. In this, one must take into account that 94 per cent of the visitors consisted of people who were already active in sports. Fifteen per cent of the visitors stated that the event had encouraged them to become (more) active in sports themselves. Of the 6 per cent of visitors that were not active in sports, only 7 per cent felt encouraged to be more active in sports.

The population of Utrecht seems to have experienced the EYOF event somewhat ambivalently. On the one side, before the event, of those that were familiar with the EYOF the majority judged it favourably (see Figure 2.3). After the event, these evaluations become somewhat less positive. More troublesome was that only 32 per cent of the local population felt they had been adequately informed on the event, and only 16 per cent stated that they felt the event had 'lived' in their direct neighbourhood (meaning that people had talked about the event, that they had witnessed expressions of the event in shops or on the streets). Especially a bit farther away from the main venues of the event, in the northern and western parts of the city (coincidentally the

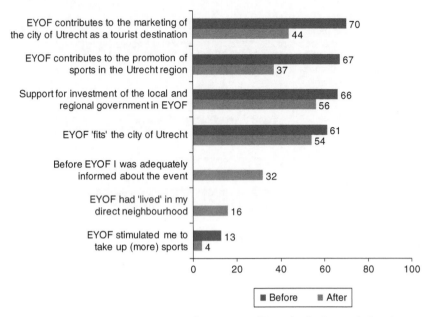

Figure 2.3 Viewpoint on EYOF 2013 by citizens of Utrecht, before and after the
event, per cent (totally) agree.
Source: Hover *et al.*, 2014.

poorer parts of the city and the parts of the city with the lowest sport participation rates), fewer people were familiar with EYOF, had 'followed' the event
or considered the event a good investment. Of the local inhabitants, a meagre
4 per cent claimed afterwards that the event had stimulated them to take up
(more) sports.

Perhaps the least positive about the event were the local sport clubs. The
survey administered shortly after the event indicated that one-third (37 per
cent) of the 300+ sport clubs of the city had been involved somehow in the
event. Of the clubs that had been involved in the organisation, 3 per cent felt
they had benefited from the event, 15 per cent felt that sport in the city had
benefited from the event and 21 per cent believed the city itself had benefited
from the event (see Figure 2.4). In general, clubs in any of the nine EYOF
sports were somewhat more positive than non-EYOF sport clubs.

The lack of enthusiasm of the local sport clubs for EYOF is to be attributed
to the organisational structure of the event. EYOF was organised by the city
of Utrecht, a special event-committee including outside professionals and a
sport marketing organisation, and nine sport federations. Attempts were made
to integrate sport clubs, or other local actors, in the process. The way this
achieved, though, was rather top-down. Meetings were organised to explain
plans and possible projects. Invitations for these meetings were sent out, as
well as letters to all sport clubs to promote EYOF. In the run-up to the event,
the mayor and the alderman used every available opportunity to publicly

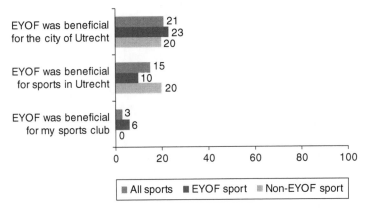

Figure 2.4 Viewpoint on EYOF 2013 by sports clubs of Utrecht that knew about
EYOF, per cent (totally) agree.
Source: Hover *et al.*, 2014.

declare the importance of the event. A former elite athlete, golden medallist
and former EYOF participant Pieter van den Hoogenband was used to boost
interest in the event.

Still, most invitations to clubs to take part in the event were sent out by mail.
More often than not, these invitations were sent out late (2–3 weeks' notice).
VSU, the spokes-group for the city's 300+ clubs, was asked to facilitate the
process and the meetings, but was not asked to actually do anything itself.
Thereby it felt not responsible for mobilising Utrecht's sport clubs. At meetings on the event, the plans on the table had in fact already been scheduled to a
great extent. There was little room for clubs, and certainly not a strong appeal
to clubs, to bring forward their own ideas, explain their needs and thoughts,
and come up with plans or projects of their own.[2] As a consequence, not a lot
of clubs developed an interest in the event, with the exception perhaps of the
clubs whose venues were to be used.

Conclusion

It seems that especially the inhabitants and the citizens of Utrecht, the organising city, were sceptical about the sport legacy of EYOF 2013. It does not seem
that the event has had a long-lasting impact upon local sport participation and
the local sport infrastructure.

In defence of the event, it must be admitted that the EYOF is complex. It
is a multi-sport event, like any Olympic event. The lack of experience in this
matter was a serious drawback. It is much easier to organise a football event or
a basketball event, with just one federation involved, than to organise an event
involving nine federations and seven very different venues.

Budgets to organise the event were rather low. There was virtually no
money to promote the event in the city (using flags, billboards and setting up

side events at non-venue places in the city). Thus, it should not come as a surprise that apart from the venues and the people who were directly involved in the event, knowledge of and interest in the event were low. Also, being an event for young, developing talented players rather than for elite, well-known sportsmen, media-interest could be expected to be lower than for a regular sports event. Strategically, it appeared to not have been a good choice to use different names for the main event (EYOF) and for the side events (Achmea High Five Challenge). The general public, as well as the media, found this confusing and did not recognise this as being a single project.

Still, the general idea is that more could have been accomplished if local organisations, especially schools and sports clubs, had been involved more in the process. The top-down nature of the project seriously hindered opportunities for local parties to be and feel involved. As a consequence, the energy that the event generated – and the positive reactions to the event of participants, volunteers and visitors all indicate that the event did generate a lot of enthusiasm – could hardly be put to use in generating social impacts and a sporting legacy. Neither the elite event nor the side events that children found to be so appealing seems to have translated into higher sports participation rates, not locally and certainly not nationally.

As for the results, the EYOF case is not an isolated case. In the London 2012 Olympic Games – a much bigger event in almost any possible way – the enthusiasm of visitors, volunteers and media seems not to have led to a lasting increase in sports participation. This is not to say that investments in elite sport events are a waste of money from the viewpoint of sports development. Elite sport events do appear to stimulate those that are already active in sports to do more sports (or to switch to another sport). What it also does *seem* to do (no formal research to our knowledge has been carried out to back this up with empirical data), is that elite sport events serve to revitalise sport infrastructures: the need to organise the event and the desire to perform before a home-crowd mobilises a sport and generates perspective and hope for those involved. As such, the prospect of the event and especially of the many media opportunities that come with it, draws the attention of politicians and sponsors to sports. And with politicians and sponsors come budgets (at least, sometimes); budgets that would not always have been available without the event.

To conclude, elite sport events do seem to be of importance for the sport sector itself. Elite sport events generate interests from politicians and sponsors, and help generate media attention and funds. In addition, the event is a boost to the sport infrastructure (federations, elite athletes, practitioners and – potentially – clubs). Success at elite sporting events boosts national morale and a sense of national pride, at least temporarily.

This all falls under the heading of what Houlihan calls the 'magic dust' of elite sporting events, the unexplainable way that people feel inspired by elite sports. What appears to be much more difficult is to translate all this elite sport capital into a lasting legacy for grass-roots sports. It is one thing to bring together elite athletes and their audience into a stadium for a once-in-a-lifetime experience, it is quite another thing to take that experience outside the stadium into the city, towards the organisations that need to get involved in order to reach a wider audience. It appears that this translation, from the event towards mobilising local parties and altering people's habits, is one that is much more difficult. We need to be more realistic about what we can achieve. To put it in Coalter's words (2007, p. 7), there is a need 'to think more clearly, analytically and less emotionally about sport and its potential'.

Elite sporting events, with their strict deadlines and media attention, suck up all the energy of the organisation and favour top-down approaches. In that sense, elite sporting events can be considered 'greedy institutions'. Generally, these are not conditions that are favourable to generating social legacies. More often than not event managers underestimate (or downright neglect) the investments that need to be made in order to generate a lasting legacy. If grass-roots sport is to benefit from elite sport events, more emphasis needs to be placed on these social processes. Event managers and politicians need to take account of the fact that elite sport events are not about a stadium, in a time frame between an opening and a closing ceremony. In fact, the event stretches out much further, both in time (days and years beyond the event) and in space (away from the stadium, into inner-cities and suburbs). It is this lesson that elite sports needs to learn if it aspires to function as a tool for stimulating grass-roots sports.

Notes

1 One example of this is that each time the Flame relay started off in another city, a child would be asked to 'do' the first lap (usually half a mile or so; the very first lap was done by the Mayor of Utrecht). In one city, the first lap was done by Koen, a child who was a member of the local athletics club. The chairman of the athletic club, who was there when Koen was about to set off for his lap, admitted that the organisation had asked him for a youth member to be involved, but only days before the event. At that time, the only thing he could do was to ask two trainers whether they could ask a child to do this. The trainers came up with two names, and as the other kid fell ill, Koen become the 'lucky one'. At the club, no broad attention was paid to the fact that one of their youth members participated in this Olympic event. The club trainer, Rob Druppers, runner-up at the 1983 800-metre World Championships in Helsinki, had not been involved. Koen's headmaster at school had not been aware of Koen's activities. He did recall receiving a letter informing him of the event, but that letter contained no references to Koen's activities. But as with so many letters and with it coming in quite late, he had not given it much attention.

2 As an example, one can point to the youth tennis tournament. It was agreed that the club that hosted the EYOF tennis competition (Domstad) would organise such a tournament, both as an attempt to stimulate Utrecht tennis youth and as an attempt to tie in other clubs in the process. This was done, however, at such a late stage that the tournament had to be restricted to some pre-matches on a Wednesday afternoon prior to the EYOF games, and a more formal tournament during one EYOF day. The 'tournament' involved some 20 children during the event, and took place without much notice to either the greater public or the local media, except perhaps for some of the parents involved. Apparently, no attempts were made to use local tournaments and competitions to interest youth to come to the EYOF tennis event, to give away free tickets to local champions or to ask

them to play a formal role in the EYOF tennis event. As a consequence, only 800 people bought tickets to visit the tennis tournament (the least of all the sports, leaving the galleries empty most of the time) against a tennis-playing population of some 50,000 in the province of Utrecht and 700,000 nationwide).

References

Baarsma, B. (2000). *Monetary Valuation of Environmental Goods: Alternatives to Contingent Valuation*. Amsterdam: Universiteit van Amsterdam.

Bottenburg, M. van, Brinkhof, S., Elling, A., Hover, P. and Romijn, D. (2012). *De maatschappelijke betekenis van topsport. Literatuurstudie in opdracht van het Ministerie van VWS*. Nieuwegein: Arko Sports Media/Utrecht: Universiteit Utrecht en Mulier Instituut.

Breedveld, K., Hover, P., Pulles, I., Romijn, D., Verhagen, S., Smits, F., Dijk, B. and Eekeren, F. van (2014). *European Youth Olympic Festival: Olympisch sportfeest onder de Dom: onderzoek EYOF Utrecht 2013: overall rapportage*. Utrecht: Mulier Instituut/Hogeschool Utrecht/ Universiteit Utrecht.

Carson, R., Flores, T. and Meade, N. (2001). Contingent Valuation: Controversies and Evidence. *Environmental and Resource Economics*, 19: 173–210.

Centre for Social Justice (2011). *More Than a Game. Harnessing the Power of Sport to Transform the Lives of Disadvantaged Young People: A Policy Report by the Sport Working Group*. London: CSJ Sport Working Group.

Coalter, F. (2007). *A Wider Social Role for Sport. Who's Keeping the Score?* London/ New York: Routledge.

DCMS (2010). *Plans for the Legacy from the 2012 Olympic and Paralympic Games*. London: DCMS.

DCMS (2011). *Meta-Evaluation of the Impacts and Legacy of the London 2012 Olympic Games and Paralympic Games Summary of Reports 1 and 2: 'Scope, Research Questions and Strategy' and 'Methods'*. London: DCMS.

DCMS (2012). *Creating a Sporting Habit for Life. A New Youth Sport Strategy*. London: DCMS.

Elling, A., Hilvoorde, I. van and Dool, R. van den (2014). Creating or awakening national pride through sporting success. A longitudinal study on macro effects in the Netherlands. *International Review for the Sociology of Sport*, 49: 129–151.

Frawley, S. (2013). Sport participation legacy and the hosting of mega-sport events. In W. Richards, M.P. de Brito and L. Wilks (eds). *Exploring the Social Impacts of Events*. London: Routledge, pp. 97–110.

Green, M. and Houlihan, B. (2005). *Elite Sport Development. Policy Learning and Political Priorities*. London: Routledge.

Hausman, J. (2012) Contingent valuation. From dubious to hopeless. *Journal of Economic Perspectives*, 26(4): 43–56.

Heere, B., Walker, M., Gibson, H., Thapa, B., Geldenhuys, S. and Coetzee, W. (2013). The power of sport to unite a nation. The social value of the 2010 FIFA World Cup in South Africa. *European Sport Management Quarterly*, 13(4): 450–471.

Hover, P., Pulles, I., Romijn, D. and Breedveld, K. (2014). *EYOF Utrecht 2013 : impact en beleving*. Utrecht: Mulier Instituut.

Hughes, K. (2013). *Sport Mega-events and a Legacy of Increased Sport Participation. An Olympic Promise or an Olympic Dream?* Leeds: Leeds Metropolitan University.

Ipsos MORI (2012). *Britons are Surprised by How Olympics Brought Country Together, Half Think it Will Have Lasting Effect with more Volunteering and Sport*. London: Ipsos MORI.

Kavetsos, G. and Szymanski, S. (2010). National well-being and international sports events. *Journal of Economic Psychology*, 31: 158–171.

Legacy Trust UK (2013). *Research Findings: Young People and London 2012*. London: Legacy Trust UK.

LOCOG (2012). *Inspire Legacy Book: A Record of the London 2012 Inspire Program*. London: LOCOG.

Miah, A. and García, B. (2012). *The Olympics: The Basics*. Abingdon: Routledge.

Mean, M., Vigor, A. and Tims, C. (2004). Conclusion. Minding the gap. In A. Vigor, M. Mean and C. Tims (eds), *After the Gold Rush. A Sustainable Olympics for London*. London: IPPR and Demos. pp. 129–251.

NAO (2007). *The Budget for the London 2012 Olympic and Paralympic Games*. London: NAO.

Preuss, H. (2011). A method for calculating the crowding-out effect in sport mega-event impact studies. The 2010 FIFA World Cup. *Development Southern Africa*, 28 (3): 367–385.

Richards, G. and De Brito, M. (2013). 'Conclusions. The future of events as a social phenomenon'. In W. Richards, M.P. de Brito and L. Wilks (ed.), *Exploring the Social Impacts of Events*. London: Routledge, pp. 219–235.

Sport and Recreation Alliance (2013). *Olympic and Paralympic Games. Legacy Survey*. London: Sport and Recreation Alliance.

UK Government and the Mayor of London (2014). *Inspired by 2012: The Legacy from the London 2012 Olympic and Paralympic Games. A Joint UK Government and Mayor of London Report*. London: UK Government and the Mayor of London.

Vekeman, A., Meulders, M., Praet, A., Colpaert, J. and Puyenbroeck, T. van (2013). Contingent valuation of a classic cycling race. *Journal of Sports Economics*, 11: 1–27.

Weed, M. (2009). *The Potential of the Demonstration Effect to Grow and Sustain Participation in Sport*. Canterbury: Canterbury Christ Church University (SPEAR).

Zimbalist, A. (2010). Is it worth it? Hosting the Olympic Games and other mega sporting events is an honor many countries aspire to – but why? *Finance and Development*, 47(1): 8–11.

3 Arguments and evidence of bridging elite performance and mass participation sports from an economic perspective

Christoph Breuer and Pamela Wicker

Introduction

In many countries the sport system is organised as a pyramid, with elite performance sport being at the top of the pyramid and mass participation sport at the bottom (Eady, 1993). The two areas are not only linked in a way that talented athletes move from mass sports to elite performance sports and mass sports is in turn nurtured by elite sports when, for example, former athletes provide their expertise as coaches (Sotiriadou *et al.*, 2008). They are also linked economically because of individual effects that are economically relevant (e.g. trickle-down effect; health and expenditure effects) and the cross-subsidisation between these two areas within community sports clubs. This chapter discusses the relationship between mass participation and elite performance sports from an economic perspective. In doing so, it uses economic theories and concepts that are enriched with empirical evidence. A distinction between the individual level and the organisational level (sports clubs) is made in the following sections.

Individual level

Theoretical considerations

The individual level focuses on microeconomic approaches such as the trickle-down effect, the concepts of super stars and role models and their relationship with the demand for sport, and the concept of consumption capital. Regarding the trickle-down effect, it is believed in economics that 'wealth may trickle down from the rich to the poor' (Aghion and Bolton, 1997, p. 151). The mechanism through which the poor benefit from the accumulation of wealth by the rich is borrowing and lending in the capital market because more funds are available for investment purposes (Aghion and Bolton, 1997). The idea of a trickle-down effect has been applied to sports (e.g. De Bosscher *et al.*, 2013; Wicker and Sotiriadou, in press) where this effect is also referred to as the demonstration effect (Weed, 2009) or Boris Becker effect (van Bottenburg, 2001). Following Weed (2009, p. 4), the trickle-down effect describes that 'people are inspired by elite sport, sports people or sports events to participate themselves'. It has three facets: (1) inspiration by elite performances and sporting success; (2) the personalities of elite performance athletes; and (3) hosting events in elite performance sport. These facets are explained from a theoretical standpoint in the following paragraphs.

First, elite performances and sporting success are associated with the concept of super stars (Rosen, 1981) which has received great attention in economics research. Following Rosen (1981), super stars are elite performance athletes who perform slightly better than others, but these relatively small differences in performances lead to disproportionately high differences in earnings. Previous studies across several sports and leagues confirmed that super stars (measured by superior performance) earn wage premiums (e.g. Kuethe and Motamed, 2010; Lucifora and Simmons, 2003). More important for the present chapter is the relationship between super stars and sport demand. Research has shown that super stars positively affect the demand for spectator sport (passive sport consumption) because they attract fans by outstanding field performances (e.g. Brandes *et al.*, 2008). Within the trickle-down effect, it is assumed that they can also affect active sport consumption in the sense that people are inspired to participate themselves.

The second facet relates to the personality of elite performance athletes. Elite performance athletes are role models for the wider population and specifically for children and youths (Biskup and Pfister, 1999). Following Yancey (1998), a role model is an individual that is considered commendable and worth of being imitated. Research showed that in Germany, 91.8 per cent of the population say that elite performance athletes are role models in terms of motivation, 89.4 per cent consider them role models in terms of fairness, 86.5 per cent in terms of community, and 85.4 per cent in terms of performance (Wicker *et al.*, 2012). The concept of role models is linked, with Adler (1985) stating that not only performance differences are critical, but also an elite athlete's personality and popularity. Typically, such athletes are more present in the media, which facilitates the development of consumption capital (Stigler and Becker, 1977) by the population. This means that people are presented with more information about these athletes which is not limited to sporting performance, but also includes private aspects. People build consumption capital about the athlete and the sport (knowledge of rules, other athletes and teams, performance aspects of a sport, etc.). With increasing interest in the athlete and the sport, it is also more likely that people take up sport themselves.

The third facet of the trickle-down effect is the inspiring function of hosting elite performance sport events which is associated with an experience value for the population (Preuss and Werkmann, 2011). When a major sport event is hosted on home soil, media attention increases and people have the opportunity to watch the competitions in the stadium. As a consequence of the increased presence of a sport, people are more likely to take up this sport themselves. This effect is also referred to as the participation legacy of sport events (Veal *et al.*, 2012). Yet this effect does not occur automatically since such social leverage of sport events needs to be facilitated by the organisers of the event, for example through celebration and community activities (Chalip, 2006). As with the other three facets, this effect is more likely in sports that have low entrance barriers and can be played by people of all ages across several geographical regions (e.g. tennis, football, table tennis, swimming). On the contrary, in sports like biathlon, downhill skiing and ski jumping, such effects are less likely because older people would rather not take up ski jumping and the geographical and climate conditions in some regions do not allow practising such sports.

Empirical evidence

Turning to the empirics, the methodological challenge is to isolate the trickle-down effect because individual sport participation may not only be affected by the three facets of this effect, but also by other factors including income, education, time, age, gender, migration background, and the availability of sports facilities (Downward and Rasciute, 2010; Wicker et al., 2013b). Since some studies could not provide any evidence (e.g. Weed, 2009), researchers questioned the existence of such an effect. Nevertheless, a few studies have tried to empirically examine this effect. Regarding the methodology of these studies, using secondary data should be more valid than relying on survey data (primary data) because it can be questioned whether people can accurately report in surveys the reason they took up a sporting activity. Interestingly, most studies concentrated on one facet of the trickle-down effect; only one study could be detected which examined all three facets (Weimar et al., 2014). The facets that received most attention in previous research are whether sporting success of elite performance athletes and hosting elite performance sports events affect mass sports participation. One reason for this research focus could be the availability of data, the straightforward measurement of hosting sport events (a simple yes–no variable) and sporting success (through medals and ranks), whereas it is more challenging to find measures for role models and personality.

Regarding the effect of sporting success, the evidence is mixed: Hanstad and Skille (2010) documented a positive relationship between sporting success (measured by medals won at Olympic Games or World Championships) and registered participants in a Norwegian biathlon. De Bosscher et al. (2013) could find positive relationships in Flanders, but not for all sports. Feddersen et al. (2009) even observed a paradox relationship in German tennis in the sense that memberships decreased during the sporting success period of Boris Becker and Steffi Graf. Mutter and Pawlowski (2013) showed that German football players are motivated by the success of the German national team to play more football. This finding is in line with the assumption of Weed (2009) that it is more likely that already existing participants increase their frequency of participation or switch activities rather than inactive people taking up a new sport activity. In another study, Mutter and Pawlowski (2014) documented that success of professional tennis players is positively associated with the playing frequency of players on the amateur (mass participation) level. The authors also estimated the economic significance of this effect and stated that €200 million of tennis-related expenditure on the amateur level could be related to professional tennis (elite performance sports) in Germany. Although the latter two studies used the concept of role models as a theoretical frame, the empirical measures and analysis focused on sporting success, which is a different facet of the trickle-down effect. This limitation confirms the existing challenge of finding appropriate measures for role models.

Concerning the effect of hosting events on mass sports participation, the evidence is also mixed: while Veal *et al.* (2012) could not detect a relationship for several sports events in Australia, Frawley and Cush (2011) found an effect, but only for juniors. The study of Wicker and Sotiriadou (in press) documented that 6 per cent of Australians would take up a new sport activity because of the 2006 Commonwealth Games hosted in Melbourne, Australia. Yet already-existing participants were included in this figure. The percentage of people having a more positive attitude because of Melbourne hosting the Commonwealth Games was higher (31 per cent). These findings support that hosting sports events may be more associated with emotional benefits, which has already been shown in previous research (Preuss and Werkmann, 2011; Suessmuth *et al.*, 2010).

Weimar *et al.* (2014) collected comprehensive data on memberships in German sports clubs, sporting success, athletes as stars or role models, and hosting major sports events from 1970 to 2011. Data were collected in 12 different sports that fulfil the requirements of being accessible to the wider population, using homogeneous sports fields and not being restricted to certain regions or climates (football, tennis, handball, table tennis, volleyball, badminton, basketball, judo, rowing, field hockey, boxing and fencing). Regarding the trickle-down effect variables, SUCCESS was measured by a gold medal at the European or World Championships or Olympic Games or equivalent events in boxing (World Champion in one of the boxing federations) and tennis (Grand Slams). STAR was measured using the ranks (from 1 to 3) in a specific voting in Germany which is called *athlete of the year* (over 1,000 sports journalists vote). The second German television network (ZDF) awards male and female athletes as well as teams at the end of each year. The personality aspect is more important in the election in an effort to find the best role model. Thus, this measure should be adequate to capture role models. HOME_EVENT was captured by whether Germany hosted a European or World Championship or the Olympic Games (1 = event in year t).

Two dynamic panel regression models were estimated, with the percentage change in memberships as the dependent variable (ΔSENIOR resp. ΔJUNIOR). One model was run for seniors (age >18) and one for juniors (age ≤18) because the trickle-down effect may differ between these two groups, as indicated by the importance of role models (Biskup and Pfister, 1999). Importantly, the trickle-down effect variables were also included as time lags; this means that the models also captured effects that occurred 1–5 years (L1–L5) later. This study also controlled for other factors that may also affect individual sport participation in an effort to isolate the trickle-down effect. These factors were SENIOR (total number of senior memberships in sport clubs) respectively JUNIOR (total number of junior memberships in sport clubs); GDP (German gross domestic product per year); WORKTIME (annual real time at work per employee in hours); POP_SENIOR respectively POP_JUNIOR (German male population of seniors respective to juniors); YEAR (time trend); FRG (to control for a structural break in the data due to the German reunion in 1990; $1 = $ YEAR ≤ 1989); and ADJUST (adjustment of membership numbers from t to $t + 1$ due to membership corrections, new counting methods or changes related to the inclusion of the German Democratic Republic (GDR) members into the Federal Republic of Germany (FRG) membership statistics).

The results (Table 3.1) reveal that the effect of sporting success on club memberships is lagged by four (juniors) and three years (seniors). Thus, the observed paradox by Feddersen *et al.* (2009) could also be explained by time-lagged effects, i.e. the effects do not occur in the current year, but a few years later. The role model effect is only significant for juniors with a time lag of one year, probably because it takes some time to build consumption capital. The effect of sport events on home soil is only significant in the year of the event. This implies that sports clubs should be prepared to have capacity for new members when Germany hosts a major sport event in the sports they provide. This study is among the first to provide evidence of a significant trickle-down effect in all three facets (Weimar *et al.*, 2014).

Economic relevance

If there was a trickle-down effect and mass sports participation increased because of sporting success of elite performance athletes, athletes' personalities, and/or hosting elite performance sports events – why should this effect be economically relevant? We would argue that there are at least three reasons why increased mass sports participation is relevant from an economic standpoint: (1) increased sport-related expenditure, (2) health benefits and (3) creation of social capital. These effects are explained in the following paragraphs.

First, according to the sport consumption model (Downward *et al.*, 2009), sport expenditure follows sport participation. Research shows that sport participants spend a significant amount of money on their sport: for example, German households spent a total of €11 billion on sport and leisure activities (Pawlowski and Breuer, 2011) and members of German sports clubs spent on average €1,610 on their sport per year (Wicker *et al.*, 2010). Sport-related expenditure is economically relevant; it is equivalent to approximately 3 per cent of the total gross value added of the member states of the European Union (SportsEcon Austria, 2012).

Second, sport participation is associated with health benefits (e.g. Humphreys *et al.*, 2014; Warburton *et al.*, 2006) which are of economic value. Research shows that active people are less likely to be obese or have other diseases that

Table 3.1 Results of the dynamic panel regression, 1970–2011

	ΔSENIOR	ΔJUNIOR
ΔSENIOR_L1	0.08842 (1.71)★	–
SENIOR _L1	0.00000 (–0.41)	–
ΔJUNIOR_L1	–	0.43659 (9.05)★★★
JUNIOR_L1	–	0.00000 (0.41)
SUCCESS	0.0036 (0.41)	0.00504 (0.53)
SUCCESS_L1	0.00997 (1.24)	0.0078 (0.94)
SUCCESS_L2	0.00042 (0.04)	0.00585 (0.54)
SUCCESS_L3	0.00588 (0.67)	0.02353 (2.54)★★
SUCCESS_L4	0.01797 (1.92)★	0.00315 (0.30)
SUCCESS_L5	0.01292 (1.48)	0.01106 (1.19)
STAR	–0.00261 (–0.25)	–0.00997 (–0.9)
STAR_L1	–0.0012 (–0.12)	0.02109 (2.04)★★
STAR_L2	0.00142 (0.15)	–0.01347 (–1.3)
STAR_L3	0.00138 (0.14)	–0.01516 (–1.38)
STAR_L4	–0.01058 (–1.03)	–0.0084 (–0.76)
STAR_L5	–0.00832 (–0.86)	–0.00111 (–0.11)
HOME_EVENT	0.02606 (2.49)★★	0.03934 (3.54)★★★
HOME_EVENT_L1	–0.01644 (–1.58)	0.00776 (0.7)
HOME_EVENT_L2	0.00617 (0.57)	0.00813 (0.72)
HOME_EVENT_L3	–0.01182 (–0.98)	–0.0077 (–0.61)
HOME_EVENT_L4	–0.00266 (–0.23)	0.01089 (0.89)
HOME_EVENT_L5	0.01774 (1.45)	0.01856 (1.43)
ΔINCOME	0.08986 (0.52)	0.04186 (0.23)
ΔGDP	0.49659 (2.27)★★	0.05208 (0.24)
ΔWORKTIME	–0.96003 (–2.38)★★	–0.53032 (–1.32)
ΔPOP_SENIOR	–0.99785 (–1.20)	–
ΔPOP_JUNIOR	–	0.29196 (0.75)
YEAR	–0.00089 (–1.53)	–0.0019 (–2.59)★★★
FRG	0.02832 (2.12)★★	–0.00915 (–0.52)
ADJUST	0.00214 (0.2)	0.01295 (1.16)
Within LSDV – R^2	0.22	0.38
Frees test	0.63★★★	0.23★★★
Hausman test	46.69★★★	24.65★★★

Source: Weimar *et al.*, 2014.

Note.
Displayed are the non-standardised coefficients, z-values in parentheses; ★ $p < 0.1$; ★★ $p < 0.05$; ★★★ $p < 0.01$.

represent financial burdens for health systems worldwide (e.g. Katzmarzyk *et al.*, 2000; Sander and Bergemann 2003).

Third, social capital is created when people practise sports together. Social capital 'refers to features of social organization, such as trust, norms, and networks that can improve the efficiency of society by facilitating coordinated actions' (Putnam, 1993, p. 167). The creation of social capital is particularly strong in organisational settings like non-profit sports clubs that facilitate the development of new contacts and friendships (Ulseth, 2004). A nation's stock of social capital is economically relevant because it contributes to the reduction of transaction costs (Fukuyama, 1995). Transaction costs occur when goods or personnel is exchanged; typical costs are initiation costs, agreement costs, execution costs, control costs and adjustment costs (Picot *et al.*, 2012; Williamson, 1979). When people themselves are trustworthy, trust each other and can also trust institutions, i.e. when the stock of social capital is high, then the costs of controlling each other are lower (Fukuyama, 1995). Consequently, social capital was found to be positively associated with economic development and growth (Zak and Knack, 2001).

Organisational level

On the organisational level, the focus is on non-profit sports clubs, which represent the basis of the sport pyramid in many countries. From a theoretical perspective, economic and financial aspects of these organisations (e.g. cross-subsidisation within clubs, portfolio theory and revenue diversification) are relevant. The relationship between elite performance sport and mass participation sport is documented using primary data on non-profit sports clubs that stem from the German Sport Development Report (Breuer and Feiler, 2013b; Breuer and Wicker, 2009b, 2011). For example, the results will discuss the financial challenges of promoting elite performance sports and show this promotion affects the financial structure of sports clubs.

Non-profit sports clubs have a variety of goals (Nagel, 2008). They not only provide programmes for mass participation sports and social events, they also promote elite performance sports (Breuer and Feiler, 2013b). While this is not true for all clubs, there are some clubs that have squad athletes. In Germany, 10 per cent of the clubs had squad athletes in 2012; yet this share of clubs has significantly decreased over time (Breuer and Feiler, 2013b). For example, two years earlier 14.6 per cent of the clubs had squad athletes (Breuer and Wicker, 2011). One explanation for this decrease could be the costs associated with promoting elite performance sports. Research shows that organisational problems related to the financial situation of the sports clubs in general and the costs of sports competitions are significantly higher in clubs that have squad athletes (Breuer and Feiler, 2013a; Breuer and Wicker, 2009a). With regard to specific expenditure categories, it was found that clubs with squad athletes have significantly higher sport-related expenditure related to coaches, sports equipment and sports events. Also, expenditure in other areas, including administrative personnel, membership fees to other sports organisations, taxes and insurances, are significantly higher in those clubs (Breuer and Wicker, 2009a). Thus, engaging in the promotion of elite performance sports is not only a matter of philosophy, but also a matter of finances. The financial consequences are discussed in the next paragraphs.

A more detailed analysis reveals that particularly multi-sports clubs have squad athletes (Breuer and Wicker, 2009a). As shown above, elite performance sport is relatively costly and these costs cannot only be covered by the membership fees of the elite athletes themselves. At this point it is important to mention that sports clubs provide *club goods* (Buchanan, 1965); members pool their resources and finance the club's activities from this resource pool. This sharing of resources implies that the members' utility increases with increasing club memberships because more resources are available while some fixed costs do not increase. For example, a coach is not paid more if he/she has one member more in the sports programme. Yet, members' utility only increases up to a certain point because at some stage the club becomes too crowded and therefore utility decreases from this point on (Sandler and Tschirhart, 1997; Wicker *et al.*, 2014). The sharing of resources also allows cross-subsidisation. This means that some members pay higher membership fees which are used to finance the activities of members who pay lower fees. Typically, adults pay higher membership fees than juniors (Breuer and Feiler, 2013b) while being more oriented towards mass participation sports, which is not as costly as elite performance sport that is typically practised by juniors and adolescents. The presence of several sports and club size also facilitate cross-subsidisation. Thus, participants of mass sports finance elite performance sports within non-profit sports clubs.

Elite performance sports is not only a financial challenge for clubs, it also represents an opportunity for them to generate revenues in more areas. From the viewpoint of financial stability it is critical that clubs do not only have high total revenues, but also a revenue portfolio (Kearns, 2007). The idea of revenue diversification is rooted in portfolio theory, which stems from the generic finance sector, but has also been applied to non-profit organisations (Kingma, 1993) including sports clubs (Wicker *et al.*, 2013a). In short form, organisations can decrease their financial risk by diversifying their revenue portfolio and relying on revenues of different risk levels. Revenue diversification is important because it was found to be positively associated with financial stability (Carroll and Stater, 2008). Within sports clubs, research showed that clubs promoting elite performance sports have higher levels of revenue diversification than clubs which do not promote it (Wicker *et al.*, 2013a). Thus, promoting elite performance sport opens opportunities for clubs to generate revenues from more sources, including various types of subsidies and sponsorships. On the contrary, focusing on mass participation and health sports or having a more commercial orientation is associated with lower levels of revenue diversification (Wicker *et al.*, 2013a). Consequently, clubs promoting elite performance sports should exploit the financial opportunities associated with it to cover the relatively high costs. Overall, the members practising mass participation sport will also benefit from increased financial stability of their club due to a higher level of revenue diversification.

Conclusion

This chapter showed that elite performance sport and mass participation sport are interrelated economically, both on the individual level and on the organisational level. On the individual level, the trickle-down effect describes that people are inspired to participate in sport themselves by the sporting success of elite performance athletes, the personality of elite performance athletes (role models) and the hosting of major elite sport events. Thus, elite performance sport affects mass participation sports, and this relationship is economically relevant because of increased sport-related expenditure, health benefits and the formation of social capital. On the organisational level, members practising mass participation sport finance elite performance athletes within non-profit sport clubs. On the other hand, clubs promoting elite performance sport have opportunities to generate more diverse revenues which in turn positively affect the club's financial stability. Thus, the promotion of elite performance sport is not only a financial challenge for clubs, also an opportunity.

References

Adler, M. (1985). Stardom and talent. *The American Economic Review*, 75 (1): 208–212.

Aghion, P. and Bolton, P. (1997). A theory of trickle-down growth and development. *Review of Economic Studies*, 64: 151–172.

Biskup, C. and Pfister, G. (1999). I would like to be like her/him. Are athletes role-models for boys and girls? *European Physical Education Review*, 5 (3): 199–218.

Brandes, L., Franck, E. and Nüesch, S. (2008). Local heroes and superstars. An empirical analysis of star attraction in German soccer. *Journal of Sports Economics*, 9(3): 266–286.

Breuer, C. and Feiler, P. (2013a). Finanzielle Situation und ökonomische Bedeutung des Vereinssports. In C. Breuer (ed.) *Sportentwicklungsbericht 2011/2012. Analyse zur Situation der Sportvereine in Deutschland*. Cologne: Sportverlag Strauß. pp. 48–71.

Breuer, C. and Feiler, P. (2013b). Spor*t Development Report 2011/2012. Analysis of the situation of Sports Clubs in Germany*. Abbreviated version. Cologne: Sportverlag Strauß.

Breuer, C. and Wicker, P. (2009a). Leistungs- und Hochleistungssport im Sportverein. In C. Breuer (ed.), *Sportentwicklungsbericht 2007/2008. Analyse zur Situation der Sportvereine in Deutschland*. Cologne: Sportverlag Strauß. pp. 108–131.

Breuer, C. and Wicker, P. (2009b). Sports clubs in Germany. In c. Breuer (ed.), *Sport Development Report 2007/2008. Analysis of the Sports Clubs' Situation in Germany*. Abbreviated Version. Cologne: Sportverlag Strauß. pp. 5–50.

Breuer, C. and Wicker, P. (2011). *Sports Development Report 2009/2010. Analysis of the Situation of Sports Clubs in Germany*. Abbreviated Version. Cologne: Sportverlag Strauß.

Buchanan, J.M. (1965). An economic theory of clubs. *Economica*, 32 (125): 1–14.

Carroll, D.A. and Stater, K.J. (2008). Revenue diversification in nonprofit organizations. Does it lead to financial stability? *Journal of Public Administration Research and Theory*, 19: 947–966.

Chalip, L. (2006). Towards social leverage of sport events. *Journal of Sport and Tourism*, 11 (2): 109–127.

De Bosscher, V., Sotiriadou, P. and van Bottenburg, M. (2013). Scrutinizing the sport pyramid metaphor. An examination of the relationship between elite success and mass participation in Flanders. *International Journal of Sport Policy and Politics*, 5 (3): 319–339.

Downward, P. and Rasciute, S. (2010). The relative demands for sports and leisure in England. *European Sport Management Quarterly*, 10 (2): 189–214.

Downward, P., Dawson, A. and Dejonghe, T. (2009). *Sport Economics. Theory, Evidence and Policy*. Oxford: Butterworth-Heinemann.

Eady, J. (1993). *Practical Sports Development*. London: Pitman.

Feddersen, A., Jacobsen, S. and Maennig, W. (2009). Sports heroes and mass sports partici- pation – the (double) paradox of the 'German Tennis Boom' [online]. Available from: www.hced.uni-hamburg.de/WorkingPapers/HCED-029.pdf (accessed 22 October 2012).

Frawley, S. and Cush, A. (2011). Major sport events and participation legacy: the case of the 2003 Rugby World Cup. *Managing Leisure*, 16: 65–76.

Fukuyama, F. (1995). *Trust: The Social Virtues and the Creation of Prosperity*. New York: The Free Press.

Hanstad, D. and Skille, E. (2010). Does elite sport develop mass sport? *Scandinavian Sport Studies Forum*, 1: 51–68.

Humphreys, B.R., McLeod, L. and Ruseski, J.E. (2014). Physical activity and health out- comes. Evidence from Canada. *Health Economics*, 23 (1): 33–54.

Katzmarzyk, P.T., Gledhill, N. and Shepard, R.J. (2000). The economic burden of physical inactivity in Canada. *Canadian Medical Association Journal*, 163 (11): 1435–1440.

Kearns, K. (2007). 'Income portfolios'. In Young, D.R. (ed.) *Financing Nonprofits*. Plymouth: AltaMira Press. pp. 291–314.

Kingma, B.R. (1993). Portfolio theory and nonprofit financial stability. *Nonprofit and Voluntary Sector Quarterly*, 22 (2): 105–119.

Kuethe, T.H. and Motamed, M. (2010). Returns to stardom. Evidence from U.S. Major League Soccer. *Journal of Sports Economics*, 11 (5): 567–579.

Lucifora, C. and Simmons, R. (2003). Superstar effects in sport. Evidence from Italian soccer. *Journal of Sports Economics*, 4: 35–55.

Mutter, F. and Pawlowski, T. (2013). Role models in sports. Can success in professional sports increase the demand for amateur sport participation? *Sport Management Review* (in press). DOI:10.1016/j.smr.2013.07.003.

Mutter, F. and Pawlowski, T. (2014). The monetary value of the demonstration effect of professional sports. *European Sport Management Quarterly*, 14 (2): 129–152.

Nagel, S. (2008). Goals of sports clubs. *European Journal for Sport and Society*, 5: 121–141.

Pawlowski, T. and Breuer, C. (2011). The demand for sports and recreational services. Empirical evidence from Germany. *European Sport Management Quarterly*, 11 (1): 5–34.

Picot, A., Dietl, H., Franck, E., Fiedler, M. and Royer, S. (2012). *Organisation. Theorie und Praxis aus ökonomischer Sicht*. 6th edn. Stuttgart: Schäffer Poeschel.

Preuss, H. and Werkmann, K. (2011). Erlebniswert Olympischer Winterspiele in München 2018. *Sport und Gesellschaft*, 8 (2): 97–123.

Putnam, R.D. (1993). *Making Democracy Work. Civic Traditions in Modern Italy*. Princeton, NJ: Princeton University Press.

Rosen, S. (1981). The economics of superstars. *The American Economic Review*, 71: 845–858

Sander, B. and Bergemann, R. (2003). Economic burden of obesity and its complications in Germany. *European Journal of Health and Economics*, 4 (4): 248–253.

Sandler, T. and Tschirhart, J. (1997). Club theory. Thirty years later. *Public Choice*, 93: 335–355.

Sotiriadou, K., Shilbury, D. and Quick, S. (2008). The attraction, retention/transition, and nurturing process of sport development. Some Australian evidence. *Journal of Sport Management*, 22: 247–272.

SportsEcon Austria (2012). Study on the contribution of sport to economic growth and employment in the EU [online]. Available from: http://ec.europa.eu/sport/library/ studies/study-contribution-spors-economic-growth-final-rpt.pdf (accessed 26 May 2014).

Stigler, G.J. and Becker, G.S. (1977). De gustibus non est disputandum. *The American Economic Review*, 67 (2): 76–90.

Suessmuth, B., Heyne, M. and Maennig, W. (2010). Induced civic pride and integration. *Oxford Bulletin of Economics and Statistics*, 72 (2): 202–220.

Ulseth, A.-L.B. (2004). Social integration in modern sport: Commercial fitness centres and voluntary sport clubs. *European Sport Management Quarterly*, 4 (2): 95–115.

van Bottenburg, M. (2001). *Global Games*. Urbana and Chicago, IL: University of Illinois Press.

Veal, A.J., Toohey, K. and Frawley, S. (2012). The sport participation legacy of the Sydney 2000 Olympic Games and other international sporting events hosted in Australia. *Journal of Policy Research in Tourism, Leisure and Events*, 4 (2): 155–184.

Warburton, D.E., Nicol, C.W. and Bredin, S.S. (2006). Health benefits of physical activity. The evidence. *Canadian Medical Association Journal*, 174 (6): 801–809.

Weed, M. (2009). The potential of the demonstration effect to grow and sustain participation in sport. Review Paper for Sport England. Canterbury Christ Church University: Centre for Sport, Physical Education and Activity Research (SPEAR).

Weimar, D., Wicker, P. and Prinz, J. (2014). Membership in sport clubs. A dynamic panel analysis of external organizational factors. *Nonprofit and Voluntary Sector Quarterly* (in press). DOI: 10.1177/0899764014548425.

Wicker, P. and Sotiriadou, P. (in press). The trickle-down effect. What population segments benefit from hosting major sport events? *International Journal of Event Management Research*.

Wicker, P., Breuer, C. and Pawlowski, T. (2010). Are sports club members big spenders? Findings from sport specific analyses in Germany. *Sport Management Review*, 13: 214–224.

Wicker, P., Hallmann, K., Breuer, C. and Feiler, S. (2012). The value of Olympic success and the intangible effects of sport events. A contingent valuation approach in Germany. *European Sport Management Quarterly*, 12 (4): 337–355.

Wicker, P., Feiler, S. and Breuer, C. (2013a). Organizational mission and revenue diversification among non-profit sports clubs. *International Journal of Financial Studies*, 1 (4): 119–136.

Wicker, P., Hallmann, K. and Breuer, C. (2013b). Analyzing the impact of sport infrastructure on sport participation using geo-coded data. Evidence from multi-level models. *Sport Management Review*, 16 (1): 54–67.

Wicker, P., Breuer, C., Lamprecht, M. and Fischer, A. (2014). Does club size matter? An examination of economies of scale, economies of scope, and organizational problems. *Journal of Sport Management*, 28 (3): 266–280.

Williamson, O.E. (1979). Transaction cost economics. The governance of contractual relations. *Journal of Law and Economics*, 22: 233–261.

Yancey, A.K. (1998). Self-image building in adolescents in foster care. The use of group process interactions with role models. *Adolescence*, 33: 253–267.

Zak, P.J. and Knack, S. (2001). Trust and growth. *The Economic Journal*, 111: 295–321.

4 The question of the trickle-down effect in Danish sport

Can a relationship between elite sport success and mass participation be identified?

Rasmus K. Storm and Trygve Laub Asserhøj

Introduction

Politicians and sport leaders around the globe often argue that elite sport has a positive effect on mass participation (Grix and Carmichael, 2012; De Bosscher et al., 2013). The idea of the so-called 'demonstration effect' or 'trickle-down effect' (Hogan and Norton, 2000; Green, 2007), seeing international pride gained by medals won in the Olympics or other prestigious sporting events as a major catalyst for mass participation, is widespread (Houlihan et al., 2009; De Bosscher and Bottenburg, 2011). Typically the concept is used strategically to push for large public investments in elite sport facilities or to justify the use of money to attract major international sporting events (Mahtani et al., 2013; Hamer et al., 2014). It is also used as an argument to support elite sport because it is thought that international athletic success motivates children, youth, adults and older people to take part in sport themselves (van Bottenburg, 2002; Vigor et al., 2004; Murphy and Bauman, 2007; Kavetsos and Szymanski, 2009). However, this idea of a trickle-down effect is as equally unclear and vaguely documented as it is widespread (Nicholson et al., 2011; Grix and Carmichael, 2012). It has become an established truth, a dominant idea or discourse. But does the promise of enhanced mass participation from elite sport success warrant a closer examination?

This chapter seeks to shed some light on the matter by asking the questions: What do we know about the alleged relationship between elite sport and mass participation? Is it actually present, and how does it come into effect? The chapter seeks answers by taking on the following analytical progression: first, we give a short overview of the extent to which the idea of the trickle-down effect is diffused internationally in order to illustrate its persistence. Second, we review literature on the subject, showing that existing research remains sceptical about any direct relationship between elite sport's effect on mass participation. Third, we add to existing knowledge by presenting results from a national Danish survey together with an analysis of club membership figures in two popular Danish sports (football and team handball). This leads to the concluding part of the chapter, which sums up our findings and briefly states the implications of our findings for sport policy.

The dissemination and institutionalisation of the trickle-down effect idea

It is not easy to identify how or why the idea of the trickle-down effect has become such a dominant idea, as seems to be the case today. However, according to Donnelly et al. (2011), the idea has emerged in parallel with the evolution of the Olympic Games, which is now the largest modern international sporting event. With enormous prestige attached to hosting the Olympic Games or winning in some of its 300+ medal events, this mega-event is a prime example of where the trickle-down effect has been embraced and, as we argue, misconceived.

In response to the question of why the idea of the trickle-down effect has become so influential, Donnelly et al. (2011) argue that as bidding for and hosting major sporting events – such as the Olympics – has correlated with a massive increase in public investments over the years, the need to establish a rational argument behind bidding for or hosting the events has also risen significantly. In times of neoliberal and new public management dominance in the public sector – at least in Europe and Western countries (Schwartz, 1994; Knudsen, 2007; Sørensen, 2007; Pedersen, 2011) – using public resources on elite sport development or hosting major sports events demands tangible effects in return. These can take form as (positive) economic impacts (Horne and Manzenreiter, 2004; Whitson and Horne, 2006; Tien et al., 2011; Billings and Holladay, 2012), urban regeneration (Davies, 2012), civic pride or happiness (Wicker et al., 2012; Hallmann et al., 2013) or increased rates of mass participation that will benefit the general health of the host nation as a direct result (Grix and Carmichael, 2012).

The Olympic Movement itself has promoted the idea of elite sport's various positive externalities. Donnelly et al. (2011) point out that in the 1990s, the International Olympic Committee (IOC) proposed the existence of a 'double pyramid' of sports participation where the elite athletes rise from a broad participation base. The 'trickle-down' – or 'demonstration' – effect secures the ground from which new elite athletes rise, thus closing the 'virtuous circle of sport' containing mutual stimulation between elite sport and mass participation (Grix and Carmichael, 2012). Seeing this development as a part of a larger legacy concern for the Olympic Movement, Girginov and Hills (2008; 2009) argue that the IOC has worked actively in order to disseminate the idea that the Olympics can help build a stronger mass participation base.

Today many (Western) elite sport development systems and sport policies are, to various degrees, shaped by this idea (Grix and Carmichael, 2012; De Bosscher et al., 2013), and this does not only apply to Olympic bidders, but also to nations that are dedicated to developing elite sport in general. For example, Australian (Stewart et al., 2004; Hogan and Norton, 2000; Green and Houlihan, 2005), Japanese (Yamamoto, 2008), Canadian (Donnelly, 2010),[1] British (Grix and Carmichael, 2012), Danish (Storm, 2011) and New Zealand sport policies (Hindson et al., 1994; Collins, 2011) have over the years adhered to the central claims of the trickle-down idea. So have the politicians who have pledged their support to Olympic bids, including several British politicians during and after the successful London bid for the 2012 Olympics, and Russian President Vladimir Putin in connection to the 2014 Winter Olympics. Putin argued that one of the biggest legacies from the Sochi Winter Olympics was the boost in mass participation among young people. According to the Russian news agency RIA Novosti (2014), he said it was the Russian athletes' performances that inspired them.

Confronting the idea of the trickle-down effect

Various studies, however, show that there is no clear connection between the hosting of sports events, the focus on elite sport or international sporting success and mass participation. Many find that sport-for-all is not stimulated by elite sport in any direct way (Bottenburg *et al.* 2012; De Bosscher *et al.*, 2013). Hogan and Norton (2000), for example, find no positive correlation between elite Australian athletes' successes and developments in mass participation in the 1976–1996 period. In a study covering developments around the Sydney Olympics in Australia, Veal and Frawley (2009) only find evidence of growth in non-Olympic sports.

Other studies suggest that no effect can be found in relation to New Zealand elite sport success either. Based on a survey of 35 New Zealand clubs as well as six federations in the period after the Albertville Winter Olympics and the Summer Olympics in Barcelona, Hindson *et al.* (1994) find that only marginal positive post-Games effects could be detected. Newer data from Sport and Recreation New Zealand (SPARC) reveal that overall physical activity levels have remained relatively unchanged since 2001 (SPARC 2008). In the same period, the international competitiveness of New Zealand's elite athletes has soared significantly.

Examining membership figures in various disciplines, van Bottenburg (2002) also finds little evidence of positive effects of elite success on mass participation in Dutch sports clubs. Parallel findings are noted by Dessein and Janssens (1998) in a Belgian context and De Bosscher *et al.* (2013) confirm that these effects are hard to find in the Flanders region. In a more narrow study concerning German tennis, it is concluded that a trickle-down effect from Boris Becker, Steffi Graf and Michael Stich's unparalleled successes in the late 1980s and early 1990s did not take hold in the German population (Feddersen *et al.* 2009).

Seen from a Norwegian perspective, Hanstad and Skille (2010) show that even though there seem to be effects from international results gained by Norwegian elite athletes, such effects cannot be said to be a direct effect of the elite results themselves (Hanstad and Skille 2010). This finding only gives credence to the study conducted by Coalter (2004), who prior to the British bid for the Olympics argued that no international research has ever proven any causality in the relationship. With regard to sport-for-all in England, he points out that increases in participation have only been in disciplines or recreational activities outside the Olympic sports in which British athletes have excelled (Coalter 2004).

Danish evidence: can a relationship between elite sport success and mass participation be identified?

The research referenced above shows that the idea of the trickle-down effect can be confronted. In order to supplement existing research on the subject, the following sections present an analysis of empirical data from Denmark in order to see whether any relationship can be identified in the Danish context which opposes or aligns with international findings. Data used to query this relationship are taken from a recent study on general trends in Danish sports participation (Laub and Pilgaard 2013).[2]

As we focus on data from questionnaires in which the respondents express what they believe has motivated them to participate in sport, it is possible to analyse where trickle-down effects from elite sport to mass participation might present themselves. Supplemented by an analysis of Danish club membership figures, the analysis below aims to test whether sporting success is followed by an increase in memberships in sports in which the respondents say they are inspired by elite athletes.

Elite-inspired Danish sports participants

Figure 4.1 shows the proportion of males and females within the different age groups who answered 'mostly agree' to whether sport stars in the media influenced their own choice of sporting activity.[3] In general, around one in four children (aged 7–15) and one in ten adults (16 years and above) responded that sports stars in the media had affected their choice.

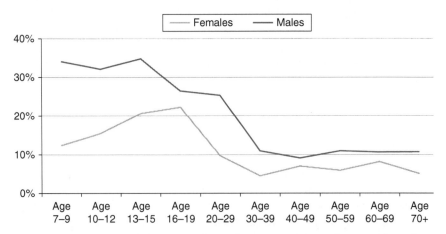

Figure 4.1 Proportion of elite-inspired Danish sports participants by age and gender.

Boys and men appear to be more inspired than girls and women by their sporting heroes, but there seems to be a negative effect on older participants among both genders.

The relationship between gender, age and elite sport inspiration is tested further through a binary regression analysis.[4] The results are shown in Table 4.1 and 4.2, representing children and adults respectively.

The results reveal that additional explanatory variables – besides age – are found to be statistically significant: gender (among children), sport media consumption, occupation (among adults) and number of children in household (among adults).

Overall, the findings suggest that if an effect of elite sports on mass participation exists in the Danish context, it is most likely to be found among boys and young men up to the age of 29 and among girls and women aged between 13 and 19. Boys and young men seem to be the main groups that tend to be affected by sports stars in the media, especially when they are consumers of sport in the media. From a broader perspective, however, only marginal inspirational effects are found. This points to the question of whether elite sport success makes a difference with regard to Danish club membership figures at all. Does the inspiration indicated by the Danish survey respondents actually materialise? In the following section we aim to answer this question.

Table 4.1 Test results, binary logistic regression – children (age: <15)

Gender: boys (1) vs girls (2)	−0.524*** (0.125)
Age: number of years, from 7 to 15	−0.069** (0.025)
Sport media consumption/week: from none (1) to 5+ hours (8)	0.437*** (0.036)
Constant	−0.480 (0.3265)
Nagelkerke R^2	0.205
N	1,548

Notes
Dependent variable: not elite-inspired (0) vs elite-inspired (1)
* $p < 0.05$; ** $p < 0.01$; *** $p < 0.001$.

Table 4.2 Test results, binary logistic regression – adults (age: >16)

Age: number of years, from 16		−0.021*** (0.006)
Occupation: reference	Retired	*
	Studying	−0.047 (0.325)
	Unemployed/on leave	0.078 (0.352)
	Employed	−0.414 (0.220)
Number of children in household: from none (0) to three or more (3)		−0.211** (0.070)
Sport media consumption/week: from none (1) to 5+ hours (8)		0.300*** (0.025)
Constant		−1.778*** (0.433)
Nagelkerke R^2		0.132
N		2876

Notes
Dependent variable: not elite-inspired (0) vs. elite-inspired (1)
* $p < 0.05$; ** $p < 0.01$; *** $p < 0.001$.

Developments in Danish membership figures in relation to sporting success

Having already shown that the trickle-down effect primarily seems to apply to a certain group of respondents, we will now narrow the scope of the analysis in order to identify the specific sporting activities the elite-inspired sporting respondents participate in. This approach entitles us to test the trickle-down effect in practice for the segments of the population to which elite inspiration seems to apply.

Unfortunately the question of which particular sports elite-inspired respondents have taken up due to inspiration falls outside the scope of the Danish survey, as it only focuses on whether 'sports stars in the media have contributed to the respondent's choice of *a* sporting activity'. The specific discipline chosen remains unspecified in the survey responses. However, by comparing elite-inspired respondents in the relevant gender and age groups with 'not elite-inspired' respondents,[5] we can get an idea of the types of sports the elite-inspired people choose to participate in.

Table 4.3 displays participation figures within five sports. The columns labelled 'Total' account for all active Danish individuals in the gender and age groups indicated. Among the active men and women in these age groups, 12 per cent of the not elite-inspired respondents (in the first 'Total' column) play handball, while 27 per cent do among the elite-inspired respondents (second 'Total' column). The adjacent columns show the participation numbers among not elite-inspired and elite-inspired respondents respectively (in per cent) within the specific gender and age groups.

The five sports are presented in descending order based on their 'elite-inspiration factor'. For instance, 12 per cent of not elite-inspired respondents and 27 per cent of elite-inspired respondents play handball, making the elite-inspiration factor (27/12) 2.22.[6] As the elite-inspired respondents (both males and females) are over-represented among people playing the sports listed, it is reasonable to assume that if inspiration is to materialise in reality, it will most likely be the case within these five specific sports and the previously specified gender and age groups (females 13–19 years and males 7–29 years).

Table 4.3 Top five sports preferred by elite-inspired respondents (Proportion active in the sport (%))

	Not elite-inspired respondents			Elite-inspired respondents		
	Total	Females (13–19 years)	Males (7–29 years)	Total	Females (13–19 years)	Males (7–29 years)
Team handball	12	14	11	27	34	25
Golf	3	2	4	7	3	8
Table tennis	7	3	9	14	2	16
Football	40	22	47	73	43	79
Basketball	5	5	6	9	7	9

Put differently, the Danish data suggest that the elite-inspired respondents are especially active in one of the five sports listed above. This points to a greater probability of identifying developments in 'real membership figures' related to elite sport success in these sports than in sports with a lower elite-inspiration factor. In the following section we will test this hypothesis.

Trickle-down effects in Danish football and team handball

Two separate case studies of the sports with high inspiration factors – focusing on the inspired gender and age groups – are thus conducted: one on Danish football and one on Danish team handball.

Football is chosen as it is the national sport in Denmark, with more than 340,000 club members under the umbrella of the Sports Confederation of Denmark (DIF) (2013 numbers).[7] The Danish (male) national team is also very popular. Football holds the position as the number-one broadcast sport on Danish television, with daily news reports and several live club matches shown throughout the week (Hedal, 2006).

Team handball is chosen as it is the number-two Danish national sport and places fifth in regard to club members, having reached 110,000 members in 2013 (DIF). With the Danish national male and female teams enjoying international success, handball has become a highly exposed sport in the Danish media and it attracts a significant amount of interest among the Danish population (Storm and Almlund, 2006).

First, we look at the overall development in membership figures in relation to international sporting success. Second, we conduct a club-level analysis to see whether elite sport success influences the number of members in clubs, both in overall terms and within the age and gender groups mentioned above.

International trickle-down analysis

Inspired by De Bosscher *et al.* (2013), we use Pearson's correlations in order to analyse the relationship between international elite sport success – measured by an Elite Sporting Index (ESI)[8] – and Danish membership figures. Membership figures are measured in three categories: (1) membership figures as a percentage of all Danish citizens (PercCit); (2) absolute membership figures (Abs); and (3) growth/fall in PercCit measured in percentage points (PercCitGF).

Assuming that a trickle-down effect from international elite sport success does not necessarily materialise immediately, we have calculated correlation coefficients for the same year (T), as well as for $T + 1$ to $T + 3$ and $T + 5$. In football, only the Danish national male team's ESI and male membership figures are analysed, as women's football receives almost no media attention at all. With regard to team handball, both combined and separate male and female calculations are done.

Table 4.4 Danish football membership figures and ESI 1988–2010 (males only)

	Correlation coefficients between success (ESI) in year T and membership figures in T, T + 1 to T + 3 and T + 5		
	PercCit	Abs	PercCitGF
T	0.370192824	***−0.567624770	0.112642530
T + 1	0.291473427	***−0.590452815	−0.169583605
T + 2	0.244571693	**−0.422760090	−0.006390336
T + 3	0.156364912	**−0.420890697	−0.021730256
T + 5	0.208097579	−0.257301681	0.103728080

Note
* $p < 0.10$; ** $p < 0.05$; *** $p < 0.01$.

Table 4.5 Danish team handball membership figures and ESI 1988–2010

	Correlation coefficients between success (ESI) in year T and membership figures in T, T + 1 to T + 3 and T + 5		
	PercCit	Abs	PercCitGF
T	***−0.555033739	***−0.494895653	0.126579096
T + 1	**−0.371718831	−0.252243088	0.205852503
T + 2	−0.234544689	−0.064146101	0.015476435
T + 3	−0.178544684	0.005886899	*−0.357165857
T + 5	−0.18882144	−0.003276615	0.122748566

Note
* $p < 0.10$; ** $p < 0.05$; *** $p < 0.01$.

The results are presented in Tables 4.4 and 4.5. These show that developments in football membership figures do not seem to follow from international sporting success. In fact, the only significant correlations are negative.

The same goes for team handball. Table 4.5 displays a correlation coefficient calculation among male and female ESIs and total membership figures (both male and female) combined. Looking at each gender separately, the same results can be found: the only significant correlations are negative.

Club-level analysis

In the club–level analysis we deploy regression analyses in order to see whether individual club success in the best Danish leagues is associated with increase in club membership figures in the period 1993–2010.

The dependent variable (membership figures) is measured in (1) absolute numbers and (2) as a percentage growth/fall in absolute numbers (relative growth). We operate with two independent variables: (1) sporting success (where the champion of the league is awarded 1 point, number two is awarded 2 points and so on),[9] and (2) inhabitants of the respective municipality in which the club has its home ground.

Two separate models are deployed: a standard OLS regression model and a panel data regression model. We add the panel model regression to the OLS regression in order to test whether the clubs have specific characteristics which are not part of the available data. The results show that the OLS and panel models reveal very similar results. However, in some cases we find differences that need to be reported. Therefore the standard OLS regression, as well as the panel model, is displayed in the below figures.[10]

Football

The relative membership growth results for football, as shown in Table 4.6, indicate a positive but insignificant effect of sporting success on membership.

Focusing on the elite-inspired group identified above, the test results are revealed in Table 4.7.

As can be seen above, both models reveal effects on membership figures from elite sport success. They are, however, marginal. An advancement of one place in the league ranking is – according to the OLS-model – followed by six (6.2) additional club members. In the RE model the effect from elite sport success is around two members (1.8) per ranking advancement.

Table 4.6 Regression test results, relative growth, males, all age groups

	OLS	Random effects
Sporting success	−0.087	−0.087
	(−0.81)	(−0.81)
Municipal inhabitants	0.0006	0.0006
	(1.28)	(0.32)
Panel data	No	Yes
N	172	172
R^2	0.005	0.003
Pseudo log-likelihood	–	–

Notes
★ $p < 0.10$; ★★ $p < 0.05$; ★★★ $p < 0.01$, *t*-values in brackets.

Table 4.7 Regression test results, relative growth, males, for elite-inspired soccer players (males aged: <24)

	OLS	Random Effects
Sporting success	−6.21	−2.82
	★★(−2.59)	★(−1.78)
Municipal inhabitants	4.048	1.615
	(0.10)	(1.12)
Panel data	No	Yes
Obs.	192	192
R^2	0.036	0.035

Notes
★ $p < 0.10$; ★★ $p < 0.05$; ★★★ $p < 0.01$

Table 4.8 Regression test results, absolute growth, males, all

	OLS	Random effects
Sporting success	−5.95	−2.53
	★★(−2.14)	(−1.34)
Municipal inhabitants	0.0	0.0
	(−7.89)	(−0.9)
Panel data	No	Yes
N	192	192
R^2	0.0997	0.005

Notes
★ $p < 0.10$; ★★ $p < 0.05$; ★★★ $p < 0.01$, t-values in brackets.

Table 4.9 Regression test results, development in absolute membership figures for elite-inspired soccer players (males age <24)

	OLS	Random effects
Sporting success	−5.982	−2.581
	★★★(−2.72)	(−1.27)
Municipal inhabitants	−0.0001	0.006
	(−0.13)	(1.00)
Panel data	No	Yes
N	192	192
R^2	0.0324	0.005

Notes
★ $p < 0.10$; ★★ $p < 0.05$; ★★★ $p < 0.01$, t-values in brackets.

With regard to developments in absolute numbers, the test results shown below only reveal a significant and positive effect from sporting success in the OLS model. As was the case above, the effect is also marginal here. An advancement of one place in the league ranking is – according to the model – followed by six (5.95) additional club members.

Switching our focus to the elite-inspired group, the test results are almost identical, as shown in Table 4.9.[11]

Team handball

For team handball, the regressions are calculated separately for each gender. The test results are displayed in Tables 4.10 and 4.11, showing relative and absolute growth, respectively.

As the figures indicate, the only significant variable affecting membership numbers is the municipal inhabitants.

The regression analysis of absolute membership figures reveals one significant relationship with regard to sporting success (males, OLS model), which can be seen in Table 4.12. However, the variable *municipal inhabitants* comes out as significant for males (OLS model) as well as for females (OLS and RE model). The estimated coefficients are, however, small.

Table 4.10 Regression test results, relative growth for elite-inspired males, team handball (relative growth)

Males	OLS	Random effects
Sporting success	−0.0002	−0.0002
	(−0.06)	(−0.08)
Municipal inhabitants	−0.0084	−0.0084
	★★★(−6.09)	★★★(−5.91)
Panel data	No	Yes
N	261	261
R²	0.0623	0.0623

Notes
★ $p < 0.10$; ★★ $p < 0.05$; ★★★ $p < 0.01$, t-values in brackets.

Table 4.11 Regression test results, relative growth for elite-inspired females, team handball (absolute growth)

Females	OLS	Random effects
Sporting success	0.0021	0.0022
	(1.25)	(1.36)
Municipal inhabitants	−0.0093	−0.0094
	★★★(−4.67)	★★★(−4.54)
Panel data	No	Yes
N	212	212
R²	0.1738	0.1738

Notes
★ $p < 0.10$; ★★ $p < 0.05$; ★★★ $p < 0.01$, t-values in brackets.

Table 4.12 Regression test results, relative growth for elite-inspired males and females, team handball

	Males		Females	
	OLS	Random effects	OLS	Random effects
Sporting success	−1.8721	0.2219	−2.2195	1.8477
	★(−1.66)	(0.23)	(−2.14)	(1.37)
Municipal inhabitants	0.0009	0.0004	0.0004	0.007
	★★★(4.36)	(1.22)	★★(2.16)	★★(2.29)
N	300	300	255	255
R²	0.0961	0.0831	0.047	0.0105

Notes
★ $p < 0.10$; ★★ $p < 0.05$; ★★★ $p < 0.01$, t-values in brackets.

No significant effects from sporting success can be found when the membership figures are separated according to the above identified elite-inspired groups (Table 4.13).

In contrast, absolute membership numbers reveal effects which can be seen in Table 4.14.

Table 4.13 Regression test results, development in relative membership figures for elite-inspired team handball players

	Males (0–24 years)		Females (0–18 years)	
	OLS	Random effects	OLS	Random effects
Sporting success	−0.0024	−0.0029	0.0021	0.0023
	(−0.80)	(−1.23)	(0.82)	(0.87)
Municipal	−0.0014	−0.0014	-0.0081	−0.0082
inhabitants	(−0.13)	(−0.25)	★★(−2.42)	★★(−2.29)
Panel data	No	Yes	No	Yes
N	252	252	212	212
R²	0.0049	0.0049	0.0271	0.027

Notes
★ $p < 0.10$; ★★ $p < 0.05$; ★★★ $p < 0.01$, *t*-values in brackets.

Table 4.14 Regression test results, development in absolute membership figures for elite-inspired team handball players

	Males (0–24 years)		Females (0–18 years)	
	OLS	Random effects	OLS	Random effects
Sporting success	−3.3740	0.1282	−1.6844	1.1514
	★(−1.85)	(0.17)	★★(−2.37)	★(1.72)
Municipal	0.0079	0.0039	0.0009	0.0032
inhabitants	★★★(4.87)	★★(2.47)	(1.35)	★★(2.50)
N	300	300	255	255
R²	0.1208	0.1011	0.0278	0.0032

Notes
★ $p < 0.10$; ★★ $p < 0.05$; ★★★ $p < 0.01$, *t*-values in brackets.

Two things should be noted, however. First, depending on the model used, the estimated coefficients switch their respective pre-sign. Somehow, the club-specific characteristics seem to change when the random effects model is used.

Second, the estimated coefficients are small. For example, advancing one place in club rankings appears to lead to three (3.4) additional male members and two (2.3) additional female members according to the respective OLS models. As mentioned above, this is a very marginal effect.

Conclusions and policy implications

This chapter has aimed to answer the question of whether a relationship between elite sport and mass participation is identifiable in Danish sport. Based on a brief review of existing research on the subject, the above analysis reveals that trickle-down effects are not generally obvious. The effects are either absent or marginal among groups that, according to their own assessments, are more likely than other Danish citizens to be inspired by elite sport stars. These findings correspond with the existing literature and studies conducted in other countries.

These results have clear implications for national sport policy. The double pyramid of sport participation is not a reliable policy platform from which politicians can develop initiatives to improve physical activity levels among their average citizens. Rather than believing in a tangible trickle-down effect from elite sport to mass participation, there should be more attention paid to other factors that encourage people to engage in physical activity. This can only come about if politicians in central positions take note of existing research on the subject and avoid developing policies based on clichéd assumptions which favour the promotion of mega-events or elite sport as tools for improving mass participation levels.

Breaking down the persistence of the trickle-down effect idea might give way to a new understanding of how elite sport and mass participation are related. Bringing this knowledge forward in political debate could also help politicians and bureaucrats form appropriate sports policies in accordance with the evidence revealed. By doing this, the likelihood of returning measurable effects from national sport policy plans will increase.

Hopefully this chapter will contribute to the development of better public policies with regard to the development of mass participation and future sport policy formulation, but only time can tell whether the myth of the trickle-down effect will keep prevailing.

Notes

1 It should be noted, though, that recent developments in Canada seem to have tipped the balance more towards sport-for-all. However, it is still being debated whether this tipping of the balance is only on the rhetorical level, considering the funding balance is still in favour of elite sport (Green, 2007).

2 The data consist of 2,000 children and 4,000 adult respondents and are statistically representative of the Danish population. Being an ongoing survey on long-term trends in Danish mass sport participation, the survey is not specifically designed to indicate whether trickle-down effects are at play among Danish citizens. However, relevant questions on the subject were included in the latest survey (Laub and Pilgaard, 2013).

3 The figure presents answers to the question: 'To which extent do you agree/disagree with the following statement: *Inspiration from sports stars in the media has contributed to my choice of a specific sporting activity!*' answered by marking the categories: 'Mostly agree', 'Mostly disagree' or 'Don't know'.

4 The figure displays the proportion of males and females within the different age groups that answered 'mostly agree' to sport stars in the media having contributed to their own choice of sports.

5 Only 'not elite-inspired' respondents who are active in sports have been included in the analysis so as not to overestimate differences between this group and the elite-inspired respondents in terms of choice of activity.

6 As numerous decimal places are included in the equation, the result is 2.22 and not 2.25, which is otherwise the result of 27 divided by 12.

7 Club sports in Denmark are organised mainly under two umbrella organisations, DIF and DGI. As DIF's role is to facilitate elite competitive sport, the analysis is narrowed down to club members organised under the umbrella of DIF.

8 ESI is defined by a top seven-point scale in the years Denmark has participated in international championships (World Cups and European Championships) in the period

1988–2010 (first place is awarded seven points, second place is awarded 6 points and seventh place is awarded 1 point).

9 Please note that by creating an inverse relationship between sporting success and membership figures, a positive development will appear with a negative pre-sign in the estimated coefficients.

10 Based on the Hausmann test, it is revealed that the random effects model in general should be used for our data instead of a fixed effects model.

11 It has not been possible to split membership data in the exact same categories as identified in the analysis of the national Danish survey data, but the division displayed in the below analysis comes close.

References

Billings S.B. and Holladay, J.S. (2012). Should cities go for the gold? The long-term impacts of hosting the Olympics. *Economic Inquiry*, 50 (3): 754–772.

Bottenburg, M., Brinkhof, S., Elling, A. and Hover, P. (2012). *The Societal Meaning of Elite Sport: A Summary Report*, Utrecht: Utrecht University School of Governance.

Coalter, F. (2004). Stuck in the blocks? A sustainable sporting legacy? In A. Vigor and M. Mean (eds), *In After the Gold Rush: A Sustainable Olympics for London*. London: The London Olympics Institute for Public Policy Research/DEMOS, pp. 93–108.

Collins, S. (2011). Sports development and adult participation in New Zealand. In B. Houlihan and M. Green (eds), *Routledge Handbook of Sport Development*. Abingdon: Routledge, pp. 231–242.

Davies, L.E. (2012). Beyond the Games: regeneration legacies and London 2012. *Leisure Studies*, 31 (3) 309–337.

De Bosscher, V. and Bottenburg, M. (2011). Elite for all, all for elite? An assessment of the impact of sports development on elite sport success. In B. Houlihan and M. Green (eds), *Routledge Handbook of Sport Development*. Abingdon: Routledge, pp. 579–598.

De Bosscher, V., Sotiriadou, P. and van Bottenburg, M. (2013). Scrutinizing the sport pyramid metaphor. An examination of the relationship between elite success and mass participation in Flanders. *International Journal of Sport Policy and Politics*, 5 (3): 319–339.

Dessein, B. and Janssens, I. (1998). *Eeen Atlanta-effect? Én Onderzoek naar de afstraling van topsportsucces op brede sportbeoefening*, Leuven: Katholieke Universiteit Leuven.

Donnelly, P. (2010). Own the podium or rent it? Canada's involvement in the global sporting arms race. *Policy Options*, December 2009–January 2010: 41–44.

Donnelly, P., Kidd, B., Houlihan, B., MacNiel, M., Harvey, J., and Toohey, K. (2011) Inspiration is not enough. Why sports mega-events always promise but rarely achieve a legacy of increased participation in sport (a class analysis). Mega-events – voices from around the world, Play the Game 2011, Cologne, Germany. www.playthegame.org/fileadmin/image/PTG2011/Presentation/Donnelly_Peter_Mega-events.pdf

Feddersen, V., Jacobsen, S. and Maening, W. (2009). Sport heroes and mass sports participation. The (double) paradox of the 'German tennis boom'. *Hamburg Contemporary Economic Discussions*, 29: 1–24.

Girginov, V. and Hills, L. (2008). A sustainable sports legacy. Creating a link between the London Olympics and sports participation. *International Journal of the History of Sport*, 25 (14): 2091–2116.

Girginov, V. and Hills, L. (2009). The political process of constructing a sustainable London Olympics sports development legacy. *International Journal of Sport Policy*, 1 (2): 161–181.

Green, M. (2007). Olympic glory or grass-roots development? Sport policy priorities in Australia, Canada and the United Kingdom, 1960–2006. *International Journal of the History of Sport*, 24 (7): 921–953.

Green, M. and Houlihan, B. (2005). *Elite Sport Development: Policy Learning and Political Priorities*, Abingdon: Routledge.

Grix, J. and Carmichael, F. (2012). Why do governments invest in elite sport? A polemic. *International Journal of Sport Policy and Politics*, 4 (1): 73–90.

Hallmann, K., Breuer, C., and Kühnreich, B. (2013). Happiness, pride and elite sporting success. What population segments gain most from national athletic achievements? *Sport Management Review*, 16 (2): 226–235.

Hamer, M., Weiler, R. and Stamatakis, E. (2014). Watching sport on television, physical activity and risk of obesity in older adults. *BMC Public Health*, 14 (10): 1–4.

Hanstad, D.V. and Skille, E. (2010). Does elite sport develop mass sport? A Norwegian case study. *Scandinavian Sport Studies Forum*, 1: 51–68.

Hedal, M. (2006). *Sport på Dansk Tv: En Analyse af samspillet mellem sport og dansk tv 1993 – 2005 [Sport on Danish Television: An Analysis of Sport on Danish Tv 1993–2005]*, København: Idrættens Analyseinstitut.

Hindson, A., Gidlow, B. and Peebles, C. (1994). The trickledown effect of top-level sport. Myth or reality? A case study of the Olympics. *Australian Leisure and Recreation*, 4 (1): 16–24.

Hogan, K. and Norton, K. (2000). The 'price' of Olympic gold. *Journal of Science and Medicine in Sport*, 3 (2): 203–218.

Horne, J. and Manzenreiter, W. (2004). Accounting for mega-events. *International Review for the Sociology of Sport*, 39 (2): 187–203.

Houlihan, B., Bloyce, D. and Smith, A. (2009). Developing the research agenda in sport policy. *International Journal of Sport Policy and Politics*, 1 (1): 1–12.

Kavetsos, G. and Szymanski, S. (2009). From the Olympics to the grass-roots. What will London 2012 mean for sport funding and participation in Britain? *Public Policy Research*, 16 (3), 192–196.

Knudsen, T. (2007). *Fra folkestyre til markedsdemokrati: Dansk demokratihistorie efter 1973 [From Public Participation to Market Let Democrazy: Danish Democrazy beyond 1973]*, 1st edn. Copenhagen: Akademisk Forlag.

Laub, T.B. and Pilgaard, M. (2013). *Sports Participation in Denmark 2011*, Copenhagen: Danish Institute for Sports Studies.

Mahtani, K.R., Protheroe, J., Slight, S.P., Demarzo, M.M.P.D., Blakeman, T., Barton, C.A., Brijnath, B. and Roberts, N. (2013). Can the London 2012 Olympics 'inspire a generation' to do more physical or sporting activities? An overview of systematic reviews. *BMJ Open*, 2013 (3): 1–8.

Murphy, N.M. and Bauman, A. (2007). Mass sporting and physical activity events: are they 'bread and circuses' or public health interventions to increase population levels of physical activity. *Journal of Physical Activity and Health*, 4: 193–202.

Nicholson, M., Hoye, R. and Houlihan, B. (2011) Conclusion. In M. Nicholson, R. Hoye and B. Houlihan (eds), *Participation in Sport: International Policy Perspectives*, Abingdon: Routledge, pp. 294–308.

Pedersen, O.K. (2011). *Konkurrencestaten [The Competition State]*, København: Hans Reitzels Forlag.

RIA Novosti (2014). Putin bestows awards upon Sochi Olympic organizers. 24 March. Available at http://en.ria.ru/sochi2014/20140324/188713957/Putin-Bestows-Awards-Upon-Sochi-Olympic-Organizers.html (accessed 14 August 2014).

Schwartz, H. (1994). Small states in big trouble. State reorganization in Australia, Denmark, New Zealand and Sweden in 1980s. *World Politics*, 46: 527–555.

Sørensen, E. (2007). Public administration as metagovernance. G. Gjelstrup and E. Sørensen (eds), *Public Administration in Transition*. Copenhagen: DJØF Publishers, pp. 107–126.

SPARC (2008). *Sport, Recreation and Physical Activity Participation among New Zealand Adults: Key Results of the 2007/08 Active NZ Survey*, Wellington: SPARC.

Stewart, B., Nicholson, M., Smith, A. and Westerbeek, H. (2004). *Australian Sport: Better by Design? The Evolution of Australian Sport Policy*, Abingdon: Routledge.

Storm, R.K. (2011). Skaber elite bredde? En analyse af aktuel forskning [Does Elite Sport Initiate Mass Participation? A Review]. *Idrottsforum.org*, 143: 1–21.

Storm, R.K. and Almlund, U. (2006). *Håndboldøkonomi.dk: Fra forsamlingshus til forretning [Handballeconomy.dk: The Development of Commercial Team Handball in Denmark]*, København: Idrættens Analyseinstitut.

Tien, C., Lo, H.C. and Lin, H.W. (2011). The economic benefits of mega events: a myth or reality. A longitudinal study on the Olympic Games. *Journal of Sport Management*, 25: 11–23.

van Bottenburg, M. (2002) Sport-for-all and elite sport. Do they benefit one another? Available at: www.vanbottenburg.com.

Veal, A.J. and Frawley, S. (2009). *'Sport-for-All' and Major Sporting Events: Trends in Sport Participation and the Sydney 2000 Olympic Games, the 2003 Rugby World Cup and the Melbourne 2006 Commonwealth Games*, Sydney: University of Technology Sydney, Australian Centre for Olympic Studies, School of Leisure, Sport and Tourism, Faculty of Business.

Vigor, A., Mean, M. and Tims, C. (2004). Executive summary. In A. Vigor, M. Mean and C. Tims (eds), *After the Gold Rush: A Sustainable Olympics for London*, London: IPPR, pp. xi–xv.

Whitson, D. and Horne, J. (2006). Underestimated costs and overestimated benefits? Comparing the outcomes of sports mega-events in Canada and Japan. In J. Horne and W. Manzenreiter (eds), *Sports Mega-events: Social Scientific Analysis of a Global Phenomenon*. Oxford: Blackwell Publishing Ltd, pp. 73–89.

Wicker, P., Prinz, J., and von Hanau, T. (2012). Estimating the value of national sporting success. *Sport Management Review*, 15 (2): 200–210.

Yamamoto, Y.-Y.M. (2008). Japan. In B. Houlihan and M. Green (eds), *Comparative Elite Sport Development: Systems, Structures and Public Policy*, Oxford: Elsevier, pp. 54–82.

5 Two Solitudes

Grass-roots sport and high-performance sport in Canada

Peter Donnelly and Bruce Kidd

When Hugh MacLennan wrote his classic Canadian novel, *Two Solitudes* (1945), the title referred to the perceived lack of communication between the English and French cultures in Canada. Today, the *two solitudes* may well refer to the divide in Canada between sport-for-all (often referred to as *grass-roots* sport) and elite sport (usually referred to as *high-performance* sport).

This chapter considers how the sport system in Canada changed, as it did in many countries, from a single system – an integrated *pyramid* where high-performance athletes emerged from a broad base of participation – to become two relatively distinct sport systems. We point to the Montréal (1976) Olympics as a key turning point where the two systems became evident; follow those changes through the development of Canadian sport policy; examine some consequences of the bipartite system; and conclude by suggesting ways in which sports policy makers might re-link the two systems to the benefit of both.

Sport in Canada: before the Montréal Olympics

The notion of a pyramid of participation may have first been proposed by Pierre de Coubertin, although rather than seeing high performance emerge from a base of sport-for-all, he suggested that high performance would 'inspire' sport-for-all:[1]

> So that a hundred may train their bodies, it needs fifty to practice sport. And in order for fifty to practice sport, twenty have to become specialized. In order to have twenty specialized, it means that five must be capable of outstanding peak performances.
> (Coubertin, 2002, cited in Müller and Poyán, 2006)

It would be naïve to suggest that, before 1976 in Canada, an idealised pyramid model of sport existed – a pyramid where a broad base of participation progressively enabled better athletes to emerge, with increasing skill and experience, to a peak formed by national team athletes. The means and opportunity to participate at a high level was always more available to those from middle- and higher-income families, and while competitive sport opportunities were available at both public (state funded) and private schools, many private schools included a wide range of competitive sport participation as a key part of their co-curricular activities.

But before the 1970s there was a relatively seamless transition from playgrounds and high schools to Olympic and professional sport, even in rural areas. There were many opportunities for athletes from lower income families to achieve prominence – through success in playground sports, interschool sports, military sports, sports clubs that were accessible to them, and through sports leagues that were a part of the feeder system for professional sports, particularly ice hockey. One of the questions to be addressed in this chapter concerns what has happened to the public feeder systems. Under the strict amateur rules of sport, which prohibited athletes and coaches from drawing income, there were practical limits to the amount of time an athlete could train and compete and a coach could dream up and attend workouts. As a result, the training requirements and performance standards were relatively low compared to today, and many more working-class and rural/hinterland youth could participate at the highest levels. To be sure, careers were short, some athletes went into debt to fund their opportunity to represent Canada internationally, and some talented individuals dropped out of sport for financial reasons. But in terms of the standards of the day, there were high-quality, inexpensive public opportunities for skill development and experience, and the costs of participation in money and time were much lower than they are today, and as result, there was a much broader basis of participation right up to the highest levels of competition.

The Montréal moment

The emergence of successful international athletes from the Soviet Union, other Eastern European countries and Cuba, in a wide range of sports, became increasingly apparent during the 1960s and into the 1970s as the Cold War began to be fought at international sport competitions. The evident success of the sport development systems in Soviet Bloc countries became widely evident in Canada during a key cultural moment – the 1972 Summit Series, an ice hockey tournament played between Canada and the Soviet Union. The 'Summit Series' is still talked about in Canada, to the extent that those who are old enough to remember can usually tell you where they were when the winning goal was scored. The tournament was planned following a series of World Championship and Olympic losses by Canadian teams. Canadians had always argued that their best players were professionals (in the capitalist cartel, the National Hockey League), and were not permitted to play against the 'shamateurs' of the Soviet Union. Many Canadians argued that 'if Canada's best players could play against the best Soviet players, Canada would always win'.

The first four games were played in Canada followed by four in the Soviet Union; the Canadian team, made up of most of the best professional players (four of the best players were left off the team because they had signed with a cartel that sought to challenge the NHL), were shocked to win only one of the first four games (the Soviet team won two and tied one). Perhaps the Canadian team had underestimated the skill and strength of the Soviet players, and they had to dig deep to tie the series after the third game in the Soviet Union. By the time Canada won the final game, 6–5, with a last-minute goal, it was clear to Canadians that there had been a shift in the world order of ice hockey. The player development and training systems in the Soviet Union were producing some of the best players in the world, and Canadian ice hockey coaches and administrators began to pay attention to the new order.

In many ways, the Summit Series foreshadowed the Montréal Olympics. Teams from the Soviet Bloc took seven out of the first ten places in the medal table in 1976, and the United States finished third, the leading medal winner not from the Soviet Bloc.[2] Canada finished 27th in the medal table, and became the first (and only) Olympic host country not to win a gold medal. While there were many striking achievements at the Montréal Games, perhaps most outstanding was the 14-year-old Romanian gymnast, Nadia Comaneci; she completed a number of very difficult routines and was awarded the first ('perfect') scores of 10.0 ever recorded in the sport. Her achievements, and the large number of medals won by other Soviet Bloc athletes, drew attention to the more scientific and professionalised sport system that had been developed.[3] Doug Gilbert (1976), a sportswriter for the *Montréal Gazette*, described the system as follows:

- Early exposure of children to physical education and a wide range of physical activities;
- A broad base of participants in sport and physical activity;
- Early identification of athletic talent; and
- Intensive and specialized training for those identified.

Note that Gilbert still acknowledged the existence of a pyramid, and the requirement for a healthy, active society and a broad base of participants as necessary to the talent identification system by which young participants were selected for 'intensive specialized training'. But the seeds of two separate sport systems were now evident – the early exposure and broad-based participation of *sport-for-all* and the talent identification and segregated specialised training of *high-performance sport*.

Although there was a great deal of uninformed criticism of the new high-performance sport development system in the media, and from Canadian athletes and sport administrators (e.g. references to children being 'stolen' from their parents to attend the specialised training schools), the success of the system also provoked a great deal of interest in the West. One of the authors of this chapter (BK) became a member of a fact-finding mission to the Soviet Union in 1973 that was conducted under the auspices of a Soviet–Canadian cultural agreement (see Kidd, 1974). Following the Montréal Olympics, similar agreements, tours and exchanges were sent to the German Democratic Republic and Cuba. Many features of the state-led, financed and monitored 'Canadian Sport System' that was established in this period were admiringly modelled on those of the Soviet Union and its allies. After Canadian athletes took the most medals at the 1978 Commonwealth Games in Edmonton, they carried Canadian sports minister Iona Campagnolo – not a multi-medalled fellow athlete or a winning coach or even the *chef de mission* – into the Closing Ceremonies on their shoulders in gratitude for the assistance that the Canadian state had provided. British journalists dubbed Canada the 'GDR of the Commonwealth'.

The first evidence of changes in sport development in Canada, reflecting the Soviet Bloc system, was a growing youth movement in a number of sports (e.g. figure skating, gymnastics, swimming and ice hockey) – earlier and earlier involvement in organised competitions and earlier specialisation in single sports, and single playing positions or events.[4] So rapid was this change that by the early 1980s, commentators such as Hart Cantelon (Queen's University) were beginning to view children's involvement in high-performance sport as 'child labour' and the participants as 'child athletic workers' (Cantelon, 1981). In 1985 Donnelly began to collect data from retired high-performance athletes about the consequences of early 'intensive specialized training'. In total, 45 former athletes were interviewed, and they reported various problems and concerns that they connected to their early intensive involvement and specialisation (Donnelly, 1993).[5] These included:

- *Family concerns* – problems such as sibling rivalry and parental pressure.
- *Social relationships* – missed important occasions and experiences during childhood and adolescence.
- *Coach–athlete relationships* – authoritarian and abusive (emotional, physical, sexual) relationships, especially in male coach–female athlete relationships.
- *Educational concerns* – any academic achievements were earned in spite of the sport and education systems, not because of them.
- *Physical and psychological problems* – injuries, stress, burnout.
- *Drug and dietary problems* – some experiences of performance-enhancing drug use, and some concern about eating disorders.
- *Retirement* – adjustment difficulties, especially when retirement was not voluntary.

Despite popular criticism of the Soviet sport system, in the language of the Cold War, especially critiques of doping and the maltreatment to which athletes were subjected, many in Canadian sport leadership were more nuanced in their views. They admired and sought to adapt what they thought to be the best features of that system to Canadian circumstances. In particular, they recognised that parents were usually honoured that their children had been selected for specialised training, children's educational needs were addressed within the specialised training programmes, and those who progressed to national teams were awarded a Master's of Sport distinction and post-competitive careers in the sport system. Against the backdrop of the inadequacies of the Canadian sport system, they looked wistfully at the way the Soviet system provided a means of upward mobility for its athletes and coaches.

In the early years, the developing Canadian sports system was more open, still associated with the pyramid: any child whose parents had the means to enrol them in an early specialisation sport programme could participate in that programme. But as the principles of talent identification became available in Canada, they enabled the emerging sport development system to become far more efficient in terms of high performance. The first, and most widely cited, paper on early talent identification in Canada was published by Tudor Bompa (1985). Bompa was a former Olympic athlete and coach from Romania who became a professor at York University in Toronto. He is credited with introducing the training principle of *periodisation* from the Soviet Union to Canada and other Western countries, and he also helped to introduce the Soviet principles of early athletic talent identification to Canada.

We are not the first to point out that, in a number of Western countries, early talent identification meant that the resources devoted to high-performance sport, and to winning medals, would not be 'squandered' on a broad base of athletes in the hope that some of them would eventually become successful (e.g. Green and Houlihan, 2005). Instead, those resources (primarily personnel and facilities) could be more efficiently concentrated on fewer individuals who had been identified as being potentially successful. Any evidence of a pyramid ended with the introduction of the new high-performance system. Now there were two systems: a poorly funded grass-roots system; and a relatively well-funded high-performance system that drew young athletes at a very early age from the grass-roots system and exposed them to intensive training and competition, employing the best available resources.

With limited federal budgets available for sport in Canada, the effect of concentrating an increasingly higher proportion of the federal sport budget on high performance has been striking (see Figure 5.1). In 1988, at the Winter Olympics in Calgary and the Summer Olympics in Seoul, Canadian athletes won a total of 15 medals (Canada sends full teams to both Summer and Winter Olympics, so the totals are combined for each Olympiad). At the 2010 Vancouver Winter Olympics and the 2012 London Summer Olympics, Canadian athletes won a total of 44 medals. Over that same period of time, participation in organised sport by Canadians over 15 years of age has decreased from 45 per cent in 1992 to 26 per cent in 2010 (as measured in four iterations of Statistics Canada's General Social Survey, the measure of sport participation in Canada with the largest sample).

We are not arguing that there is a direct or singular causal relationship between an increasing proportion of the federal sport budget being spent on high-performance sport, the consequent medal success (see de Bosscher *et al.*, 2008) and the significant decline in participation. Other factors also need to be taken into account, such as an ageing population, increasing numbers

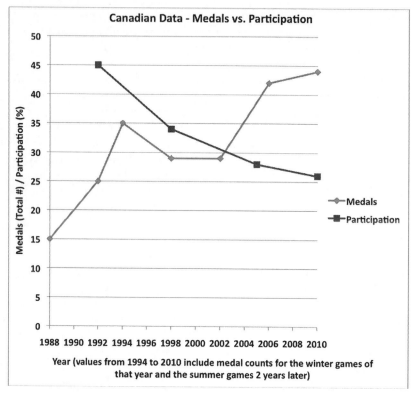

Figure 5.1 Canadian data: medals vs participation.

of immigrants in the population, and the increasing cost and privatisation of participation at a time when a large proportion of the population has seen little real increase in income. It is in fact a world-wide decline. However, it would be a mistake to discount shifting federal priorities, and the structure of Canadian sport policy has enabled this increasing investment in international sport success by decreasing investments in grass-roots participation.

Development of Canadian sport policy[6]

Since 2002, *Canadian Sport Policy* implicitly recognises the *two solitudes* – that the sport system could no longer be characterised as a pyramid – by granting equal status to 'participation' and 'excellence'. This was the culmination of over 40 years of direct federal government involvement in sport since the passage of the 1961 *Fitness and Amateur Sport Act*. However, the *Act* was motivated primarily by the lack of international sport success by Canadians, especially in ice hockey; and to a lesser extent with the fitness of Canadians. In peace time, the fitness of Canadians is a difficult issue in the Canadian confederation, where matters of health, grass-roots sport and recreation are considered to be matters of provincial jurisdiction. It was also recognised that there is far more political gain for the federal government from international success in sport than from mass sport and recreation participation.

Bifurcated federal administrative structures for high-performance sport and broadly based physical activity began to emerge as a result of the 1969 *Report of the Task Force on Sports for Canadians*. As Canada was preparing its bid for the 1976 Montréal Olympics, the *Report* recommended the establishment of a distinct administrative unit for high-performance sport. That recommendation was implemented the following year with the creation of Sport Canada; grass-roots sport, fitness and recreation, which had hitherto commanded 50 per cent of the budget, was reduced to a marketing unit called Sport Participation Canada (soon to be known by its motto, ParticipAction Canada) and a skeletal administrative unit named Recreation Canada. Without a budget to support sport participation, ParticipACTION became an arm's length promotional agency, receiving government support and funding public service announcements about health concerns and the benefits of participation in sport, exercise and recreational physical activity. Recreation Canada was replaced by Fitness Canada in 1979.

The sport system that was developed in Canada was so similar to those in Eastern Europe that, by the late 1980s the US sport historian John MacAloon (1990), began to refer to the Canadian sport system as 'the Big Red Machine' – a play on words that combined the colour of the Canadian flag and team uniforms with a reference to Communism. Development stalled in 1988 with the Ben Johnson doping scandal at the Seoul Olympic Games and the subsequent Dubin Inquiry. However, the government remained committed to high performance, and the system quickly rebounded in the 1990s with Canadian athletes beginning to win an increasing number of Olympic medals (see Figure 5.1).

In the 1990s, Sport Canada became part of the Canadian Heritage Ministry and Fitness Canada became a small part of the Health Programmes and Services Branch of the Ministry of Health (Health Canada). As the major federal agency dealing with sport and physical activity, Sport Canada's mandated focus on high performance came increasingly into question during the 1990s, with increasing concerns about physical inactivity and obesity in Canadian youth. Nation-wide consultations were carried out, leading to the development of the 2002 *Canadian Sport Policy*, and the equal status given to 'participation' and 'excellence' in the *Policy* is a direct result of those consultations. But, as noted, the clear separation of participation and excellence that is necessary in order to assign them equal status represents the final confirmation of the *two solitudes*.

Under the new *Policy*, two things became apparent. First, it became evident that Sport Canada, as a bureaucracy, was not structured in a way that it could easily change to adapt to the new responsibilities for grass-roots participation.[7] Second, the separation of powers in the Constitution Act gave the federal government an excuse to minimise its role in grass-roots sport, deferring responsibility to the provincial governments.

These questions were only partially resolved with the establishment of regular meetings of the federal and provincial/territorial (F/P-T) ministers responsible for sport and physical activity. The ministers developed a *Sport Participation Strategy* for the years 2008–2012 (the last four years of the 2002 *Canadian Sport Policy* – due to be renewed in 2012). While the ministers struggled with the difficult issue of increasing participation, and were able to develop lines of communication at the F/P-T ministerial level, the ministers were not able to prevent a continuing decline in participation rates. In 2012, a renewed *Canadian Sport Policy* was launched, again giving equal emphasis to 'participation' and 'excellence', but not seriously challenging the structures that continued to give overwhelming precedence to 'excellence' (high performance). The *Policy* gives particular prominence to a strategy that is purported to re-establish the pyramid structure of sport, namely Canadian Sport for Life (CS4L). This approach is addressed in the following section.

Some consequences of the emerging bipartite system

Increasing broad-based participation is difficult and expensive. It involves long-term planning (far more than the electoral life of a government) and the results are difficult to measure. And when large sections of corporate culture are devoted to providing and promoting 'labour-saving' and easier means of accomplishing daily tasks, public service announcements about the need for exercise have a more difficult time being heard. And determining who is responsible for providing the time, the space, and the means for people to participate in sport and physical activity is even more complicated: is it the education system? Municipal parks and recreation departments? Departments of public health? Employers? As a consequence, many governments have chosen to join the *global sporting arm's race* (de Bosscher, *et al.*, 2008; Oakley and Green, 2001) and support high-performance sport rather than broad-based participation.

On the one hand, the outcomes of high performance are very easy to measure (medals, championships), and they provide governments with tangible and media-friendly recognition of their support for high performance. Such sporting achievements also provide a perfect analogy for neoliberal capitalism – individual effort will lead to success, but only a few are able to reach the top. On the other hand, using the IOC's 'double pyramid', governments and high-performance sport administrators routinely (and erroneously) claim that the achievements of high-performance athletes will automatically *inspire* increased sport and physical activity among young people in the population. (This 'trickle-down' approach has now been widely discredited since there is so little evidence of increased participation following major Games; however, *inspiration* is still routinely used as a significant justification for public spending on such events (e.g. London 2012 Olympics). The best evidence suggests that it is necessary to invest at least as much effort and resources into increasing participation as it is into preparing high-performance athletes for success (cf. Donnelly, 2012).)

However, the decision to support high performance, often at the expense of broad-based participation in most countries other than those in the northern part of Europe, has some evident consequences for the sport system in those countries. First, national sport organisations (NSOs), the governing bodies of each sport in Canada, and especially those for Olympic and Olympic aspirant sports, have come to see high performance as their prime directive. Their budgets from Sport Canada, the Canadian Olympic Committee, *Own the Podium* (see below) and even their corporate sponsors are contingent on the international results of their athletes. Even the addition of some participation-based funding criteria as a result of the 2002 *Canadian Sport Policy* have had little effect on re-directing some NSO resources toward participation (see note 7). Second, government funding decisions began to focus on fewer and fewer sports; and third, the costs involved mean that athletes are drawn from a smaller proportion of the population. The latter two points are developed below.

Funding fewer sports. The funding efficiencies that became available as a result of the introduction of early talent identification – namely, that high-performance resources could be focused on fewer individuals who had been identified as having the potential for success – began to be replicated with the choice of sports that were to receive funding. When medals become *the* measure of success, funding is disproportionately directed toward individual sports, especially those such as boxing, swimming and track-and-field, where multiple medals are available. With only two gold medals (men's and women's) available in team sports such as basketball and field hockey, they began to receive more limited forms of support and funding. Funds also tend to follow success, and in Canada traditional success in sports such as skating and skiing is also supplemented by funding for newer sports such as snowboarding, where Canadian athletes have also been successful. Given the nature of individual sports, funding also goes to fewer and fewer athletes, with consequent limitations on participation.

Cost of involvement in high performance. In the former Soviet Bloc, and still in countries such as China and Cuba, the selection system for high performance is relatively meritocratic – children from all levels of society may be identified and recruited on the basis of their potential. They are then supported by public funds throughout their sport careers, and often following their competitive careers with jobs in coaching or sport administration. In neo-liberal societies such as Canada, with limited public support for sport in schools and communities, and where funding to support athletes from government, the Canadian Olympic Committee or other sources does not become available until they have reached a relatively high level of competition, parents are expected to assume the costs for travel, equipment, instruction and so on. As a consequence, high performance athletes are drawn from a narrowing segment of the population – mostly the aspiring middle classes who value their children's achievements in sport or other endeavours to the point where they will allocate a significant proportion of family budgets or assume debts in order to fund them. Some older Canadian data show that national team athletes tend to come from higher-income families (Beamish, 1990); more recent data from the UK suggest that a significant proportion of British Olympic team members come from the 7 per cent of the population who attended private school – including 37 per cent of the medalists in London 2012 and over 50 per cent of the medalists in Beijing 2008 (Sutton Trust, 2012).

When a focus on winning medals, funding fewer sports and the cost of involvement are combined, the result is sometimes high levels of funding for sports that have very few participants. The *Crawford Report* (2009) found that more Australian government funds were being spent on archery (an Olympic sport with relatively small numbers of participants in Australia) than cricket (a national team sport, but not an Olympic sport). In Canada, the public–private (although mostly public) funding initiative, unfortunately named *Own the Podium* (OTP), that was formed to support potential medal-winning athletes before the Vancouver 2010 Olympics, also helped to contribute to the focus on funding fewer sports and athletes. According to OTP records, the sports of bobsled, luge and skeleton received almost $3 million over and above their usual levels of pre-Olympic funding in the year leading up to Vancouver. It is difficult to imagine any sports in Canada with fewer participants. In contrast, Basketball Canada, the national sport organisation responsible for all non-professional basketball, has an annual budget from Sport Canada of approximately $3 million.

With a tightly organised high-performance sport system, and a loosely organised grass-roots sport system, with few real connections between the two, even the major high-performance funding agency, *Own the Podium*, admitted following the Sochi 2014 Olympics that there were problems: 'Our athlete pool has flat-lined so we know we need to change our approach in order to increase that pool for the longer term' (cited by Hildebrandt, 2014). It seems inevitable that the athlete pool would flat-line when athletes are being drawn from a relatively small proportion of the population rather than the entire population of a country with a population of only 34 million, and when so much funding is going to sports in which few people participate. Some ways to re-think the Canadian sport system are necessary.

Conclusion: re-building the pyramid?

We conclude by considering some ways by which the two sport systems might re-establish some connections to their mutual benefit. Of the four suggestions that follow, the first – Canadian Sport for Life (CS4L) – is already being implemented, but appears to have some real limitations. The second – participation as a legacy of hosting sports events – has been attempted several times with little success, but still retains a great deal of potential. The third involves honouring and following the *Canadian Sport Policy*, giving equal weight to 'participation' and 'excellence'. The fourth, which is in many ways connected to the third, involves attempting to re-democratise participation opportunities in Canada, re-opening and expanding the public feeder systems between grass-roots and high performance, emphasising opportunities for long-term participation and focusing more on sports that many people play in addition to those with few participants because of cost or geographical and climatic limitations.

Canadian Sport for Life. CS4L (canadiansportforlife.ca) started as an organisation called Long Term Athlete Development (LTAD), and while its intentions have always been pedagogical, its interests appear to have been more associated with early talent identification. Recognising the limitations of such a focus, the organisation changed its name, began to focus on the seven stages of LTAD and, in many ways, has attempted to re-establish the pyramid. CS4L has now been endorsed by Sport Canada, is included in the 2012 *Canadian Sport Policy*, and has developed principles that are being adopted by NSOs, other sport organisations and even schools across Canada. And yet, there is no evidence that participation has increased as a result of the implementation of CS4L. Perhaps this is because it is still a developmental organisation, assuming that most of those involved will progress through the stages of participation, with some reaching the very top. There is no evidence of attempts to advocate a broadly based, accessible system of public opportunities, let alone sustain participation among those with limited skills. If we endorse a right to play, and claim that physical activities (including sports) are a key part of our public health, then we must endorse and help to support and sustain a right to play badly. Until CS4L recognises that some people will only achieve limited 'physical literacy' and still have the right to enjoy movement and be 'active for life', the organisation will not be the answer to re-building the pyramid.

A well-planned legacy of hosting major sports events. Since legacy became a goal of investing the large amounts of money needed to host major sporting events at the start of the twenty-first century, there have been a number of attempts (e.g. Vancouver 2010; London 2012; Glasgow 2014; and Toronto 2015) to establish a legacy of participation. The examples given here have gone beyond the assumption that people will be *inspired* to participate and have attempted to plan for increased participation. The plans at both Vancouver and London foundered as a result of the budgetary and planning imperatives of hosting the Games, and were unable to follow through in any real way to establish a participation legacy. Glasgow attempted to learn from the mistakes of its predecessors, and engaged in advanced planning and investment specifically for increased participation, although it is too early to tell how successful this has been. Toronto's PanAm/Para PanAm Games organising committee talked about a participation legacy, but plans were never really made. For example, the stadium for soccer in Hamilton has been re-fitted from a professional football stadium, and will be returned to the professional team following the Games. The exception is the major swimming complex built on the campus of the University of Toronto, Scarborough, which is jointly owned by the University and the City of Toronto, with a high-performance centre as a major tenant, and has been planned to optimise use for the university community and municipal recreation, as well as high-performance sport. The use agreement has been agreed between all partners, and local citizens are already beginning to use the facility some eight months before the Games begin.

Giving equal weight to 'participation' and 'excellence'. Donnelly and Kidd (2008) designed a plan (probably too late to be implemented) that connected the athletes and facilities of the 2010 Winter Olympics to widespread initiatives to introduce and encourage people to participate in the fundamental activities (skating, skiing/boarding) that underlie most of the Winter Olympic sports. Serious planning for and commitment to grass-roots participation, perhaps even on the same order as planning, organising and preparing athletes for competition in major sporting events, would demonstrate the possibility of linking grass-roots and high performance and give equal weight to 'excellence' and 'participation'.

Sport Canada and the Canadian government could honour their commitment to the equal weight principle of the 2002 and 2012 *Canadian Sport Policies*. The policies, and the principle of equal weight, were a result of widespread consultation and were clearly recognised as a key need by the Canadian sport and physical activity community. Regular meetings between F/P-T ministers responsible for sport and physical activity are an important step, and embracing CS4L suggests that there has been an attempt to re-build the pyramid. But careful monitoring is necessary, and if resources for grass-roots and high performance are not equivalent, and there are no measurable increases in participation, then it will be necessary to seek new ways to increase participation.

Re-democratise participation opportunities in Canada. How is it possible for Canada to move from a situation in which 'the more medals we win, the fewer Canadians participate in sport' (see Figure 5.1) to a situation in which Canadian athletes achieve success, where they are drawn from a wide base of the population and are supported by an active, healthy population where many are able to participate on a regular basis. Rather than look to the past – where there was a higher rate of participation but there were also struggles involved for those with no access to the resources necessary to achieve their full potential – we should look to the future where governments may be concerned with the well-being of the entire population, and where the fetish for medals has been discarded in favour of new markers of international success in sport. Scandinavia provides an important exemplar – NSOs are funded on the understanding that their focus is on both grass-roots and high performance, and they are required to account for the ways in which their funding is spent (cf. Hanstad and Skille, 2010).

Perhaps there is no way to go now but to rebuild and re-connect the high-performance and grass-roots participation systems. It is difficult to imagine a worse situation than that in which Canada currently finds itself. At the high-performance level, despite the investment of many millions of dollars, Canadian athletes have reached a steady state in world rankings: at the last three Winter Olympics, Canadian athletes won 24 medals/fifth in the medal table (Turin), 26 medals/third in the medal table (Vancouver) and 25 medals/third in the medal table (Sochi). Participation has declined, and athletes are being drawn from a smaller and smaller pool of the population.

Gruneau (2015) cites the former head of Hockey Canada saying, 'There will never be another Gordie Howe':

> He didn't mean that we'd never see another [ice hockey] player as skilled or as effective on the ice as Gordie Howe. He meant that the days of young men from working class families in rural Canada going on to success in the National Hockey League are over. If a young male player these days isn't from a family with resources to afford power skating lessons, summer clinics, expensive equipment and a lot of travel for league games and tournaments his chances of making it to the pros are slim.
>
> (Gruneau, 2015)

Gruneau supports his case by pointing to the professionalisation of community sports clubs; deregulation, the cultural economy and the turn to sport as a strategy of community economic development (e.g. sport tourism); the erosion of public funding and the growth of privatisation; and the fact that Canada has become – in a clever word play on the professional sport code – a 'pay for play' society.

By rebuilding the public feeder systems, Canada will achieve a broader base of participation and a much deeper pool from which to draw high-performance athletes. What the British call a 'joined-up' system of sport will also be a win–win situation for sport in Canada.

Notes

1 Both positions – that high performance emerges from a broad base of participation, and that high performance *inspires* that broad base of participation – were adopted in 2000 by the IOC Sport-for-All Commission as 'the double pyramid'.
2 Soviet Union (first), East Germany (second), Poland (sixth), Bulgaria (seventh), Cuba (eighth), Romania (ninth) and Hungary (tenth).
3 Following the re-unification of Germany the release of secret documents revealed that some of the success of athletes could be attributed to a state-sponsored doping programme (*Doping for Gold*, 2008).
4 Youth involvement in high-performance sport in Canada certainly preceded the Montréal Olympics. For example, swimmer Elaine Tanner became a multiple medal winner at the 1966 Commonwealth Games at the age of 15. However, child and youth involvement started to become much more widespread after Montréal.
5 These findings have been confirmed by additional informal interviews in Canada (including some with athletes who had heard or read about Donnelly's research and approached him with their own stories) and other countries that had adopted the early involvement and specialization model, and they have been supplemented by additional research (e.g. Tymowski, 2001a,b) and reports in more popular sources (e.g. Ryan, 1995).
6 Parts of the following are adapted from Donnelly (2013).
7 Two of the initiatives that were introduced were: (1) the allocation of a significant budget, managed through the Social Sciences and Humanities Research Council, to fund research on sport (and physical activity) participation; and (2) the introduction of some

participation-based initiatives to the Sport Funding and Accountability Framework – the protocol to be followed by national sport organisations in order to receive federal funding. The former has been somewhat more successful than the latter.

References

Beamish, R. (1990). The persistence of inequality. An analysis of participation patterns among Canada's high performance athletes. *International Review for the Sociology of Sport*, 25(2): 143–155.

Bompa, T. (1985). Talent identification. *Sports Periodical on Research and Technology in Sport*. February, pp. 1–11.

Cantelon, H. (1981). High performance sport and the child athlete. Learning to labor. In A. Ingham and E. Broom (eds), *Career Patterns and Career Contingencies in Sport*. Vancouver: University of British Columbia. pp. 258–286.

Coubertin, P. (2002). 'Les assises philosophiques de l'Olympisme moderne'. In N. Müller (ed.) *Oeuvres choises de Pierre de Coubertin* (vol II). Lausanne: Comité International Olympique.

Crawford Report (2009). *The Future of sport In Australia*. Australian Government: Independent Sport Panel.

de Bosscher, V., De Knop, P., van Bottenburg, M., Bingham, J. and Shibli, S. (eds) (2008). *The Global Sporting Arms Race. Sports Policy Factors Leading to International Success*. Brussels: Meyer and Meyer.

Donnelly, P. (1993). Problems associated with youth involvement in high performance sports. In B. Cahill and A. Pearl (eds), *Intensive Participation in Children's Sports* (pp. 95–126). Champaign, IL: Human Kinetics.

Donnelly, P. (2012). Inspiration is not enough. Why sports mega-events always promise but rarely achieve a legacy of increased participation in sport. Paper presented at the World Congress of Sociology of Sport (International Sociology of Sport Association), Glasgow, Scotland, 14–18 July.

Donnelly, P. (2013). Sport participation. In L. Thibault and J. Harvey (eds), *Sport Policy in Canada*. Ottawa: University of Ottawa Press. pp. 177–213.

Donnelly, P. and Kidd, B. (2008). Opportunity knocks! Increasing sport participation in Canada as a result of success at the 2010 Vancouver Olympics. A CSPS position paper. Centre for Sport Policy Studies. Available at: www.physical.utoronto.ca/docs/csps-pdfs/CSPS_Position_Paper_2_-_Increasing_Sport_Participation_in_Canada_as_a_Result_of_Success_at_the_Vancouver_Olympics.pdf?sfvrsn=0.

Doping for Gold (2008). A Firefly Production for Thirteen/WNET New York and ITVS International in association with Five, Channel Four International, and History Channel (UK).

Gilbert, D. (1976). *Little Giant of World Sports. Sports Comparison Study, GDR-Canada.* Toronto: Kontakt Press.

Green, M. and Houlihan, B. (2005). *Elite Sport Development. Policy Learning and Political Priorities*. New York: Taylor and Francis.

Gruneau, R. (2015, in press). Goodbye Gordie Howe. Sport participation and class inequality in the 'pay for play' society. In D. Taras and C. Waddell (eds), *How Canadians Communicate V: Sport*. Edmonton: Athabaska University Press.

Hastad, D.V. and Skille, E.A. (2010). Does elite sport develop mass sport? A Norwegian case study. *Scandinavian Sport Studies Forum*, 1: 51–68.

Hildebrandt, A. (2014) *Own the Podium* sets sights on 2018, 2022 Olympic medalists. Challenges ahead as Canada seeks to keep up with rival countries. *CBC Sports*, 24

February. Available at: http://olympics.cbc.ca/news/article/own-the-podium-sets-sights-2018–2022-olympic-medallists.html (accessed 26 February 2014).

Kidd, B. (1974). Growing athletes in the Soviet hothouse system. *Canadian Dimension*, November.

MacAloon, J.J. (1990) Steroids and the state: Dubin, melodrama and the accomplishment of innocence. *Public Culture* Spring, 2(2): 41–64.

MacLennan, H. (1945). *Two Solitudes*. Toronto: McClelland and Stewart.

Müller, N. and Poyán, D. (2006), 'Olympism and "Sport-for-All"', *11th World Sport-for-All Congress*. Available at: www.coubertin.ch/pdf/sport_tous.pdf (accessed 2 May 2008).

Oakley, B. and Green, M. (2001). Still playing the game at arm's length? The selective re-investment in British sport, 1995–2000. *Managing Leisure*, 6(2): 74–94.

Ryan, J. (1995). *Little Girls in Pretty Boxes. The Making and Breaking of Elite Gymnasts and Figure Skaters*. New York: Doubleday.

Sutton Trust (2012). Press release: Over a third of British Olympic winners were privately educated. 14 August. Available at: www.suttontrust.com/newsarchive/third-british-olympic-winners-privately-educated.

Tymowski, G. (2001a). Rights and wrongs. Children's participation in high performance sports. In I. Berson, M. Berson and B. Cruz (eds), *Cross Cultural Perspectives in Child Advocacy*. Greenwich, CT: IAP (Information Age Publishing). pp. 55–93.

Tymowski, G. (2001b). Pain, children, and high performance sport. A justification of paternalism. *Journal of Professional Ethics*, 9(3–4): 121–152.

6 The problem with the pyramid

Why most models of talent development are flawed

Richard Bailey and David Collins

Introduction

Most chapters in this book have examined the relationship between elite sport and sport-for-all with a focus on supposed 'trickle down effects' from the former to the latter. Our interest in this contribution is with the reverse. While our colleagues explore sport from the top levels downwards, we look at it from the lower levels up. Our specific concern is talent development. Despite evident differences in the ways talent is identified and developed around the world, most share broadly the same assumptions about the underlying logic of the ways in which progressively reducing numbers of players rise from mass participation settings, such as community sports clubs and physical education classes, to higher levels of competition. The preferred metaphor chosen to represent this logic is the pyramid (see Figure 6.1).

Pyramids, trickle down and foundation stones

We have argued elsewhere that there exists a 'Standard Model of Talent Development' (SMTD) that represents and summarises the most common principles underlying policies and practices in the field. Not only are these principles widely shared across national and sporting boundaries, but they are usually considered so self-evident that they rarely warrant critical examination at all (Bailey and Collins, 2013). The defining logic of this model is usually represented by a pyramid, although other metaphorical phrases like 'trickle down' and 'foundation stones' are also used (Kirk and Gorily, 2000). The model operates as follows:

- a broad base of mass participation lies at the lowest level;
- successively high levels involve fewer and fewer players;
- since higher levels have capacity for fewer players, progress to these levels necessarily requires the removal of players from the system.

So, the SMTD is inherently a selective procedure, characterised by selection, progression and exclusion.

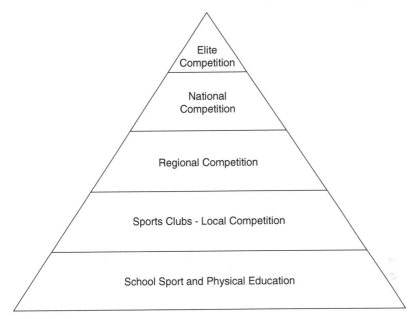

Figure 6.1 The pyramid model of sports development.
Source: Tinning *et al.*, 1993.

We call this the 'standard model' because it is the established way of thinking about talent development, especially in the West (Klentrou, 1993; Régnier
et al., 1993). Subsequently, Houlihan (2000) has suggested that versions of the
pyramid model characterise many sports development policy statements, while
Kirk *et al.* (2005) argue that its influence can be seen in numerous international
sports participation models and that 'the assumptions underpinning the pyramid
model continue to have a powerful residual influence on thinking about junior
sport participation and sport development in sport policy' (p. 2). Moreover, the
language of a UK government-sponsored research report into elite dance development is interesting in part because of its explicitness: 'Constructing a Pyramid
of Progression for Talent in Dance' (Schmidt, 2006). It seems that the pyramid
model is firmly entrenched in thinking about talent development.

What does the SMTD look like in practice? Indicative characteristics are as
follows:

- The focus is solely on progressing those identified as talented, and not on
  the wider group of players, even though others may meet the necessary
  standards later.
- Progression from one level to the next involves removal of large numbers
  of players from the system (and possibly also from the sport).
- 'Formal' threshold measures (e.g. county-/state-level representation for
  some, 'ideal' body proportions for others) are often in place that select or
  de-select players for progression.

- Once a player has been de-selected from a talent route, it is often difficult or impossible to return to it.
- Early specialisation in one or a small number of activities is seen as necessary in order to achieve high performance.
- It is presumed that early ability in an activity (which enables progression up the pyramid) is indicative of later success (Bailey *et al.*, 2011)

The SMTD has face validity and is compatible with common sense notions of gifts and talent (Bailey *et al.*, 2004; Lohman, 2006), and perhaps this, combined with the absence of alternative theories, explains its wide acceptance. However, we suggest that its apparent success is based on an illusion based on a version of what statisticians call the 'survivorship bias', in which inappropriate attention is placed on the winners of a system, while forgetting the huge number of losers (Taleb, 2004). The illusion is powered by the fact that some players succeed because it is a selective system, and some are bound to succeed within it. However, the SMTD is insidious because, as we will argue, there are reasons to doubt that talent alone determines success within the system, and that luck plays a much larger role than most realise or will admit, especially those who benefit from its continued existence. In fact, there is no way of knowing who might have succeeded through different systems, and who were de-selected from the system but might have, under different circumstances, gone on to achieve high performance. Indeed, since those cut from systems are rarely, if ever, the focus of study or attention, it is unlikely that much evidence for the SMTD's lack of efficacy will be available. Furthermore, the equivocal predictive validity of these models is further compounded by the demotivating consequences of early elimination of almost all players within the system.

The presumption of early specialisation

At the heart of the SMTD is a presumption that it takes a considerable amount of time and energy to achieve high performance in a specific domain. According to Régnier *et al.* (1993, p. 308), 'the underlying method is to provide space and equipment for a number of athletes, let them practice for 10 years, and then skim the cream from the top'. The allusion here is to the association suggested by some researchers between the amount of practice and the level of achievement (Ericsson *et al.*, 1993; Ericsson, 2013; cf. Gladwell, 2008). Indeed, in the motor learning literature, practice is generally seen as the variable having the greatest influence on skill acquisition (Vaeyens *et al.*, 2008).

The most influential contemporary statement in favour of the importance of early and sustained training is the theory of 'deliberate practice' developed by Ericsson and colleagues (Ericsson *et al.*, 1993; Ericsson and Charness, 1994). This work introduced an important distinction that had been missing from earlier models: not all forms of practice differentiate individual performance. The key is the specific form and volume of training, as summarised by Colvin (2008, pp. 68–70):

deliberate practice requires that one identify certain sharply defined elements of performance that need to be improved, and then work intently on them. ... High repetition is the most important difference between deliberate practice of a task of performing and the task for real, when it counts. ... Top performers repeat their practice activities to stultifying extent. ... It isn't much fun. ... Deliberate practice is not inherently enjoyable.

Ericsson *et al.* (1993) also argue that it is not simply the accumulation of hours of deliberate practice that lead to superior levels of performance, but that the accumulation must coincide with critical periods of biological and cognitive development (before puberty). On the one hand, they suggested that early specialisation is vital for future success because the earlier players commit to a strict training regime, the quicker they will attain the desired level of skill. On the other hand, someone starting serious training at a later age would be unable to 'catch up' with those who started earlier.

While research has offered broad support for the importance of deliberate practice in the development of expertise (Ericsson *et al.*, 2006; Starkes and Ericsson, 2006), a number of studies have raised serious questions regarding the detail of the theory, and especially its universal application (Abernethy *et al.*, 2003). Significantly, studies have empirically refuted the claim that expert performance requires an average of 10,000 hours of deliberate practice (van Rossum, 2000; Baker *et al.*, 2003; Bullock *et al.*, 2009). Côté and Fraser-Thomas (2007, p. 18) identify three testable tenets that they claim are at the foundation of the deliberate practice framework, which apply equally to the SMTD:

1   Elite players specialise in their main sport at a younger age than sub-elite players.
2   Elite players start deliberate practice at a younger age than sub-elite players.
3   Elite players accumulate more deliberate practice hours than sub-elite players throughout their career.

The clearest support for the first tenet comes from so-called 'early specialisation' sports (e.g. female gymnastics and figure skating), but this relationship is tautologous as the competition framework also occurs very early in the performer's life. In other words, *all* performers in these activities are relatively young, and generalising from them to sport *per se* is invalid. Moreover, studies have demonstrated that elite performers from many sports actually participated in a wide range of activities throughout their childhood (Côté *et al.*, 2009; MacNamara *et al.*, 2011). Research shows that many elite performers did not specialise early in their chosen activity, nor did their early experiences reflect those of deliberate practice (especially the assertion that training not to be inherently enjoyable). In fact, what evidence is available across a number of eventual elites suggests that early specialisation is negatively correlated with eventual success (Gullich, 2011). Successful players often describe their early sporting experiences as playful and varied (Carlson, 1988; Côté *et al.*, 2007).

Evidence in favour of the second tenet also comes primarily from early specialisation sports. Some have hypothesised the existence of biologically determined 'critical periods' during childhood when physiological and movement development are optimised (Balyi and Hamilton, 2003). However, recent comprehensive reviews have concluded that the case for the existence of such critical periods is, at best, unconvincing (Bailey *et al.*, 2010; cf. Ford *et al.*, 2011).

Finally, the third tenet appears to be more defensible, at least with regards to comparisons of practice time between elite and sub-elite players (Côté and Fraser-Thomas, 2007). However, evidence suggests that the most marked differences between groups of elite and sub-elite players do not occur until after childhood (Strachan *et al.*, 2009). In fact, we would expect such differences to arise within a pyramid-like system as, in addition to higher levels of motivation and commitment, elite players are more able to accumulate more training hours, anyway. It does not follow that deliberate practice will not be needed at a later stage. On the contrary, it becomes progressively more important as players move into adolescence and adulthood (Côté *et al.*, 2009), but this does seem to undermine the claim that early, specialised practice is a necessary condition of later high performance. Furthermore, as shown by a recent meta-analysis of studies in this area (Macnamara *et al.*, 2014), the contribution of deliberate practice to eventual success may be much lower than previously thought, with figures of 26 per cent of the variance in eventual game performance accountable to this generally ubiquitous element. In summary, it appears that the basic tenets of the SMTD are coming under increasing challenge.

Developmental concerns of early specialisation

Given the lack of evidence for the requirement of early specialisation, it is worthwhile noting concerns raised by researchers of physical and psycho-social risks associated with early intensive sports training (Baker, 2003). The most obvious risks are linked to intensive training at early periods of development and over-use injuries. Serious training during childhood can increase susceptibility to a number of serious conditions involving irritation and inflammation of growth plates, which produce new bone tissue and determine the final length and shape of bones in adulthood (Dalton, 1992).

The literature also points to psychological risks of early intensive training (Boyd and Yin, 1996). Some of these concerns relate directly to the immaturity of the players, and the subsequent dangers of pressure, frustration and a sense of failure (Martens, 1993). Further psychosocial concerns linked to early specialisation include compromised social development, sport drop-out, burnout and eating disorders (Baker, 2003). In addition to the inherent undesirability of these outcomes, they are also associated with the reduction or even prevention of adherence to physical activity in later life (Collins *et al.*, 2012).

Talent development as developing abilities

There is an increasing acceptance among sport scientists and coaches that performance in all forms of sport necessarily involves the development of a range of skills and abilities (such as physical fitness, movement competence, non-cognitive skills) (Vaeyens *et al.*, 2008; Williams and Ford, 2008). For example, Simonton (1999) proposed that multiple components contribute to the development of ability within any area and that these components interact in a multiplicative rather than an additive way. He offered four implications of this multiplicative model:

1   The area in which an individual displays ability will not be determined by any single, specialised component, but rather by the weighted multiplicative integration of the contributing components.
2   All talented performers will all have some ability of each necessary component, but individual levels within any area will vary.
3   Many otherwise talented players will be limited in their performance because of the absence of one of these components, even if they excel in others.
4   The number of components necessary for elite performance will vary from domain to domain, and some will be extremely complex.

Success in sport is rarely determined by a narrow range of characteristics, and this is especially the case in those activities requiring high levels of tactics, decision making and problem solving. Even sports that seem to place particular reliance on a relatively small number of physical characteristics (such as rowing or body-building) place considerable demands on psychological and social competence as well (Abbott *et al.*, 2002). Different roles within a particular sport mean that the necessary skills and abilities are not evenly distributed across all positions, although players at the highest levels are likely to possess a fundamental competence in all areas (Vaeyens *et al.*, 2008). Nevertheless, the inherent complexity of almost all sports suggests the necessity of measuring a number of dimensions (Régnier and Salmela, 1987), rather than single measures. Interestingly, even the comparatively simple, objective performance or CGS sports (results measured in centimetres, grams, seconds – Moesch *et al.*, 2011) seem to benefit from a later specialisation, so giving the multiplicity of talents time to evolve, establish and impact.

Potential and performance

Despite the widespread reliance on unitary conceptions of talent development, the conflation of potential and performance is a fundamental conceptual error (Abbott *et al.*, 2002; Bailey and Morley, 2006; Vaeyens *et al.*, 2008). One of the most uncontested lessons learned from the developmental sciences is that individual development is the result of an interaction between inherited abilities and social and cultural learning (Oyama, 2000). At a minimum, this suggests that any understanding of development needs to be cognisant of the influences of experience, and performance in any domain is the result of a complex choreography between various causal influences (van Rossum and Gagné, 2005). This is why it is wise 'to distinguish between determinants of performance and determinants of potential/skill acquisition' (Abbott *et al.*, 2002, p. 26).

Consider, for example, the family characteristics associated with elite sports performance (Bailey and Morley, 2006):

- parents achieved high standards in their domain;
- relatively high socio-economic status;
- ability and willingness to financially support participation and specialist support;
- ability and willingness to invest high amounts of time to support the child's engagement in the activity;
- parents as car owners;
- relatively small family size;
- two-parent family;
- attendance at an independent school.

Of course, the family is only one of a large number of variables that significantly influence (and could potentially inhibit), such as the availability and quality of coaching, the availability and quality of facilities, access to funding and choice of sport. Since young players can hardly be held responsible for the type of their families, schools, cities, etc., it seems fair to say that, to some extent, their sporting achievement (or simply engagement) is mediated by 'blind luck' (Bailey, 2007), irrespective of their ability in a sport.

In addition, some have highlighted the subjective nature of many talent assessment procedures (Burwitz *et al.*, 1994), whereby players find themselves removed from a system for rather arbitrary reasons. A striking example of such arbitrariness is the effect of relative age on performance (Roberts and Fairclough, 2012).

Numerous studies have shown that players born early within a selection year have a considerable advantage over those born later. This seems in part because of the relative physical size and strength and further matured coordination of players who can be up to one year older than their peers (Helsen *et al.*, 2000). Ward and Williams (2003) found that 'elite' football players as young as eight had better skills due to extra opportunities rather than any genetic advantage. Those with the benefit of extra months of development are more likely to be identified as talented and progress to the next level of the pyramid, where they would be expected to receive better coaching, play with a higher standard of team-mates and opposition and compete and train more frequently (Gladwell, 2008). Despite this advantage, however, recent work suggests that the actual achievement of elite status is proportionately higher in supposedly disadvantaged, late birth children (McCarthy and Collins, 2014), perhaps because of the extra challenge (and consequent growth) that these performers have had to overcome (cf. Collins and MacNamara, 2012).

In fact, many organisational and environmental factors influence the developing ability of students. To base a judgement of talent on current performance, therefore, is to confuse those things that are within the student's control and those that are not (Bailey, 2007), and to mistakenly believe that talent development is merely a probabilistic enterprise (Vaeyens *et al.*, 2008). Current performance can be a poor indicator of ability since it rewards things other than talent. It is simply naïve to overlook the real-world gap between the abilities an individual brings to an activity and the sports player, athlete or dancer who emerges at the end of the process.

Development and inclusion

Implicit within the SMTD is a conception of development and performance in physical activities as linear and predictable (Abbott *et al.*, 2005). It also presumes that successful progression from one level to the next is indicative of later or emergent ability. Both of these presumptions are mistaken. Some skills and knowledge that are important for later performance success, although they can be trained and improved at early ages, do not become fully developed or explicitly apparent until later (Abernethy and Russell, 1987; Tenenbaum *et al.*, 2000). Furthermore, the determinants of performance do not characterise success through the different age groups (Régnier and Salmela, 1987), and skills and physical qualities likely to result in short-term success may become redundant a year later. For example, hard running and physical maturity may be key to rugby success at the age of 12, but as players get older size and strength become progressively less important, and decision making and anticipation become more important for success (Abbott and Easson, 2002). So, short-term talent identification strategies run the risk of expelling potentially talented players because their current performance does not match simplistic expectations.

In this context, it is perhaps not surprising that the single most significant element that distinguishes evidence-related approaches (Abbott *et al.*, 2002; Bailey and Morley, 2006; Côté and Hay, 2002; van Rossum and Gagné, 2005) from the SMTD is their promotion of long-term engagement and development, and their rejection of short-term identification (Bailey *et al.*, 2010). A host of factors undermine the central importance given to talent identification, as opposed to its development (Vaeyens *et al.*, 2008), such as relative age effect (Helsen *et al.*, 2000; Musch and Grondin, 2000), the unpredictability of childhood-to-adult physical measures and childhood-to-adult performance standards (Abbott *et al.*, 2002) and the subjective or arbitrary nature of most talent assessment procedures (Abbott *et al.*, 2002). In fact, some researchers have suggested that many of the qualities that distinguish elite adult performers in the physical domain do not appear until late in adolescence, therefore invalidating the talent selection methods premised on pre-adolescent selection practices altogether (French and McPherson, 1999; Tenenbaum *et al.*, 2000; Williams and Franks, 1998).

Evidence of this sort implies the need for a radical departure from standard talent practices. At the least, it stresses the need for a strict distinction between valid and invalid identification measures, accompanied by an abandonment of developmentally inappropriate methods of assessing young people. More generally, it de-emphasises identification and selection and promotes an emphasis on appropriate development activities and environments (Martindale *et al.*, 2005).

Despite the plethora of evidence for the importance of development, it is notable and concerning that so many in sport still speak in the language of the SMTD and pursue the Holy Grail of selection/identification. As we stated earlier, there are telling arguments from both a performance and a participation perspective that better options are available. More positively, research supports talent development that: (1) is multi-factorial, involving the development of different abilities; (2) allows opportunity for playful sampling of a range of sports during the early stages, after an essential and sound preparation; (3) progressively introduces time and resources necessary for sustained play and practice; (4) addresses the gap between a child's potential and the player (or spectator or couch potato) they turn out to be as an adult; and (5) recognises that some young people grow up in environments that make it extremely difficult for them to realise their talents, unless an external agent (like a committed coach or teacher) or agency (such as a non-government organisation or national governing body) breaks the pattern of exclusive opportunity that has traditionally characterised elite sport in the SMTD.

We suggest that the best way in which these messages may be advertised and applied is through coordinated government action, focused on the educational system when all are available for influence. It is concerning, therefore, that current policy, at least in the UK, ignores much of this evidence. At the participation level, sports are rewarded on the numbers registered, in a clear misapplication of the SMTD. In the meantime, school PE has become focused on ensuring the activity levels of the children in the short term, rather than evolving an integrated and progressive system of physical education then movement to clubs for a lifelong involvement. In elite circles, sports systems, perhaps understandably given their sole focus, attend to the development of sport-specific skills at earlier ages, ignoring the demonstrated need for more general and broad ranging development (cf. Giblin *et al.*, 2014a,b).

A Darwinian conclusion

Many commentators have suggested that the SMTD has the character of a Darwinian process of selective retention. For example, Kirk *et al.* (2005, p. 1) write that the pyramid model is 'informed by a Social-Darwinist notion that the "fittest" (in this case the most talented) survive to reach the top of the pyramid'. They are partly correct. However, the analysis is flawed by its implication that selection is determined by talent. This chapter has provided evidence that this is not the case.

Furthermore, the nature of the selection processes are significantly different between these two cases. Darwinian selection takes place within context-specific niches (Ruse and Ruse, 1986). Our claim is that it is erroneous to assume that survival and progression within the niche of the SMTD is determined wholly, or even largely, by superior talent. Talent is, no doubt, an important factor. However, so also are a host of social, economic and psychological variables that are not necessarily related to talent at all. In other words, survival is not just of the fittest (or fastest, strongest or most skilful), but also of the luckiest. Parental income and support, schooling, gender, social class and a host of other factors that are independent of sporting ability characterise the context of the talent development niche. For this reason, the SMTD is not really a model of talent development at all, but rather a model of luck (lucky genes, but also lucky geography, lucky opportunities, lucky family).

References

Abbott, A. and Easson, B. (2002). The mental profile. In B.D. Hale and D. Collins (eds), *Rugby Tough* (pp. 17–33). Champaign, IL: Human Kinetics.

Abbott, A., Collins, D., Martindale, R. and Sowerby, K. (2002). *Talent Identification and Development. An Academic Review.* Edinburgh: Sport Scotland.

Abbott, A., Button, C., Pepping, G.-J. and Collins, D. (2005). Unnatural selection: Talent identification and development in sport. *Nonlinear Dynamics, Psychology and Life Sciences*, 9: 61–88.

Abernethy, B. and Russell, D.G. (1987). Expert–novice differences in an applied selective attention task. *Journal of Sport Psychology*, 9: 326–345.

Abernethy, B., Farrow, D. and Berry, J. (2003). Constraints and issues in the development of a general theory of expert perceptual motor performance. A critique of the deliberate practice framework. In J.L. Starkes, and K.A. Ericsson (eds), *Expert Performance in Sports. Advances in Research on Sport Expertise* (pp. 349–369). Champaign, IL: Human Kinetics.

Bailey, R.P. (2007). Talent development and the luck problem. *Sport, Ethics and Philosophy*, 1: 367–376.

Bailey, R. and Collins, D. (2013). The standard model of talent development and its discontents. *Kinesiology Review*, 2, 248–259.

Bailey, R.P. and Morley, D. (2006). Towards a model of talent development in physical education. *Sport, Education and Society*, 11, 211–230.

Bailey, R., Tan, J.E.C. and Morley, D. (2004). Talented pupils in physical education: secondary school teachers' experiences of identifying talent within the 'Excellence in Cities' scheme. *Physical Education & Sport Pedagogy*, 9(2): 133–148.

Bailey, R.P, Collins, D., Ford, P., MacNamara, Á., Toms, M. and Pearce, G. (2010). *Participant Development in Sport: An Academic Review.* Leeds: Sports Coach UK.

Bailey, R.P., Leigh, J., Pearce, G. and Reeves, M. (2011). National *Impact Evaluation of the Gifted and Talented Physical Education and Sport Programme.* Loughborough: Youth Sport Trust.

Baker, J. (2003). Early specialization in youth sport. A requirement for adult expertise? *High Ability Studies*, 14: 85–94.

Baker, J., Côté, J. and Abernethy, B. (2003). Sport-specific practice and the development of expert decision-making in team ball sports. *Journal of Applied Sport Psychology*, 15: 12–25.

Balyi, I. and Hamilton, A. (2003). Long-term athlete development update: trainability in childhood and adolescence. *Faster, Higher, Stronger*, 20: 6–8.

Boyd, M.P. and Yin, Z. (1996). Cognitive–affective sources of sport enjoyment in adolescent sport participants. *Adolescence*, 31: 383–395.

Bullock, N., Gulbin, J., Martin, D., Ross, A., Holland, T. and Marino, F. (2009). Talent identification and deliberate programming in skeleton. Ice novice to Winter Olympian in 14 months. *Journal of Sports Sciences*, 27: 397–404.

Burwitz, L., Moore, P.M. and Wilkinson, D.M. (1994). Future directions for performance-related sports science research. An interdisciplinary approach. *Journal of Sport Sciences*, 12: 93–109.

Carlson, R.C. (1988). The socialization of elite tennis players in Sweden. An analysis of the social development. *Sociology of Sport Journal*, 5: 241–256.

Collins, D. and MacNamara, Á. (2012). The rocky road to the top. Why talent needs trauma. *Sports Medicine*, 42 (11): 907–914.

Collins, D., Bailey, R., Ford, P.A., MacNamara, Á., Toms, M. and Pearce, G. (2012). Three worlds. New directions in participant development in sport and physical activity. *Sport, Education and Society*, 17(2), 225–243.

Colvin, G. (2008) *Talent is Overrated: What Really Separates World-class Performers From Everybody Else*. New York: Penguin.

Côté, J. and Fraser-Thomas, J. (2007). Youth involvement in sport. In P. Crocker (ed.), *Introduction to Sport Psychology: A Canadian Perspective* (pp. 266–294). Toronto: Pearson Prentice Hall.

Côté, J. and Hay, J. (2002). Children's involvement in sport. A developmental perspective. In J. Silva and D. Stevens (eds), *Psychological Foundations of Sport* (pp. 484–502). Boston, MA: Allyn and Bacon.

Côté, J., Baker, J. and Abernethy, B. (2007). Practice and play in the development of sport expertise. In R. Eklund and G. Tenenbaum (eds) Handbook of Sport Psychology (3rd edn, pp. 184–202). Hoboken, NJ: Wiley.

Côté, J., Horton, S., MacDonald, D.J. and Wilkes, S. (2009). The benefits of sampling sports during childhood. *Physical and Health Education*, Winter: 6–11.

Dalton, S.E. (1992). Overuse injuries in adolescent athletes. *Sports Medicine*, 13: 58–70.

Ericsson, K.A. (2013). Training history, deliberate practice and elite sports performance. An analysis in response to Tucker and Collins review – what makes champions? *British Journal of Sports Medicine*, 47(9): 533–535.

Ericsson, K.A. and Charness, N. (1994). Expert performance. Its structure and acquisition. *American Psychologist*, 49, 725–747.

Ericsson, K.A., Krampe, R.T. and Tesch-Römer, C. (1993). The role of deliberate practice in the acquisition of expert performance. *Psychological Review*, 100: 363–406.

Ericsson, K.A., Charness, N., Feltovich, P.J. and Hoffman, R.R. (eds). (2006). *Cambridge Handbook of Expertise and Expert Performance*. Cambridge: Cambridge University Press.

Ford, P., De Ste Croix, M., Lloyd, R., Meyers, R., Moosavi, M., Oliver, J., Till, K. and Williams, C. (2011). The Long-Term Athlete Development model. Physiological evidence and application. *Journal of Sports Sciences*, 29(4): 389–402.

French, K.E. and McPherson, S.L. (1999). Adaptations in response selection processes used during sport competition with increasing age and expertise. *International Journal of Sport Psychology*, 30: 173–193.

Giblin, S., Collins, D. and Button, C. (2014a). Physical literacy. Importance, assessment and future directions. *Sports Medicine*, 44: 1177–1184.

Giblin, S., Collins, D., MacNamara, A. and Kiely, J. (2014b). The third way. Deliberate preparation as an evidence-based focus for primary physical education. *Quest*, 66: 385–395.

Gladwell, M. (2008). *Outliers: The Story of Success*. London: Penguin.

Gullich, A. (2011). Training quality in high-performance youth sport. Invited keynote at the Science for Success Conference, Research Institute for Olympic Sports (KIHU), Finland, 11–12 October.

Helsen, W., Hodges, N., Van Winckel, J. and Starkes, J. (2000). The roles of talent, physical precocity and practice in the development of soccer expertise. *Journal of Sports Sciences*, 18: 727–736.

Houlihan, B. (2000). Sporting excellence, schools and sports development: The politics of crowded policy spaces. *European Physical Education Review*, 6: 171–193.

Kirk, D. and Gorely, T. (2000). Challenging thinking about the relationship between school physical education and sport performance. *European Physical Education Review*, 6: 119–134.

Kirk, D., Brettschneider, W.-D. and Auld, C. (2005). *Junior Sport Models Representing Best Practice Nationally and Internationally. Junior Sport Briefing Papers*. Canberra: Australian Sports Commission.

Klentrou, P.P. (1993). *Gymnastics Talent: A Review of Literature*. Gloucester, ON: Canadian Gymnastics Federation.

Lohman, D.F. (2006). Beliefs about differences between ability and accomplishment. From folk theories to cognitive science. *Roeper Review*, 29(1): 32–40.

MacNamara, Á., Collins, D., Bailey, R.P., Ford, P., Toms, M. and Pearce, G. (2011). Promoting lifelong physical activity and high level performance. Realising an achievable aim for physical education. *Physical Education and Sport Pedagogy*, 16, 265–278.

Macnamara, B.N., Hambrick, D.Z. and Oswald, F.L. (2014). Deliberate practice and performance in music, games, sports, education, and professions. A meta-analysis. *Psychological Science*, DOI: 10.1177/0956797614535810

Martens, R. (1993). Psychological perspectives. In B.R. Cahill and A.J. Pearl (eds), *Intensive Participation in Children's Sports* (pp. 9–18). Champaign, IL: Human Kinetics.

Martindale, R., Collins, D. and Daubney, J. (2005). Talent development. A guide for practice and research within sport. *Quest*, 57: 353–375.

McCarthy, N. and Collins, D. (2014). Initial identification and selection bias versus the eventual confirmation of talent: evidence for the benefits of a rocky road? *Journal of Sports Sciences*, DOI: 10.1080/02640414.2014.908322.

Moesch, K., Elbe, A.-M., Hauge, M.-L.T. and Wikman, J.M. (2011). Late specialization: the key to success in centimeters, grams, or seconds (CGS) sports. *Scandinavian Journal of Medicine and Science in Sports*, 21(6): e282–e290.

Musch, J. and Grondin, S. (2001). Unequal competition as an impediment to personal development. A review of the relative age effect in sport. *Developmental Review*, 21: 47–167.

Oyama, S. (2000). *Evolution's Eye. A Systems View of the Biology–Culture Divide*. Durham, NC: Duke University Press.

Régnier, G. and Salmela, J. (1987). Predictors of success in Canadian male gymnasts. In B. Petiot, J.H. Salmela and T.B. Hoshizaki (eds), *World Identification Systems for Gymnastic Talent* (pp. 143–150). Montreal: Sport Psyche Editions.

Régnier, G., Salmela, J. and Russell, S. (1993). Talent detection and development in sport. In R.N. Singer, M. Murphy and L.K. Tennant (eds), *Handbook on Research on Sport Psychology* (pp. 290–313). New York: Macmillan.

Roberts, S.J. and Fairclough, S.J. (2012). The influence of relative age effect in the assessment of high school students in physical education in the United Kingdom. *Journal of Teaching in Physical Education*, 31(1): 56–70.

Ruse, M. and Ruse, M. (1986). *Taking Darwin Seriously: A Naturalistic Approach to Philosophy.* Oxford: Blackwell.

Schmidt, B. (2006). *Constructing a Pyramid of Progression for Talent in Dance.* Coventry: National Academy for Gifted and Talented Youth.

Simonton, D. (1999). Talent and its development. An emergenic and epigenetic model. *Psychological Review*, 106, 435–457.

Starkes, J.L. and Ericsson, K.A. (eds). (2006). *Expert Performance in Sports.* Champaign, IL: Human Kinetics.

Strachan, L., Côté, J. and Deakin, J. (2009). 'Specializers' versus 'samplers' in youth sport. Comparing experiences and outcomes. *The Sport Psychologist*, 23: 77–92.

Taleb, N. (2004). *Fooled by Randomness: The Hidden Role of Chance in Life and in the Markets.* New York: Random House.

Tenenbaum, G., Sar-El, L. and Bar-Eli, M. (2000). Anticipation of ball locations in low and high skilled performers. A developmental perspective. *Psychology of Sport and Exercise*, 1: 117–128.

Vaeyens, R., Lenoir, M., Williams, A.M. and Philippaerts, R. (2008). Talent identification and development programmes in sport. Current models and future directions. *Sports Medicine*, 38: 703–714.

van Rossum, J. (2000). Deliberate practice and Dutch field hockey. An addendum to Starkes. *International Journal of Sport Psychology*, 31: 452–460.

van Rossum, J. and Gagné, F. (2005). Talent development in sports. In F. Dixon and S. Moon (eds), *The Handbook of Secondary Gifted Education* (pp. 281–316). Waco, TX: Prufrock Press.

Ward, P. and Williams, A.M. (2003). Perceptual and cognitive skill development in soccer. The multidimensional nature of expert performance. *Journal of Sport and Exercise Psychology*, 25: 93–111.

Williams, A. and Ericsson K.A. (2005). Perceptual-cognitive expertise in sport. Some considerations when applying the expert performance approach. *Human Movement Science*, 24: 283–307.

Williams, A.M., and Ford, P.R. (2008). Expertise and expert performance in sport. *International Review of Sport and Exercise Psychology*, 1(1): 4–18.

Williams, A.M. and Franks, A. (1998). Talent identification in soccer. *Sport, Exercise and Injuries*, 4: 159–65.

7 Opportunities for 'all' versus 'gold' for sport and country

A South African discourse

Cora Burnett

Introduction

South Africa has a well-documented colonial past, with much scholarly work focusing on the apartheid government (1948–1994), during which time the country faced political and sporting isolation. In 1964 the International Olympic Committee banned South Africa from taking part in the Olympic Games and global sporting and political powerhouses were soon to follow. After more than 30 years of international sporting isolation because of the country's apartheid regime, democracy emerged for South Africans in the early 1990s and they re-entered the global arena of competitive sport. Not only did first world countries unite in the opposition against apartheid, but other African countries lobbied for change at multiple global forums. In the 1960s, the trend of de-colonisation gained momentum and several African countries made their presence known in the United Nations and in FIFA (*Fédération Internationale de Football Association*). Since the mid 1990s, South Africa has been a symbol of African prowess by bidding for the Summer Olympic Games in 1995, hosting several international sporting competitions and being the host nation for the 2010 FIFA World Cup (Meulders *et al.*, 2012). In the game of political power and national prestige, elite sport came to dominate national politics, strategies and sporting structures.

Capturing the different sectors of sport in the South African context in 2014, four years after the FIFA World Cup, and after the national elections in May this year, is no easy feat. In his 2014 State of the Nation address, President Jacob Zuma communicated a positive narrative, yet acknowledged that there are major poverty-related challenges facing the government. He acknowledged the high level of unemployed youth; extreme economic inequality; 'dismal education'; 'misguided transformation'; a high HIV-prevalence rate (for people between 20 and 64 years; and a worsening score on the Human Development Index (HDI) (Sethlatswe, 2014).

At the core of such inequality lies racially based class division, with a large proportion of black South Africans (41.9 per cent) and coloureds (24.5 per cent) still living in relative poverty ($2 per day or R524 per month per person at 2008 currency values), compared to 11.1 per cent Indians and 0.8 per cent whites (Alexander, 2013, p. 345). Social sport policies have been encapsulated by the first Sport and Recreation Plan for South Africa, which mainly focuses on addressing these inequalities and establishing sport as a basic human right and constitutional imperative, with reciprocal effects on poverty alleviation (Sport and Recreation South Africa, 2013a).

Poverty as a key factor of social exclusion underpins people's lack of access in terms of four basic systems: democracy, welfare, the labour market and family and community (Collins, 2004; Cortis, 2009). Poverty also exacerbates other forms of exclusion and marks class differences (Sugden and Tomlinson, 2000, p. 319). With the concentration of resources among certain ethnic populations, city-based schools and clubs, the rural black population ('ethnic black'), women and persons with disabilities are earmarked for fast-track development in addressing the 'apartheid-layering' of disenfranchisement.

The chapter addresses the policy framework and the discourse of sport development within the broader societal structures and context of poverty.

South Africa's sport policy frameworks

From the 1950s onward, South Africa's apartheid policies not only excluded the majority of its population from participation in elite sports, but also left communities and schools without quality sporting infrastructure (Booth, 1997). International isolation and global anti-apartheid activism succeeded in isolating the country from international competitions – first by being banned by the IOC (International Olympic Committee), and then by FIFA in the 1960s (Laverty, 2010). Re-entry into the global sports arena in the early 1990s represented a bold move by a young democracy, despite existing inequalities. Scholars and political activists who masterminded a successful campaign for, first, banning South Africa from global sporting events and, then, negotiating for the return, advocated for global redress and inclusion. In this regard, Kidd (2011, p. 158) advocated for levelling of the playing field between developed (the Global North) and developing economies (the Global South), and for erasing 'the patriarchal, middle-class, heterosexist and Europeanist character' of modern Western sporting practices. If neo-colonial and liberal practices took 300 years to become entrenched in South African society, global expectations to have 'normal sport in a normal society' established in the space of 20 years is an illusion. Makhenkesi Stofile (2006, p. 10), Minister of Sport and Recreation in the early 1990s, reflected on the ideological (apartheid) baggage of South African sport and argued for fighting 'politics with politics' and for political intervention, as market forces favour the environment of strong, well-established white-dominated sport:

> Sport is a reflection of the class of those truly in power. Clearly in our situation the power matters, economic power continues to reside in a few hands. The same hands as in the past! Access to a lucrative sports industry continues to reflect that... It does not mean nothing happened since 1992.

Indeed a lot of change is taking place at the juniors' level. Equity does not only refer to jobs, it also refers to sport as a fundamental human right. Let us all strive to make that attainable. Our children must be the beneficiaries of our sacrifices. We dare not fail.

The language of 'redress' became the prominent political narrative and deviated from an initial focus of nation-building through reconciliation – a process driven by President Mandela, the first democratically elected president of South Africa (Pillay and Bass, 2008; Maguire, 2011). As a peacemaker, Mr Nelson Mandela provided the inspiration for the first National Sport and Recreation Plan, drafted in 2011; a quote from his speech delivered at the Laureus World Sports Awards Ceremony in 2000 provided the inspiration. It reads:

> Sport has the power to change the world. It has the power to inspire. It has the power to unite people in a way that little else can. Sport can awaken hope where there was previously only despair.
>
> (Sport and Recreation South Africa, 2011, front page)

Since then, a sense of entitlement has become evident, and this message inspired a quest for an equitable dispensation by the political majority. For this majority, freedom without opportunity means systemic marginalisation. It is up to the government to provide the political framework, the political will, the structural alignment and resources that will guide societal transformation and optimal inclusive sporting practices (Sport and Recreation South Africa, 2013a).

Odendaal (2006) provides a historical overview of how change and transformation of sports like rugby and cricket not only carry colonial ideology, but also became an inherent part of the cultural practices of white Afrikaans- (rugby) and English-speakers (cricket). It found a foundation in hegemonic structures that is difficult to change, and for political reasons became the symbol of white male colonial domination to be 'dismantled'. The question was: who would do the 'dismantling' and on whose terms?

When Margaret Talbot (2007) wrote about the 'politics of sport and physical education', she referred to Harold Lasswell's book *Politics: Who Gets What, When, How?* Political leaders do not always safeguard the rights of minorities or acknowledge space for agency from individuals or groups. Governments often fund and drive their own strategic thrusts, focusing on achieving political goals in the national, continental (e.g. Pan-African) and global playing fields. Hoberman (2007) referred to the policy drive for sportive nationalism as evidence of political pathology, as it ties into the success of national athletes and teams in international competitions. Political goals may be highly ambitious (medal count at the Olympic Games or hosting sport mega-events) or scaled down to compare with performances of similar-income countries. In this case, South Africa could be compared to other African countries (All Africa Games Competitions), or compete against its middle-income counterparts, as in the other BRICS countries (Brazil, Russia, India and China) (Tomlinson *et al.*, 2011). The Cape Town Olympic Games bid and the 2010 FIFA Football World Cup had special significance for the African continent as it was the first one on African soil and vividly marketed under the slogans of *Ke Nako* (Tswana for 'It's Time') and *Simunuye* ('We are one') (Kersting, 2007). It meant 'time for Africa' on which the public media built a convincing case for South Africa's recognition as a player on the global stage of sport and political power in Africa.

The relatively poor performance of South African athletes at the 2000 Sydney Olympics motivated the appointment of a Ministerial Task Team to transform the entire sport system in order to deliver the country an international competitive edge. Seven umbrella bodies were restructured into two: the Department of Sport and Recreation to deal with mass participation, and a non-governmental organisation (the South African Sports Federation and Olympic Committee or SASCOC, established in 2004) to coordinate elite sport. Within these two paradigms, Sport and Recreation South Africa's White Paper identifies transformation and reconciliation as national priorities, while also integrating global direction (e.g. IOC, FIFA and the UN), and regional policies (e.g. the Supreme Council for Sport in Africa, now the African Union Sports Council) (Sport and Recreation South Africa, 2013b).

The National Sport and Recreation Plan

The National Sport and Recreation Plan (NSRP) provides implementation direction for the national sport policy. For elite sport, the key successes relate to the winning of the IRB Rugby Union World Cup in 1995 and 2007, as well as the hosting of the 2010 FIFA Football World Cup, which served as a directive (Burnett, 2012a). Alongside the framework of Long Term Athlete Development, the *Case for Sport* (Sport and Recreation South Africa, 2009) underpins the rationale for mass participation and life-long physical activity. It is captured in a differential concept, namely 'Long-Term Participant Development', loosely associated with the sport-for-all phenomenon. Two diverse sport development phenomena are recognised in policy documents and structures, which are interlinked (Sport and Recreation South Africa, 2013a). National development priorities favour the provision of optimal opportunities for participation through structured club and school sport as a foundation for the development of successful elite athletes and teams reflective of the country's (racial) demographics (BauNews, 2006).

The NSRP adheres to the democratic principles enshrined in the Constitution that award the minister legislative powers to oversee the development and delivery of sport and recreation by the state and its strategic partners to all corners of the country. His/her role and responsibilities are guided by a legal framework, with the most prominent Acts, being:

- Occupational Health and Safety Act, 1993 (Act No. 85 of 1993);
- Public Service Act, 1994 as amended by Act 30 of 2007;

- Public Finance Management Act, 1999 as amended by Act No. 29 of 1999;
- Preferential Procurement Policy Framework Act (PPFA), 2000 (Act No. 5 of 2000);
- Broad-Based Black Economic Empowerment Act 2003 (Act No. 53 of 2003);
- Division of Revenue Act where SRSA coordinates financial allocations to provincial departments responsible for sport through the Mass Participation and Sport Development Grant.

Two key sport-specific Acts include:

- The South African Institute for Drug-free Sport Act, 1997 (Act No. 14 of 1997 as amended) with key responsibility placed on SRSA to ensure that sport in South Africa is practised free from the use of prohibited substances or methods intended to artificially enhance performance;
- The National Sport and Recreation Act, 1998 (Act No. 110 of 1998 as amended) with key responsibility placed on SRSA to ensure that sport and recreation, from a national perspective, is administered and governed in the best interests of the stakeholders in sport and recreation in South Africa (Sport and Recreation South Africa, 2013b).

Other legislation also refers to the South African Boxing Act, 2001 (Act No. 11 of 2001); the Safety at Sports and Recreation Events Act, 2010. (Act No. 2 of 2010); the South African Combat Sport Bill, 2014; Fitness Industry Bill, 2014; Intergovernmental Relations Framework Act, 2005 (Act No. 13 of 2005); Lotteries Act 1997 (Act No. 57 of 1997); and SA Schools Act, 1996 (Act No. 84 of 1996) (Sport and Recreation South Africa, 2013b).

With a vision (2030) of delivering *An Active and Winning Nation*, the NSRP identified 31 strategic objectives, of which only six have a non-elite sport focus, by referring to health-related activities (including campaigns), physical education, recreation and sport-for-development initiatives (Sport and Recreation South Africa, 2013b). It is against these strategic drives that the elite sport paradigm dominates and supports the government's quest for transforming South African society as guided and measured by a Transformation Charter and a multi-dimensional score card system (Sport and Recreation South Africa, 2013b).

The following section provides an overview of the South African Sport Ministry's key strategic thrusts. Recognising Houlihan's (2005) criticism of ana-lysing sport policies from a top-down approach, some institutional-level arguments and public debates serve as reflections and inductive retrospection.

Mass participation in sport

Creating a well-resourced sport environment with optimal alignment of all stakeholders to provide opportunities for participation at all levels is aimed at broadening the pool of talent for identification and specialisation. In 2004 the government's priority was to provide mass participation opportunities in activities such as aerobics, various ball games, athletics (big walk/fun run) and indigenous games (selected traditional games from the major ethnic populations) (Burnett and Hollander, 2006). The community-based programme, *Siyadlala* (a Zulu word meaning 'Let us Play') delivered on that mandate, but took on the trappings of modern sports, as rules were standardised and competitions offered at all levels – including national competitions.

With the critical mass of participants at school, the School Mass Participation Programme was launched in 2008 and additional (priority) codes such as rugby, cricket, netball and football were introduced to different age groups in impoverished schools across the country (Burnett and Hollander, 2008). Yet the lack of school facilities and inadequately trained teacher-coaches provided unique challenges for the successful implementation and delivery of talented athletes.

Since 2004, consecutive Ministers of Sport set targets for school sport development on the 'physical education and winning model' of Cuba. They developed legislation that would increase their involvement and mandated involvement in school, university and club sport (Coetzee, 2004). In 2012, a R233 million National School Sport Programme was launched, and although educators welcomed this initiative for developing life skills, Minister Fikile Mbalula envisaged the programme to deliver mainly sporting talent (Mkhwanazi, 2012). In his budget speech, the Minister announced the allocation of 40 per cent (R525 million) of the Ministry's total budget to mass participation, with the expectation that the School Sport Programme would increase the talent pool and improve the international performance of South African athletes (O'Connor, 2012). He also announced the return of 'Magnificent Wednesdays', which would ensure the re-establishment of school leagues in a variety of sports, including indigenous games (such as *marabaraba* – a board game). He also envisaged that the memorandum signed between the two national departments (Sport and Recreation and Basic Education) would lead to the reintroduction of physical education as a cornerstone for developing 'sporting competencies'. Sport, arts and culture MEC Tebogo Modise (Seemise, 2013, p. 23) shared this vision, saying:

> Our schools are the basis for which to identify and develop talent. Time at school is a critical period in a pupil's life in which to groom and nurture talent for the development of our future stars.

The minister argued for compulsory sport participation and motivated a facility audit with expected implications of spending billions (of rands) on infrastructure development, where schools and communities could share sporting facilities (Ndaba, 2013; Potgieter, 2012). A hybrid model for talent development would be enhanced by developing 100 (additional) specialised centres for talented athletes, as well as introducing a feeder scheme, by talent scouts from sport federations, at school level across 16 priority sports (Edwards, 2011). Elite sport profiling is further reflected in national school sport competitions presented as 'school-level Olympics' – thus structuring mass participation clearly on exclusionary lines.

Elite sport and mass participation blurred the less tangible educational outcomes associated with sport-for-all and non-competitive physical activities. On the one hand, developing elite sport in South Africa is based on a sport development framework of developing clubs, building school and community sport facilities and having a vibrant competitive school sport system. On the other hand, a human development framework is followed for structuring 'life orientation' content, while also providing school-based programmes to increase access to sport and structured physical activities. Basic Education Minister Angie Motshekga published the Draft School Sport Policy in the 9 December 2011 *Government Gazette*. It commented on the 'benefits of healthy physical activities for the child, the community and the country' with reference to 'a nation's capacity to compete and grow in a global economy' (Jones, 2011, p. 4). Concern about excessive government interference in structuring school sport as a production line for competitive sport and elite athlete development had little impact on the strategic drive of the government machinery (Smit, 2009).

Both ministers (Sport and Recreation and Education) share the ideal of transforming South African sport by developing talent at grass-roots level with the aid of 'formative subjects' such as physical education. Since life orientation replaced physical education in public schools in the early 1990s, learners had very limited access to (practical) physical activities. In addition to transformation in sport to foster 'racial inclusion' in competitive sport teams, unemployed youths were offered one-year contracts, first as School Sport Assistants (School Sport Mass Participation Programme) and then as Extra School Sport Programme coaches in an attempt to alleviate poverty among the South African youth (Burnett and Hollander, 2008; Burnett, 2014). Minimal training workshops hardly equipped them, or, in some cases, the teacher-coaches, with the skills to deliver quality sport programmes. It seems that poverty alleviation became a key driver, as about 42.7 per cent of the youth contributed to the survival of their households. The programme had systemic flaws and compromised sustainable quality service delivery, yet it provided the 'blueprint' for the current practice (Burnett, 2010). The current system offers short-term contracts to relatively more 'unemployed' youth, resulting in a higher turnover rate and a low level of training. The absence of evidence-based research and validated monitoring and evaluation further compromises policy implementation and reflective learning from school-based mass participation in sporting activities (Coalter, 2013).

The slow process of bottom-up sport development and inclusive sport practices translated into coercive top-down tactics, such as implementing racial quotas in high-profile sports such as rugby, cricket and netball – from school to national levels.

Elite sport

South African sporting triumphs marking the development of a young democracy include the national soccer team (Bafana Bafana) winning the African Cup of Nations in 1996 and their rugby counterparts winning the IRB Rugby World Cup in 1995 and 2007. However, democracy and broad 'human rights' came into question through the over-representation of white players in rugby and cricket, and black players in soccer. In the 2010 FIFA World Cup not one white player played for the national football team (Anon, 2010). Elite South African sport offers a window onto the social fabric of the broader society and shows complex internal and external influences and changes. After the Mandela era of reconciliation, the racial cracks and resistance to transformation from the 'white elite' frustrated politicians. In 2010 the then Minister of Sport and Recreation (Makhenkesi Stofile) and long-serving parliamentary sports portfolio committee chairman Butana Khompela reverted to 'apartheid tactics' by threatening to withhold the Springbok team's passports if it did not represent the racial makeup of the country (Anon, 2010).

Public debate about implementing 'racial quotas' at all levels of competition centred around the sporting success of the national teams (particularly Rugby Union), while displaying a demographic profile of its team 'for 'nation-building' (Isaacs, 2011). At the National Sport and Recreation Indaba that laid the foundation of the National Sport and Recreation Plan, arguments in favour and against 'racial quotas' went on for hours, with resolutions on 'transformation' such as the following being accepted:

> The quota system still has a role to play in the transformation of South African sport. This will be implemented using a developmental approach as continued in the revised Transformation Charter.
>
> As the time goes, the quota system needs to be reviewed within a process of creating an enabling environment for a winning nation that will support merit in the long run.
>
> (Sport and Recreation South Africa, 2011, p. 12)

Sport and Recreation Minister Fikile Mbalula launched a transformation commission of inquiry, warning that 'no sporting code is safe', but focused on rugby union and cricket, saying that he wanted to 'see multiracial rugby and cricket teams by the end of the year' (Ntloko, 2012, p. 20). The argument of 'transformation versus merit' was voiced in 2005 by the then Minister of Sport and Recreation, who said: 'you can't use merit, because merit assumes that all people have equal opportunities' (Shafto, 2005, p. 15). In 2013, he announced incentives and punitive measures to sport bodies for driving transformation and meeting pre-set targets. The targets would measure change, yet were resisted by a dominantly white labour union (AfriForum), which challenged the quotas as 'unlawful under the Constitution of the International Rugby Board' (Mdhelela, 2013, p. 15).

Acting as host country for the 2010 FIFA World Cup came at the cost of a huge financial investment, with the main returns being measured in the multiple effects of nation-building, (questionable) poverty-reduction strategies and South Africa emerging as a recognised continental power (Pillay and Bass, 2008; Burnett, 2010). Maguire (2011) reflected on media debates and 'images of South Africa through the lens of the FIFA World Cup' in addressing 'Afro-pessimism' through public diplomacy, nation-building and engaging in strategic partnerships for poverty alleviation and 'social capital'. Research confirmed the success of the mega-event in the rebranding of the country and in its imagery of nationhood (Bolsmann and Brewster, 2009; Lepp and Gibson, 2011). The repeated failure of the national football team to compete at continental and global levels elicited a public outcry and severe criticism from the Minister of Sport and Recreation:

> I think first and foremost we need to concede that we have a crisis of monumental proportions. This tournament was just one journey that proved that and laid it bare. What I saw there was not a problem of coaching, it was a bunch of losers who don't have any respect for this country. I saw a team that was South African in the second half, fighting to win.
>
> Nigeria was shocked, the coach even stood up. They thought they were going to meet the lions whose stadium was filled to capacity to come and fight for their country. But what did they come to meet? Just a bunch of unbearable, useless individuals.
>
> (Anon, 2014, p. 22)

The minister argued that transformation and elite sporting success (in this case, Bafana Bafana at least qualifying for the African Cup of Nations) lies in the implementation of a competitive school and club sport system. He pushed for the professionalisation of institutionalised sport. Providing an 'enabling environment' became a strategic thrust, with the focus on building public sport facilities. The ministry, through its delivery agent of elite sport, South African Sports Confederation and Olympic Committee (SASCOC), adopted a 'coaches framework' to ensure that sport coaches obtained the minimum qualifications and offered them a pathway to specialisation to equip them for athlete development. Through the coaches, the aim was to improve talent selection from 90 per cent rather than the estimated 30 per cent of the total population, which made the schools the most obvious 'feeder system' (Gunning, 2002). This had implications for football, which is currently selecting one school per province for competitions, compared to other sporting codes that have player rather than institutional representation at regional competitions (Ntloko, 2012).

It was envisaged that funding national Olympic-style competitions for 16 sporting codes, as well as for indigenous games with follow-up monitoring (athlete tracking) at club and university levels, will deliver global sporting success and sporting idols. Successful elite sports attract sponsorships, which up to now still favour able-bodied and male sport teams, despite the announcement that netball (the most popular sport for females) is running semi-professional leagues. With government spending focused on the elite sport delivery system, positive social outcomes of mass participation programmes are relatively under-reported.

Public debate about health concerns for young athletes' use of steroids and performance-enhancing substances (Waterworth and Skade, 2010), disabling sport injuries and excessive pressure on young athletes to perform (even resulting in suicide) are to some extent marginalised in the quest to deliver in the 'fame and fortune' model of competitive sport (Miti, 2011). Schools are also in a race to 'buy' athletes, with fierce competition among the top sport schools provoking controversial media debate (Fengu, 2011). Elite sport overshadows 'sport for health', although from time to time academics drive incentives to create awareness and address issues such as obesity (Nagel *et al.*, 2008). Professor Tim Noakes, a high-profile sport scientist and medical doctor, has warned against an elitist approach and current funding models. He said:

> The more a country spends on nurturing its elite athletes, the greater the chances are that its athletes will succeed. But this concentration of resources on the talented few is probably to the detriment of the majority.
>
> (Ardé, 2005, p. 4)

The lack of service delivery on broad-based sport participation opportunities to foster health and quality of life outcomes in the absence of physical education provides a gap for non-governmental organisations to offer school-based programmes.

Sport-for-development

Early in 2000, the then Minister of Education, Kader Asmal, and Minister of Sport and Recreation, Ngconde Balfour, emphasised 'the importance of physical education and sport in the development of the child', and identified schools as the place 'where the foundation for healthy living practices should be laid' (*Soweto Reporter*, 2000, p. 9). Their joint vision was to reinstate physical education in schools and provide competitive and recreational activities, as well as utilise sport as a vehicle for crime prevention and HIV/AIDS advocacy programmes.

In addition to identifying sporting talent, the rationale for mass participation in sport was to utilise it as a tool for addressing 'social deviance'. In 2007, Sam Bopape, the then spokesperson of the National Department of Education, subscribed to the vision that 'a child in sport is a child out of court', when talking about introducing the School Sport Mass Participation programme:

some objectives were to foster pride and respect amongst the youth by enhancing social cohesion, nation-building and turning schools into functional learning institutions. We also aim to strategically link schools to national interventions such as HIV and Aids awareness campaigns, crime prevention and substance abuse.

(Visagie, 2007: 5)

The 2013 White Paper also recognises the UN stance on sport and recreation, where sport is recognised as a fundamental human right; it subscribes to utilising sport as a tool towards achieving the Millennium Development Goals, while also harnessing the power of sport for development and peace objectives (Sport and Recreation South Africa, 2013a). With the current Deputy Minister of Sport and Recreation serving as chair of the Executive Board of the SDP IWG, this would remain a strategic drive, as would a partnership with loveLife (an international non-governmental organisation), and other corporate stakeholders delivering HIV and AIDS education (Sport and Recreation South Africa, 2013b; Burnett, 2014).

Social entrepreneurs, sponsored by the corporate or development sectors, offer thousands of projects at schools across the country without the real synergy of being guided by a policy framework (Coalter, 2013). Kidd (2011, p. 161) reports on this emerging phenomenon as follows:

During the last two decades, national and international corporations, foundations, non-governmental organizations (NGOs), sports organizations and professional and Olympic athletes have responded to the inadequacy of public schools and recreation centres that once provided accessible opportunities for sport and physical activity by creating their own organizations and programmes.

Possibly one of the most ambitious projects of this kind was the GIZ-YDF programme implemented in ten African countries, including South Africa, from 2007 to 2013 (Burnett, 2013). GIZ (German Development Cooperation) offered a Youth Development through Football (YDF) programme in partnership with SRSA and mainly NGO partners and networks. Funding came from the German Federal Ministry of Economic Cooperation and Development (BMZ) and the EU (European Union), and delivered sport-for-development activities to 40,344 South Africans between 7 and 25 years old.

Robust research has informed the programme design and implementation, while providing evidence of positive social outcomes (Burnett, 2012b). It also attracted Nike South Africa for funding capacity-building of the Sport for Social Change network – currently having 54 NGO members in Southern Africa and being the only 'recreation body' funded by SRSA (Burnett, 2013; 2014). Nike South Africa is embarking on a 'running programme' for the most disadvantaged youth in Alexandra Township, informed by their global 'Designed to Move' initiative (Burnett, 2014).

Conclusion

National governments find it challenging to balance expenditure between sport-for-all and elite sport, and this is exacerbated in developing countries when resource allocation skews toward competitive sport, compromising spending on sport-for-all sectors (including physical education, mass participation and sport-for-development initiatives) (Skille, 2011). Another challenge is the blurring of boundaries between sport phenomena such as competitive sport being used for both entertainment and nation-building, and the demarcation of the sport-for-all policy ethos which may also be socially engineered for nation-building (Green, 2006). It seems that sport is socially constructed and politically manipulated to reach myriad objectives. It can also be made to fit the argument of conceptual engineers advocating for their causes at all levels of engagement (Coalter, 2013). No sporting policy or practice thus escapes the ideological and political baggage engrained in its DNA.

Poverty and the lack of resources, coupled with competition-driven motives, negatively impact on the notion of universal access and the sport-for-all ethos (Skille, 2011). The structuring of school sport as an elitist activity in the context of scarce resources may result in 'cherry-picking' and pooling pockets of talent, rather than educating children and providing options for an active and healthy lifestyle (Miranda *et al.*, 2011).

Elite sport, which is entrenched in professionalism and nation-building, absorbs public funding and national strategic drives at the cost of offering choices for preferred participation. In South Africa, the interplay between reconciliation and transformation causes polarised and fragmented delivery of 'sport-for-all' as defined by myriad roles.

References

Alexander, G. (2013). Assets and Incomes. In J. Kane-Berman (ed.) *South Africa Survey*. Johannesburg: South African Institute of Race Relations, pp. 291–348.

Anon. (2010). Editorial comment. Mbalula sport on over sports quotas. *Weekend Post*. 13 November, p. 8.

Anon. (2014). Sport minister takes off the gloves and comes our fighting. *City Press*. 26 January, p. 22.

Ardé, A. (2005). Why school sport is so vital. *Saturday Star*. 6 August, p. 4

BauNews. (2006). Children must take part in sport. *Express*. 22 December, p. 18

Bolsmann, C. and Brewster, K. (2009). Mexico 1968 and South Africa 2010. Development, leadership and legacies. *Sport in Society*, 12(10): 1284–1298.

Booth, D. (1997). The South African Council on sports and the political antinomies of the sports boycott. *Journal of Southern African Studies*, 23(1): 51–67.

Burnett, C. (2010). The role of the state in sport for development. A South African scenario. *African Journal for Physical Education, Health Education, Recreation and Dance (AJPHERD)*, 16(1): 42–55.

Burnett, C. (2012a). In Africa for FIFA and sons. In B. Segaert, M. Theeboom, C. Timmerman and B. Vanreusel (eds), *Sports Governance, Development and Corporate Responsibility.* London: Routledge, pp. 17–29.

Burnett, C. (2012b). GIZ/YDF as a driver of sport for development in Africa. *Journal of Sport and Development,* 9(1): 1–11.

Burnett, C. (2013). GIZ/YDF and youth as drivers for sport for development in the African context. *Journal of Sport for Development* [online], 1(1): 1–10. Available from: www.jsfd. org/publications (accessed 26 April 2014).

Burnett, C. (2014). Report on the pilot of Alex Butterflies Programme. (Unpublished report). University of Johannesburg, Department of Sport and Movement Studies.

Burnett, C. and Hollander, W.J. (2006). *Report of the mid-impact phase of the Mass Participation Project (Siyadlala) of Sport and Recreation South Africa.* Johannesburg: University of Johannesburg, Department of Sport and Movement Studies.

Burnett, C. and Hollander, W.J. (2008). *The Pre-impact Assessment of the School Sport Mass Participation Project.* Johannesburg: University of Johannesburg, Department of Sport and Movement Studies.

Coalter, F. (2013). *Sport for Development: What Game are we Playing?.* London: Routledge.

Coetzee, G. (2004). SA se 'Olimpiese agterstand', skole in visier. Kabinet hersien sportbeleid. [SA's 'Olympic backlog', schools aimed at. Cabinet reviews sport policy]. *Beeld.* 18 August, p. 2.

Collins, M. (2004). Sport, physical activity and social inclusion. *Journal of Sports Sciences,* 22: 727–740.

Cortis, N. (2009). Social inclusion and sport. Culturally diverse women's perspectives. *Australian Journal of Social Issues,* 44(1): 91–106.

Edwards, G. (2011). Minister se groot plan vir sport op skool. [Minister's ambitious plan for sport at schools]. *Beeld,* 3 February, p. 3.

Fengu, M. (2011). Heat on schools for poaching sports stars. *Daily Dispatch,* 28 May, p. 4

Green, M. (2006). From 'sport-for-all' to not about 'sport' for all? Interrogating sport policy interventions in the United Kingdom. *European Sport Management Quarterly,* 6(3): 217–238.

Gunning, E. (2002). Balfour takel skolesport. [Balfour attacks school sport]. *Rapport,* 1 December, p. 2.

Hoberman, J. (2007). Sportive nationalism. In A. Tomlinson (ed.), *The Sport Studies Reader.* London: Routledge, pp. 124–129.

Houlihan, B. (2005). Public sector sports policy. Developing a framework for analysis. *International Review for the Sociology of Sport,* 40(2): 163–185.

Isaacs, Z. (2011). Transformation is about more than colour quotas. *Business Day,* 24 November, p. 31.

Jones, M. (2011). After-school sport to be compulsory. Education department plans to get pupils fit and healthy. *Pretoria News,* 30 December, p. 4

Kersting, N. (2007). Sport and national identity: A comparison of the 2006 and 2010 FIFA World Cups. *Politiko,* 34(3): 277–293.

Kidd, B. (2011). Epilogue. The struggles must continue. In R. Field and B. Kidd (eds), *Forty Years of Sport and Social Change, 1968–2008.* London: Routledge, pp. 157–166.

Laverty, A. (2010). Sports diplomacy and apartheid South Africa [online]. Available from: http://theafricanfile.com/politicshistory/sports-diplomacy-and-apartheid-south-africa (accessed 16 June 2014).

Lepp, A. and Gibson, H. (2011). Reimaging a nation. South Africa and the 2010 FIFA World Cup. *Journal of Sport and Tourism,* 16(3): 211–230.

Maguire, J. (2011). *Invictus* or evict-us? Media images of South Africa through the lens of the FIFA World Cup. *Social Identities*, 17(5): 681–694.

Mdhelela, J.-M. (2013). We need racial quotas to redress SA's past imbalances, Mr Kriel. *The New Age*, 10 December, p. 15.

Meulders, B., Vanreusel, B., Bruyninckx, H., Keim, M., and Travill, A. (2012). A governance perspective on sport mega-events. sports governance, development and corporate responsibility. In B. Segaert, M. Theeboom, C. Timmerman and B. Vanreusel (eds). *Sports Governance, Development and Corporate Responsibility*. London: Routledge.

Miranda, E.G.E., Armstrong, E., Lambert, V. *et al.* (2011). Physical fitness of South African primary school children, 6 to 13 years of age. Discovery vitality health of the nation study. *Perceptual and Motor Skills*, 113(3): 999–1016.

Miti, L. (2011). Lives being destroyed in the name of sport. *Daily Dispatch*, 21 June, p. 7.

Mkhwanazi, S. (2012). More to sport than soccer, sir. *Citizen*. 30 March, p. 13.

Nagel, G., Rapp, K., Wabitsch, M., *et al.* (2008). Prevalence and cluster of cardiometabolic biomarkers in overweight and obese schoolchildren: results from a large survey in south-west Germany. *Clinical Chemistry*, 54(2): 317–325.

Ndaba, B. (2013). Bid to do away with all work and no play for pupils. *Star Tuesday*, 4 June, p. 7.

Ntloko, M. (2012). Transformation inquiry looms. *Business Day*, 25 January, p. 20.

O'Connor, M. (2012). Skolesport is nou prioriteit [School sport is now a priority]. *Burger*, 12 May, p. 2.

Odendaal, A. (2006). Sport and liberation. The unfinished business of the past. In C. Thomas (ed.), *Sport and Liberation in South Africa*. Alice: University of Fort Hare. pp. 11–38.

Pillay, U. and Bass, O. (2008). Mega-events as a response to poverty reduction. The 2010 FIFA World Cup and its urban development implications. *Urban Forum*, 19: 329–346

Potgieter, M. (2012). Hoofde verwelkom planne vir skolesport [Principals welcome plans for school sport]. *Burger*, 15 March, p. 4.

Seemise, P. (2013). School sports to become a way of life for every pupil. *The New Age*, 12 September, p. 23.

Sethlatwe, B. (2014). Reflecting on twenty years. *FastFACTS*, 4(272): 1–21.

Shafto, M. (2005). Right place to start transformation is in schools. *Independent*, 5 March, p. 15.

Skille, E.Å. (2011). Sport-for-all in Scandinavia. Sport policy and participation in Norway, Sweden and Denmark. *International Journal of Sport Policy and Politics*, 3(3): 327–339.

Smit, M. (2009). Bid to marry schools with federations. Sam says move will not interfere with autonomy of institutions. *Business Day*, 16 April, p. 19.

Sowetan Reporter (2000). School sport policy. *Sowetan Reporter*. 23 February, p. 9.

Sport and Recreation South Africa (SRSA). (2009). *A Case for Sport*. Pretoria: Department of Sport and Recreation South Africa.

Sport and Recreation South Africa (SRSA). (2011). *Declaration and Resolutions of the National Sport and Recreation Indaba*. Pretoria: Department of Sport and Recreation South Africa.

Sport and Recreation South Africa (SRSA). (2013a). *White Paper on Sport and Recreation*. Pretoria: Department of Sport and Recreation South Africa.

Sport and Recreation South Africa (SRSA). (2013b). *National Sport and Recreation Plan*. Pretoria: Department of Sport and Recreation South Africa.

Stofile, M. (2006). Sport is a human right. Opening of conference address by the (then) Minister of Sport. In C. Thomas (ed.), *Sport and Liberation in South Africa*. Alice: University of Fort Hare, pp. 3–8.

Sugden, J. and Tomlinson, A. (2000). Theorising sport and social class. In J. Coakley and E. Dunning (eds), *Handbook of Sport Studies*. London: Sage, pp. 309–321.

Talbot, M. (2007). The politics of sport and physical education. In A. Tomlinson (ed.), *The Sport Studies Reader*. London: Routledge, pp. 150–156.

Tomlinson, R., Bass, O. and Bassett, T. (2011). Before and after the vuvuzela. Identity, image and mega-events in South Africa, China and Brazil. *South African Geographical Journal*, 93(1): 38–48

Visagie, N. (2007). Government departments unite to promote school sport participation. *Diamond Fields Advertiser*, 14 March, p. 5

Waterworth, T. and Skade, T. (2010). Why steroid abuse is rife in schools. Boys putting their lives at risk. *Independent on Saturday*, 20 November, p. 2

8 The Paralympic Movement and sport-for-all

Elite, recreational and inclusive sport for development[1]

Mary A. Hums and Eli A. Wolff

This chapter focuses specifically on issues of inclusion, sport-for-all and the participation of athletes with disabilities within the Paralympic Movement. The chapter will examine the elite, recreational and inclusive sport for development dimensions of the Paralympic Movement.

The Paralympic Movement

The Paralympic Movement does much to promote sport and physical activity for people with disabilities around the world. The Movement operates on various levels. The Paralympic Games showcase elite talent. Other sectors of the Paralympic Movement foster recreational grass-roots-level sport.

The Paralympic Games

The Paralympic Movement has been growing at a steady pace since the first competitions were held for people with disabilities (IPC, 2012). Although sport and physical activity for people with disabilities existed earlier, the first recognised competition occurred in 1948 at Stoke Mandeville Rehabilitation Hospital. The hospital served as a healing space for wounded veterans from the Second World War. Many of those receiving care there were young people whose lives were altered instantly by an explosion or gunfire. A physician at the hospital, Dr Ludwig Guttmann, recognised that true healing involved more than dressing wounds or stitching injuries. True healing took place in a more holistic sense – including the mind, body and spirit.

Many people at the hospital were active prior to acquiring their injuries, and physical activity was a part of their lives. Knowing this, Guttmann decided to incorporate physical activity, including sport, into the rehabilitation programmes for the people being treated there. Think for a minute. Many of you reading this are athletes and enjoy physical activity. If the opportunity to enjoy those activities was taken away from you by injury or illness, you would naturally feel less than yourself – less than whole. As we realise now, sport is a human right. It is like enjoying music or creating art. It makes us more fully human. If you lost the ability to participate, you would welcome the opportunity to be active again.

> Sir Ludwig came up with the revolutionary idea of using sport as a key part of rehabilitation – this, combined with his positive attitude towards patients, was the key to his success in treating them. Under his care, people were encouraged to try activities including wheelchair polo, wheelchair basketball and archery, which proved popular, as paraplegics could compete with able-bodied counterparts.
>
> (Bushby, 2011, paras. 5–7)

In 1948, Guttmann staged the first Stoke-Mandeville Games for wheelchair athletes. That event, symbolically opening on the same day as the Opening Ceremonies of the Olympic Games being held in London, saw 16 men and women compete in archery (Bushby, 2011). Four years later, athletes from the Netherlands would join in, and the first recognised international competition for athletes with disabilities became a reality.

Slowly but surely, athletes with disabilities began to compete in increased numbers and the Paralympic Movement progressed. The first event officially using the Paralympic Games moniker took place in Rome in 1960, the same year the Summer Olympic Games were staged in that same city. There, 400 athletes representing 23 countries competed in eight sports – archery, athletics, dartchery, snooker, swimming, table tennis, wheelchair basketball and wheelchair fencing. Sweden hosted the first Winter Paralympic Games a few years later, in 1976. Just under 200 athletes from 16 countries competed in alpine skiing and cross-country skiing in those first Winter Games (IPC, n.d.).

Over the years, the Paralympic Games evolved. Sports were added to both the Summer and Winter Paralympic Games programmes and the number of National Paralympic Committees (NPCs) sending delegations from their countries increased. At the Summer Games in Beijing in 2008, the Games met a long strived-for goal, as the number of athletes competing topped the 4,000 mark, with female athletes comprising 35 per cent of all competitors. Looking forward to Rio de Janeiro in 2016, the addition of two new sports, para-canoe and para-triathlon, will bring the total number of sports on the programme up to 22 (Rio 2016, n.d.).

The Paralympic Games are a showcase for elite athletes who represent their countries at the highest level of international competition, but the Paralympic Movement is more all-encompassing. The road to becoming a Paralympian is long, and not everyone has the abilities to be an elite athlete, just as is the case in able-bodied sport. So what opportunities are there for people with disabilities who want to participate in sport and physical activity? And how does the Paralympic Movement help generate these opportunities?

Recreational sport opportunities

In its current Strategic Plan, the IPC addresses athlete development on the grass-roots level. The organisation's Strategic Goal 2 is Athlete Development. Two stated Strategic Priorities are to 'develop strategies to maintain the effective and efficient promotion of sports activities for Para athletes from grass-roots to elite level focusing on those countries and organisations most in need' and 'develop athlete pathway programmes starting from the grass-roots to the elite level boosting athlete participation and career development' (IPC, 2011, p. 19). The IPC's vision includes athlete development, but what might a local example of this in action look like?

One example of promoting Paralympic sport on the grass-roots level is an organisation called Blaze Sports. Founded as a legacy from the 1996 Atlanta Summer Paralympic Games, Blaze Sports has served over 13,000 children and adults with disabilities since it began operation. The stated goals of the organisations are as follows (Blaze Sports, 2014):

> To provide sport, recreation and physical activity opportunities for people with physical disability in sport comparable to those provided non-disabled, nationally and internationally.
> To foster character development, productive lives, healthy lifestyles and self-sufficiency for people with physical disability through sport.
> To use cutting-edge training, distance learning opportunities, and fresh ideas as a vehicle to build the capacity of local service providers.
> To build positive perceptions of people with physical disability.
> To promote peace building, human rights and equity through sport.

Blaze Sports sponsors a number of activities, including programmes in adapted water sports, canoe/kayak, climbing, swimming, athletics and wheelchair basketball. They also organise camps and have been vital in the Dixie Games, a multi-sport disability sport event, for 35 years. Their educational programming includes a certification whereby one can become a Certified Disability Sport Specialist (CDSS).

Blaze Sports provides a best-practices model for sport administrators and coaches who want to partner with the Paralympic Movement to create athletic opportunities for young people with disabilities. Other avenues exist outside the Paralympic Movement to foster recreational sport participation for people with disabilities and these will be discussed further into this chapter. In its quest to provide opportunities from the grass-roots level upwards, the Paralympic Movement faces a number of challenges and issues. These are addressed next.

Issues facing the Paralympic Movement

In attempting to further the growth and development of Paralympic sport, the Paralympic Movement will encounter challenges along the way. Two of these are (a) providing sport in developing countries and (b) constantly evolving technology.

Providing sport in developing countries

As the reader is well aware, in these times a great disparity exists among nations in our world. The so-called developed countries have stronger sport and non-sport infrastructures. As the IPC states (2014, p. 18):

> in developing nations sport infrastructure is sometimes poor with few facilities, limited supply of equipment and little government support. In between you find a wide range of organizational models, resource levels and capabilities with cultural and language differences contributing to the mix. Hence, initially motivated Para athletes are often struggling to find the right starting point at the grass-roots level and miss coaching and career assistance to become elite. They feel deprived of 'their right to practice sports' as stated in the UN Convention on the Rights of Persons with a Disability.

The IPC initially established the Organizational Development Initiative (ODI), followed by the International Paralympic Foundation (IPF) as a means to help smaller NPCs grow Para-sports in their countries. These initiatives indicate that the IPC is committed to 'grow and sustain athlete participation at all levels by providing quality competition opportunities and skilled human resources (coaches, officials, administrators) as the foundation for the pathway from initiation to high performance sport' (IPC, 2014, p. 18).

Athletes in developing countries need these boosts to help them access sport. In countries where conflict and natural disasters have played a major role, many people with disabilities are without the basic necessities of life, much less access to sport and physical activity. Yet, sport and physical activity contribute to the health and well-being of people in such circumstances. As stated by the IOC in its Olympic Charter, the practice of sport is a human right (IOC, 2013). This right is not limited to those living in the developed world. The practice of sport is a human right for all people, regardless of ability or situation. One factor that can hinder athletes, however, is access to the necessary equipment. This will be addressed in the next paragraphs.

Equipment and technology

Many sports, whether designed for able-bodied people or people with disabilities, require a certain amount of equipment. For people with disabilities, the cost of this equipment can be prohibitive, especially for people in developing countries. Success in competition may require costly state-of-the-art sports equipment (Brittain, 2010; Hambrick *et al.*, in press). A beginner's sledge hockey sled costs $500, recreational handcycles start around $2,500 and low-level mono-skis can cost upwards of $3,000 (Freedom Factory, 2011; Mobility

Sports, 2013). Oftentimes, athletes are required to use shared equipment in order to participate. This results in 'down-time' – waiting for a piece of equipment to be open – and also more wear and tear on the equipment that is available. While sharing equipment is certainly far better than having no equipment at all, it does present a barrier to those who wish to take part in healthy, recreational activity.

In our rapidly changing technology environment, it is not just social media, communications, and transportation that are evolving. Sports equipment technology is advancing as well. Prosthetics and racing wheelchairs are getting lighter. Rugby wheelchairs are being built to take bigger hits while being easier to manoeuvre. Archery and shooting equipment enables athletes to be more precise with their aim. But at what point does technology take over and the human element diminish?

There is also, of course, the ongoing debate over whether a prosthetic device provides an advantage for an athlete with a disability over an able-bodied athlete. While we are all too familiar with the battle Oscar Pistorius had to wage to compete for a chance on the South African Olympic squad, the discussion does not end there. Just this past summer (2014), German Paralympic long jump champion Markus Rehm was left off the German team for the European Athletics Championship, saying 'the athlete's carbon-fiber prostheses gives him an unfair advantage' (Starcevic, 2014, para. 1). Rehm had won the long jump competition at the German Nationals, beating out numerous able-bodied jumpers. Officials from the German athletics federation (DLV) opted to drop him from the squad on the basis that jumping off a prosthetic device provided him an unfair advantage (Starcevic, 2014).

The discussion over creating opportunities for people with disabilities to participate or compete in sport and physical activity continues, in different sports and on various levels, from grass-roots to elite. The next section continues this discussion, focusing on sport for development and peace.

Inclusive sport for development and peace

In addition to elite and grass-roots dimensions of sport directly within the Paralympic Movement, sport for people with disabilities also takes place on a very local level, with small organisations leading the charge to get people with disabilities active and living a healthy life. These organisations often fall under the category of sport for development and peace (SDP).

When you hear the term sport for development and peace, what comes to mind? In a nutshell, it is utilising the power of sport to accomplish social good. This power of sport can take three forms: (1) the power to inform, (2) the power to empower and (3) the power to transform (Hums and Wolff, 2014). According to Sport Matters, an SDP organisation based in Australia (2014, para. 1–2):

> Access to sport and physical activity is a fundamental human right. Sport is well recognised internationally as a low-cost and high-impact tool for development and a powerful agent for social change. It is a cultur-

ally accepted activity that brings people together and unites families, communities and nations. Effective sport-for-development programs combine sport and play with other non-sport outcomes to achieve the desired development objectives. The focus is not on mass participation or performance in elite sport. This requires a purposeful, professional and socially responsible intervention that is tailored to the social and cultural context.

The United Nations Office of Sport for Development and Peace (UNODSP) recognises the power of sport as offering the following (UNOSDP, n.d., para. 5–6):

Fundraising, advocacy, mobilization and raising public awareness: in particular by appointing celebrity athletes as 'Ambassadors' or 'Spokespersons' and leveraging the potential of sports events as outreach platforms. The mobilising power of sport is often used as a 'door-opener' to convey crucial messages about HIV/AIDS, child's rights, the environment, education, etc.

Development and peace promotion: in grass-roots projects sport is used in an extremely wide range of situations – whether as an integrated tool in short-term emergency humanitarian aid activities, or in long-term development cooperation projects, on a local, regional or global scale.

So how does sport for development and peace relate to people with disabilities? A few examples will illustrate this point.

One successful SDP organisation is Sport4Socialisation (S4S). Headquartered in the Netherlands, S4S operates on the ground in Zimbabwe, utilising sport to help achieve its goals of assisting people with disabilities. The organisation does this by strategies which include:

- Strengthening them [people with disabilities] through rehabilitation services, adapted physical activity, provision of medication and assistive devices;
- Increasing access to quality education;
- Connecting them with both able-bodied and disabled peers;
- Teaching them valuable life skills and to stand up for themselves in society;
- Educating their families on dealing with disability and create opportunities to fend for themselves economically;
- Inspiring, encouraging and coaching their communities to change attitudes on disability.

(Sport4Sociaisation, 2014, para. 3)

Next, we have the organisation Disability Is Not Inability (DINIP). DINIP started in 2011 in Burera, Rwanda. In that country, women with disabilities are not valued because they are seen as a source of shame and objects of charity. DINIP began offering football opportunities for these women, achieving a solid level of success. 'Our project has focused on disabled women rights through football tournaments and the project has been able to have tangible impacts because more than 250 women with disabilities knew their rights to education and inheritance' (Beyond Sport, 2014, para. 1).

SDP organisations take different shapes and identify differing social needs depending on where they operate. One common theme for these organisations is the emphasis on grass-roots participation rather than elite competition. These types of organisations and their programmes help people with disabilities access local sport and physical activity opportunities on the level appropriate for their interests and abilities. They may also ignite an interest in a sport for someone with a disability who may wish to pursue competition on a higher level.

The way forward

This chapter has served to provide a very basic overview of some of the participation and competition opportunities enjoyed by people with disabilities in sport. From elite to grass-roots levels, people with disabilities are moving into the greater sporting arena. The goal is to find a place for everybody – a place where sport-for-all truly means *all*, including people with disabilities. Where to look for guidance on this? The United Nations Convention on the Rights of Persons with Disabilities provides a global framework for sport-for-all in Article 30.5, stating that persons with disabilities have a right to 'participate on an equal basis with others in recreational, leisure and sporting activities' (United Nations, 2006). Given the relationship and intersection between the Olympic and Paralympic Movement, one could also look to the IOC's Sport-For-All Commission which includes the following statement:

> Sport-for-All is a movement promoting the Olympic ideal that sport is a human right for all individuals regardless of race, social class and sex. The movement encourages sports activities that can be exercised by people of all ages, both sexes and different social and economic conditions.
>
> (IOC, 2014, para. 3)

So where in here is disability? Of course, as this chapter illustrates, providing opportunities for people with disabilities in sport is not the sole responsibility of the IOC. Or for that matter the IPC, although many look there for instruction. Creating opportunities can happen locally, nationally or internationally. But mostly, creating opportunities happens one sport at a time, one person at a time, one gymnasium or swimming pool at a time. It happens one wheelchair, one football, or one flashing light at a time. Change happens when people in sport open their minds to creative possibilities for participation by all!

Note

1 The authors wish to dedicate this chapter to a long-time Paralympic friend and colleague who recently passed away – Mr. Jon McCullough. May we always remember his friendship, his dedication to inclusion for all, and his mantra for life: 'Share the love.'

References

Beyond Sport. (2014). Disability is not inability. Retrieved from www.beyondsport.org/project/d/disability-is-not-inability-project-dinip

Blaze Sports. (2014). Our purpose. Retrieved from www.blazesports.org/about/our-purpose

Brittain, I. (2010). *The Paralympic Games Explained*. New York: Routledge.

Bushby, H. (2011). London 2012: How Stoke Mandeville put the Paralympics on the map. BBC News, 15 September. Retrieved from www.bbc.com/news/uk-14896776

Freedom Factory. (2011). Semi-custom recreational equipment. Retrieved from www.freedomfactory.org/pricing.htm

Hambrick, M.E., Hums, M.A., Bower, G.G. and Wolff, E.A. (in press). Examining elite para-sport athletes with sport involvement and sports equipment. *Adapted Physical Activity Quarterly*.

Hums, M.A. and Wolff, E.A. (2014, April 3). Power of sport to inform, empower, and transform. *Huffington Post*. Retrieved from www.huffingtonpost.com/dr-mary-hums/power-of-sport-to-inform-_b_5075282.html?utm_hp_ref=sportsandir=Sports

IOC (2013). *Olympic Charter*. Lausanne: IOC.

IOC (2014). Sport-For-All Commission. Retrieved from www.olympic.org/sport-for-all-commission

IPC. (n.d.). IPC historical results database. Retrieved from www.paralympic.org/results/historical

IPC. (2011). *International Paralympic Committee Strategic Plan 2011–2014*. Bonn: IPC.

IPC. (2012). Foundations for Paralympic Movement's recent growth were laid in Spain in 92, says IPC president. Retrieved from www.paralympic.org/news/foundations-paralympic-movement-s-recent-growth-were-laid-spain-92-says-ipc-president

IPC. (2014). *International Paralympic Committee Strategic Plan 2011–2014*. Bonn: IPC.

Mobility Sports. (2013). Program sleds. Retrieved from www.mobilitysports.com/#!/~/category/id=1500942andoffset=0andsort=normal

Rio2016. (n.d.). Paralympic Games. Retrieved from www.rio2016.org/en/the-games/sports/Paralympic

Sport Matters. (2014). Why sport? Retrieved from www.sportmatters.org.au/why_sport.php

Sport4Socialisation. (2014). Welcome to S4S. Retrieved from www.sport4socialisation.org/home

Starcevic, N. (2014, July 31). Track and field: German long-jump champion, an amputee, left off team. *Columbus Dispatch*. Retrieved from www.dispatch.com/content/stories/sports/2014/07/31/german-long-jump-champion-an-amputee-left-off-team.html

United Nations. (2006) Convention on the Rights of Persons with Disabilities, 2006. Retrieved from www.un.org/disabilities/

UNOSDP. (n.d.). Why sport? Retrieved from www.un.org/wcm/content/site/sport/home/sport

9 Elite sport and sport-for-all

Tales of a small country

Uri Schaefer

Introduction

The power of sport and physical activity as a social tool and as a unique and most important platform for the development of every child was well presented by researchers and is well known to politicians. However, in Israel sport and physical activity have not yet received the expected attention and, as a result, the proper resources thus remain in the past, undeveloped. The huge potential of sport is not used – not as a social vehicle to integrate the people, to enhance public health, to build bridges between the Jews and the minorities, nor as a basic right of every individual to maximise his/her potential or to compete on the world's sport stages like World Championships or Olympic Games in order to increase national pride, sympathy, etc.

Many reasons contributed to this situation: the ongoing need to continue to fight for our independence; the Jewish heritage and culture, which is known as 'The people of the book', didn't see sport and physical activity as an important element that needs special attention; the necessity to build and develop the country and face many social and economic crises first.

We should note, however, that all along the years, since our independence (1948) physical education has been mandatory in schools (two hours per week to each class), and Israel does have some outstanding achievements (in 1977 Maccabbi Tel Aviv basketball team won for the first time the European Basketball Championship, and in the 1992 Barcelona Olympic Games we won our first two Olympic medals: a bronze in Judo for men and a silver for women in the same). Up to the London 2012 Olympic Games Israel had won seven medals.

It is for this reason that we, the Ministry of Culture and Sport under the leadership of Minister Limor Livnat, decided in 2009 to change the status of sport in the country.

Overview

The Sport Authority is responsible for the field of sport in the Ministry of Culture and Sport. The Sport Authority is in charge of the sport policy and strategy in Israel. Its role is to promote, oversee and deal with sport-related issues in Israel, in both the fields of elite, competitive sport and sport-for-all. It aspires to develop and promote sport culture and competitive sport in Israel on every level, through the development and fostering of excellence, support and assistance in sport-related activities in the framework of local authorities and non-governmental bodies like the National Governing Bodies (NGBs) and promotion of an active lifestyle throughout the country's population with the help and coordination of relevant stakeholders (i.e. the communities).

Among others, the Sport Authority strives to establish a strategic policy for sport in Israel and to promote supporting legislation. It oversees different sport bodies while offering financial support, advice, consultancy and professional guidance to sport bodies and institutions, as well as to sport administrations in local authorities. In addition, the Sport Authority represents the government, inside Israel and outside of it, in every sport-related issue.

General: establishing a strategy

The Ministry of Culture and Sport, through the work of the Sport Authority, started a re-organisation process in 2008, recognising the importance of sport for the citizens and the country, as well as the need to elevate elite and competitive sport and the value of sport culture.

The process was composed of several stages which were executed hierarchically in terms of importance, in consultancy with relevant stakeholders and personnel. The initial step was to determine the vision.

Setting the vision and the objectives

The Israel Sports Authority strives to implement the culture of sport in Israel as a part of the life cycle of every citizen and promote achievement-oriented sports excellence, aiming at attaining top sport accomplishments on the international level, while creating national pride and promoting ethical values and standards in sport.

SWOT analysis

We performed a SWOT – strengths, weaknesses, opportunities and threats – analysis soon afterwards. In order to do that efficiently, we isolated our weaknesses (such as poor facilities, weak coaching education structure, etc.), and identified possible opportunities (such as appointment of a new Minister for Culture and Sport, a new Sport Authority Director, etc.). With the aim of finding an edge over the competition, as opposed to resorting to playing catch-up, we have established our own comparative advantages aimed to serve us competitively in the future. The analysis was performed by a team consisting of Sport Authority members and a focus group which represented our main partners: sport organisations and NGBs, local authorities, Wingate Institute and the Schools' Sports Federation. We had to address four main weaknesses which were identified through the SWOT analysis, and at the same time use our existing opportunities and strengths, such as the size of the country, the traditional success in sailing and judo, the Sport Law, the new Minister and Sport Authority Director.

The main weaknesses include coaching and coach education, sport infrastructures (facilities and grass-roots-level athletes) and sport administration, among others.

While developing the strategy, we were assisted by the late Prof. Feigenbaum, who was a renowned business administration specialist, Vice Dean of the famous Academic Institution, The Teknion, and a former star of our national Volleyball team. As a result, we presented our strategy, which is based on three main principles:

1   Cooperation with key partners: NGBs, Olympic, non-Olympic and Paralympic sport organisations, local authorities.
2   Strategic capabilities within the Sport Authority (finance, legislation, administration, marketing, etc.).
3   Evaluation, feedback and control; all of which were labelled by us as the 'Strategic House'. (see Figure 9.1)

The strategic plan's main objective was, and still is, to improve the quality of life of the citizens of the state, and thus aimed to address and fight chronic diseases such as overweight and obesity, especially among the young generation; diabetes, etc., and also to increase our medal count in major sporting events, namely Olympic and Paralympic Games, European Championships and World Championships and the World Games in Non-Olympic Sports.

The strategy

What is the strategy? It consists of four layers (as presented in Figure 9.1).

A   **The PRODUCT**: adopted from the business terminology. In principle, we are 'selling' (and focusing on) three products:
    1   Competitive and elite top sports – in cooperation with NGBs, Olympic and Paralympic Committees, Non-Olympic Sport Association, Local Authorities, etc.
    2   Sport-for-all and traditional games – in cooperation with local authorities.
    3   Infrastructure – building new sport facilities and redevelopment of sport facilities.
B   **The CLIENTS**: stakeholders and strategic partners, without whom reaching the objectives we have set is impossible (NGBs, local authorities,

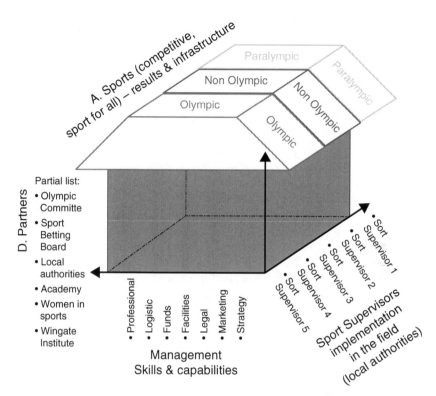

Figure 9.1 The goal is to promote competitive sports (A). This could be done through building management capabilities (B), implemented in local authorities via sport supervisors (C). Cooperation between partners is necessary (D).

Israeli Olympic and Paralympic Committees, Non-Olympic Association, Wingate Institute, etc.).

C   **SUPERVISION**: After implementing the strategy with the help of seven Sport Authority supervisors distributed across seven districts (North, Haifa, Tel Aviv, Center, Jerusalem and the vicinity, South, ethnic minorities).

D   **STRATEGIC CAPABILITIES**: professional, logistics, facilities-related, financial, regulation, marketing and administration issues, among others.

The strategic plan was introduced to the Sport Authority staff, and it received unanimous plaudits and support. The plan was also introduced to all Sport Department Directors in the local communities participating in the yearly Sport Administrators Conference (which is held annually in cooperation with the Center of the Local Authorities; in Israel there are 253 local communities and the Sport Authority is cooperating and advising 240 of them), to sport organisations, the Wingate Institute and the School Sports Federation.

During the strategic development process, structural changes within the Sport Authority took place.

Structural changes

For the first time, a Deputy to the Sport Director was appointed in the field of sports for all, in addition to the deputy of competitive and elite sports, who was appointed beforehand. The aim was to ensure both 'products' would receive adequate attention and care. Furthermore, we see both as a tree that has the same roots, but once grown has different branches.

As part of the new structure, the Diving Authority – in charge of supervising the 46 scuba diving training schools in Israel (we have about 30,000 divers who dive annually) – is inclusive in 'sports for all', while the new Motorsport Authority (founded in 2007) belongs to 'competitive sports'.

At the same time, a directorate consisting of six members was established to the Sport Authority. The six members are the director, the two deputies, the head of the Motorsport Authority, the head of the Diving Authority and the head of Women Sports (who is a former Olympic swimmer) in order to ensure women's representation.

Executing the strategy

Transparency: ISO9002

Once it became clear that one of the biggest weaknesses in Israeli sport is the management level within NGBs and sport departments across local authorities, we recommended they adopt ISO9002 as a basis for transparent administration, which offers, among others, swift answers to public complaints and references, and ensures supervision and control over those. In that framework, an NGB which decides to adopt ISO9002 is rewarded financially as part of our policy.

Striving for excellence: EFQM

In order to be justify demanding organisations adopt the model, the Sport Authority adopted the EFQM (European Foundation for Quality Management). We are delighted to point out that the Sport Authority won the 2013 prize on behalf of the Prime Minister for excellent administration, and was awarded a silver medal – category one star! The ceremony was held at the Bible Museum in Jerusalem in September 2014.

The Sport Authority strives to continue its mission, and it has set defined areas for further improvements with the intention of transforming the efficiency of our work while offering improved products for our clients. In addition, we are encouraging local authorities to appoint people with academic backgrounds in management (business administration, public administration, etc.) as Sport Department directors, while an academic background in sport serves as an advantage (yet not a necessity, as opposed to how it was prior to the changes).

Finding the balance in regulation

In the regulation field, the Sport Authority constantly operates in order to, on the one hand, ensure the functionality of the sport system within our educational, social and sport values, with the budget allocation as a main concern, and on the other hand to reduce regulation as much as we can.

Generic Code of Ethics

With the above in mind, we initiated the Generic Code of Ethics. We contacted the Ethics Center in Jerusalem, and together with NGBs and the Olympic, Paralympic and Non-Olympic Committees, we started a development plan which took about two years. The Generic Code requires the NGBs not only to adopt it, but to instil its principles among referees, athletes, coaches, directors and board members. It should be noted that the code was developed with the help of a steering committee, in which the Olympic Committee of Israel, the Paralympic Committee and the Non-Olympic Association were involved. Once the Olympic Committee realised it needed to adopt the code to include a section which specifically related to conflict-of-interest situations, it rejected the process and requested the adoption of the International Olympic Committee code. The Sport Authority did not oppose that request, so long as the Generic Code would be the minimum requirement for every NGB. Today the Sport Authority and the Olympic Committee are looking for a solution for that part of the code.

As of 2013, every NGB in the country was due to adopt the Generic Code as a precondition to receive any financial support from the Sport Authority or from the Sport Betting Board, and to act based on its values, subject to the NGBs' legal adviser. The Sport Authority is insistent on morality and transparency, specifically over major and significant issues such as conflict of interests.

Equality in women's representation

As part of our Ministry Sport policy, we initiated a process which led to a change in the Sport Law and in the criteria for being eligible to receive financial support from the Sport Authority and the Sport Betting Board. The new condition states that every NGB board will have to either be made up of 30 per cent women or the percentage of female athletes in the specific sport, whichever is the lowest.

Coaching

The obligation to be certified as a coach is part of the Israeli Sport Law (1988). Until 2000, the Wingate Institute was the only body offering such qualifications. As a result of a petition to the High Court of Justice, the area became open for competition. Over 40 bodies are operating as coach education bodies in the country today. As a result, the quality of the teaching process has decreased significantly; the entrance and final examinations are on a low level and control over the schools is very limited.

Due to the most important role of the coach in the development process of the athletes, from grass-roots level to the podium, as of 2012 the Sport Authority has opened a department responsible for coaching qualifications, coaching excellence and coaching education. An amendment of the current law is being discussed. The objective is to use a different model based on the ICCE and EC (the International Council for Coaching Excellence and the European Committee) four-stage model. Training methods are transformed in order to provide coaches with utmost professionalism, with coaches having to go through a refresher course as a precondition for renewing their licence. The final examinations of levels 3 and 4 will be performed by external experts in full cooperation with the given NGBs.

Equality: promoting women in sport

The Ministry of Culture and Sport believes sport serves as a significant educational tool, consisting of valuable virtues in the development of health and well-being for all citizens, regardless of their faith, gender, ethnicity or age. Women deserve an equal platform to men, and as such they shall receive the required opportunities to take part. In order to ensure that happens, a Council for the Advancement of Women in Sport has been established with the responsibility of providing women with equal rights through funding and, more importantly, through legislation. In 2005 the Israeli government took the decision of establishing the Council, which promises equal participation and rights for women. The Council's initial budget was 80 million NIS for a period of eight years. As of 2015, a decision was made to allocate 20 million NIS per year in order to enhance the development of female sports for the years to come (namely from 2015 on, every year the council will receive 20 million NIS). As of 2013, women constitute 20 per cent of the active athletes in the country (versus 6 per cent in 2005), while they make close to 50 per cent of the Israeli Olympic teams. In 2013, Israel had two world champions in its ranks: Lee Kurzits in windsurfing and Yarden Gerbi in kudo (60 kg). In 2014, Israel won one silver medal for women in the World Judo Championships and one bronze medal for women in windsurfing in the World Championship. In addition, the Israel women's artistic gymnastic team won – for the first time – the silver medal in the World Championship, to name just a few achievements.

Fair play

Professionalism and competitiveness notwithstanding, our achievements will be dealt a massive blow if the platform on which they exist is filled with negativity and violence. In order to tackle violence in sport, especially in football and basketball, all stakeholders have legislated a law named 'The Law against Violence in Sport' (2008), in addition to the Safety in Public Places Law (1962). The law is designed to have police forces outside stadiums and arenas, placing them in the second circle of the sport zone while enforcing control over the spectators using civil guards. As a result, we are hopeful of witnessing improved law enforcement which would eliminate violence and racism. According to explanatory notes of the Bill, the need for a separate law that will regulate violence in all areas of team sports was triggered by repeated incidents of expressions of violence and racism in team sports and events, with an emphasis on football and basketball. Last year police authorities reported that there was a decline in the frequency of violence during ball-based matches. However, the intensity of the incidents has grown worse. In addition, no solution has been found yet to the racism during matches. As a result, the Sport Minister appointed a Special Committee headed by a former high-ranked police officer named Zur, who provided a very detailed plan as to how the ministry and all the stakeholders should cooperate in order to reduce those negative social events as quickly as possible. Today we are still operating to implement the Zur Committee's recommendations (including installing high-tech cameras in all stadiums, arenas and halls, demanding every spectator be identifiable once they enter the stadium).

Amendment of the Israeli Sport Law in the field of integrity

The institution for scrutiny of judges' and referees' ethical qualifications began its activities in 2012, as part of the ministry's fight against corruption in sport, following legislation of an amendment to the Sport Act, and is chaired by a retired judge. Its purpose is to prevent the appointment of field referees or judges or attorneys at the NGBs' courts and disciplinary tribunals if they have criminal records or other ethical issues. In 2013–2014 more than 3,000 judges were scrutinised. About 20 were found as having a problematic record, but only three were disqualified due to their criminal records.

Establishment of 'National Sport Council' (Amendment Number 6)

In 1998, the Levin's Committee recommended the formation of a National Sport Council. However, throughout the last 15 years no one actually advanced the establishment of the Council. However, our Sport Minister and the Director of the Sport Authority were successful in promoting the Council. In 2013, the Law of the National Sport Council successfully passed at the Knesset (Israel's parliament) ruling and it was officially established. The Council has three main goals:

1   To advise the Sport Minister about the National Sport proposed policy and strategy.

2   To advise the Sport Minister on how to distribute the financial funds to NGBs and to sports clubs based on a public committee's recommendations.
3   To advise the Sport Minister as to the policy and financial means concerning the National Plan of building sport facilities.

   The Council consists of 19 members who are representatives of stakeholders such as the Olympic Committee, popular sport fields (football and basketball), non-Olympic sports and Paralympic fields, women in sports, local authorities, governmental partners (Ministry of Culture and Sport, Ministry of Finance and Ministry of Justice) and public representatives. It is a public council whose role is to advise the minister with regards to the aforementioned issues.

The Wingate Law

As part of our ever fertile collaboration with the Ministry of Finance, the Ministry of Justice and the prestigious and renowned Wingate Institute (winner of the highest prize in the country – the Israel Award), a decision has been made concerning the latter's role as the National Institute of Sport. With that in mind, the Wingate Institute has developed a recuperation programme, working with a top-class accountant, in order to cover its accumulated deficits. Furthermore, an upgrade of the existing facilities will take place to ensure professionalism and perfection. The initiated 'Wingate Institute Law' will establish and determine the institute's main activity according to its designated aims; serving Israel as its national institute for excellence, and will be funded accordingly by the government in the following fields: Elite Sport Unit, National School for Coach Education, Academy for Young Athletes, Sports Sciences and Research and Sport Medicine department.

Database

In order to establish the decision-making process based on reliable and up-to-date data, the Sport Authority started a systematic collection of data in its field of work. Up to now, surveys and results have been collected in the follow subjects:

1   Mapping of facilities 2010 (to be repeated in 2015).
2   Mapping of active athletes over the age of 13 (with the exception of gymnastics and figure skating (over the age of 6) and swimming (over the age of 8)) on a yearly basis distributed by gender and community criteria.
3   Mapping of the activities across the country in both competitive sports and sport-for-all, including the financial investments and efforts put into sport in each community out of the 253 in the country.
4   A 2012 survey of physical activity and sport habits in Israel for the population over the age of 18.

5   A 2014 survey of physical activity and sport habits in Israel for children aged 9–18.

6   Strategic plans for the 12 sport fields: football and basketball, the popular sports, as well as the 10 prioritised sports chosen by a public committee (for the purposes of increasing the chances to reach World and European Championship achievements).

7   Two satisfactory surveys for the Sport Authority's 'clients': NGBs and Sport Department Directors in local communities.

Strategic plan to increase the number of athletes in Israel

On 8 December 2013, the Israeli government decided to support the 'National Program to Promote and Enhance Sport Among Children' – 'Sport Flourishes'. As part of the project, an unprecedented sum of 371 million NIS (approximately €80 million) will be invested by the 'Sport Betting Council', the Ministry of Finance and the Ministry of Culture and Sports over a period of five years. The main aim is to increase the number of registered athletes (13+) by 50,000 until 2019. The project's aim and expected outcome, among other things, is expanding the exposure of children to sport, and instilling the principles of passion for sport, fun and well-being. In addition to that, the project aims to encourage children to engage in competitive sport in targeted disciplines across the local municipalities. Reducing the costs of participating in sports, and reducing the costs of operating sport clubs is also essential for the project's success. For the project to bear fruit there is also a need to register children to NGBs from the age of 10 (instead of 13), while strengthening the cooperation between NGBs, local communities and the clubs.

In addition, with football being the most popular sport in the country, a decision was made to contact one of the top football clubs in Europe, with the hope of forming a unique bond which will allow us to cooperate in nurturing young talent, aiming to recruit 20,000 young football players over five years (out of an overall target of 50,000 registered athletes (+13) goal in the entire Sport Flourishes project, mentioned above).

Trigger-Foresight

In order to self-examine our situation compared to different European countries, Trigger-Foresight, a leading Israeli strategic and business consulting firm – were hired by the Sport Authority. The changes we have enforced and implemented are crucial to the development of sport, but we have come to recognise the importance of keeping up to date with current successful models. Through constant research and development a comparative database, Trigger-Foresight will ensure we are up there with the most advanced countries in terms of structure, strategies and responsibilities.

Conclusion

This chapter describes a new approach, commonly used in strategic management areas of competitive bodies. The approach highlights the importance of setting the goals (what needs to be done) and laying the implementation methods to support them, while prioritising a long-term strategy over a short-term one. Needless to say, the probability of reaching all of the objectives is relatively modest, but they constitute a platform for pragmatic and dynamic dialogues between stakeholders as has never been done before. The Ministry of Sport acknowledged its need to have close contacts with the Betting Council, the Competitive Sports Unit and different national governing bodies. Both competitive sport and sport-for-all are incredibly important for a small country striving for international success. Unfortunately, achievements such as Olympic medals and Maccabi Tel Aviv's Euroleague win are rare at this point. On the other hand, they prove success is possible, and we will make sure it happens.

Israel's success in the fields of medicine, agriculture, communications and high-tech tell us there is no reason not to expect better in sports. We have set the foundations needed to achieve success, and results are already visible to an extent. The belief in our ability to overturn the sport culture in Israel, as well as to reach the top sport level, is essential. We certainly believe the tide is turning. Last but not least, in 2013 the overall public budget allocated for sport was 420 million NIS (approximately €87.5 million), versus close to 700 million NIS (approximately €145.8 million) in 2015. This ongoing change enabled us to believe that we shall meet our goals.

10 Sexual exploitation in women's sport

Can female athletes respond to it?

Stiliani 'Ani' Chroni

Real stories and the choices athletes have for responding

> For seven years – from the age of just 10 – Karen Leach was abused by her swimming coach. She had hoped to swim for Ireland in the Olympics and spent hours training at the pool every day before and after school. It was her life. However, infamous paedophile coach Derry O'Rourke shattered her dreams and her childhood. O'Rourke did not only destroy Karen's life. His actions literally cost a life. Karen's mother died by suicide just days after telling her daughter how much she loved her and how sorry she was for failing to look after her. Garda [Irish police] found her body in a canal. There have also been times when life became unbearable for Karen and she too tried to take her own life but her young son has now given her a strong reason to live and a future together to fight for.
>
> (Karen Leach; Torney, 2011)

> I felt I had done something wrong and he was going to jail. I should be in trouble. That it took two to tango. I thought it had been a real relationship – and that I loved him and he loved me. I thought I was going to marry him. ... When you're in a situation like I was – training at a high level – you do have to be close to your coaches. And from the time I was eight years old until I was 16 Daniel Doyle was my sun. My world revolved around him and I wanted to do nothing but please him.
>
> (Kayla Harrison, USA judo Olympian; Lawton, 2012)

Karen was raped by her coach and Kayla was in love with her coach – two different stories presented here exposing how the coach–athlete relationship may veer away from the professional one it should be and become complicated. The stories reveal two different painful experiences from two female elite athletes. Karen hated what happened to her from the start; Kayla initially thought she had a true loving relationship, expecting to marry her coach. Both women struggled for a long time. Karen endured the sexual exploitation for seven years in the hope to make it to the Olympic Games, then tried to end her life due to the rape experiences. Kayla, who worshiped her coach for many years, eventually moved to work with another coach at a new training environment to finally live her Olympic dream in 2012, while she still questioned what she had done wrong for her former coach to go to jail.

As sexual exploitation exists in the realm of sport (Chroni *et al.*, 2012), stories like Karen's and Kayla's are everyday stories lived worldwide (also by male athletes, as sexual exploitation sees no gender; however, only cases of male coach–female athlete are addressed here). Some of these stories make the headlines and we get to hear what the athletes experienced, while others are never heard – possibly they do not report the incident as under-reporting is one of the barriers in the fight against sexual exploitation in sport and in society at large (Csáky, 2008; Di Martino *et al.*, 2003; Fasting *et al.*, 2011; 2014). Brackenridge exposed the magnitude of the problem over a decade ago, 'Everyone talks about the perils of doping, but if there were 100 drugs cases under investigation in football, 60 in swimming 40 in tennis, there would be uproar. Yet that's the scale of the problem with sex abuse today' (quoted by Downes, 2002). Today, as sexual exploitation cases make the headlines and find their way to courts around the globe, national sport stakeholders are establishing laws, policies and procedures against it to safeguard the participants. The culture of sport still resists change, and authority figures such as coaches groom (see Brackenridge, 1997; 2001 for the term groom that describes the trapping of an athlete in a coercive and manipulative process, where one slowly gains the trust of the athlete before systematically breaking down interpersonal barriers) young and older female athletes, the parents and sport clubs to consent to the power abuse expressed through various forms of sexual exploitation as part of the athlete's journey to success (ranging from the light form of gender discrimination to the severe one of rape; see Brackenridge, 1997; 2001 for the sexual exploitation continuum). As Brackenridge (1997) and Cense (1997) described, too often athletes socialised in the elite sport culture accept and tolerate sexual harassment, because it is viewed as a part of the masculine culture of sports and something that 'one just has to live with'. Recently, Katie Kelly (US swimmer) attested to this experience in her interview: 'abuse and sexual harassment … was something you had to learn how to deal with. … And so there was much more tolerance. … This tolerance of treating women and girls like what happened to them is incidental and not a big deal' (Trucks, 2014a). International sport stakeholders, like the International Olympic Committee (2007), have declared any form of sexual exploitation being at minimum unwanted, wrongful and unethical, as well as illegal depending on a country's legal system (see Lang and Hartill, 2014 for safeguarding structures in various countries).

While Karen's rape experience is a straightforward one to be classified as an unwanted, wrongful, unethical and illegal act from the coach, oftentimes the 'what doesn't kill you makes you stronger' or 'all good, no harm, no foul' mentalities prevail, particularly in cases of successful performances obtained by the athletes. Consequently, people often miss the harm done to the athlete as well as the problem in such cases. Starr (2013a), founder of the watchdog non-profit organisation 'Safe4athletes' that supports male and female athlete victims of sexual exploitation, explains:

> When the emotionally immature athlete does not cry 'foul', is a successful performer and the coach is winning, the rule appears to be 'all good, no harm, no foul'. A sexually abused athlete may not be able to deal with the reality of such a relationship until twenty years after the fact. During that period, only that athlete suffers a pain that is so great, they cannot discuss it with anyone. When the dust settles and the truth of the destruction of the athlete's life is revealed, the artful acquaintance paedophile still receives sympathy from those who respect his success as a coach.

In the case of Kayla, however, who consented to the intimate relationship with her coach, one may question whether her lived experience is an unwanted, wrongful, unethical, illegal one. How does one come to view such a relationship as consensual when it involves a young athlete with no power and an adult coach with all forms and shapes of power concentrated on him; when it involves a female athlete who is instructed in every step and a coach who orders these instructions on a day-to-day basis? Areas where the power and control relation within the coach–athlete relationship may be manifested are training, knowledge, team selection, playing time, access to facilities and competition, diet and weight control, as well as influence over interpersonal relationships (Bringer, *et al.*, 2002; Tomlinson and Yorganci, 1997). Female athletes who were victimised by their coaches respond that this is not possible: 'I guess, rumors with my situation started when I was 14, that I was having an affair with my coach. And nowadays, and being a parent, I know that a 14-year-old isn't even capable of having an affair' (*Debra Denithorne-Grodensky, US Olympic swimmer,* Trucks, 2014b).

> There is nothing consensual about a minor athlete falling in love with their coach, a significant power figure whose coaching attention can make the difference between an Olympic medal or national record and failure. The notion of an acceptable consensual romantic relationship between a teacher and student or coach and athlete violates every legal, moral and ethical principle in our society. Yet these relationships and their acceptance are commonplace in our competitive sports environment especially with our female athletes. While this is something that everyone would openly say is appalling and should be stopped at all costs especially when the relationship begins with an underage athlete (under the age of 18). Yet there are such famous athletes as Lindsay Vonn who started dating her coach at the age of 16, whom she went on to marry.
>
> (Starr, 2012)

The concentration of power empowers the coach and disempowers the athlete, and this coaching style (that is merely prescriptive, the coach has total control, the athlete has no say, decisions and priorities are centred to what the coach thinks is best) has given permission to many coaches to exploit their power while taking away choice and control from the athlete (Kidman and Lombardo, 2010; Tomlinson and Yorganci, 1997). For a long time this authoritarian or coach-centred coaching has been considered as the ideal style of coaching and it is still a commonly used one by many coaches, especially when winning is the main focus (Kellett, 2002; Kidman and Lombardo, 2010; Lombardo, 2010). Coach-centred coaching attempts to control athlete behaviour on and off the court (Kidman and Lombardo, 2010). According to Sand *et al.* (2011), the coach's power capital as well as how this power is carried out is the central point in the coach–athlete relationship, and the overuse of power appears to be the case in the athlete stories discussed here.

The male coach–female athlete relationship can be viewed as a grey area, if lived and interpreted or misinterpreted through loose ethical rules and standards. To this day, research-wise we lack the knowledge from the coaches' point of view. Burton-Nelson (1994) shares one of the few extracts that voice the coach perspective on this topic:

> When you have someone you spend hundreds of hours with, when they give you blood, sweat, tears, their lives, you become close. You become attached to them. And it's really difficult to put parameters on the attachment. I think that's human nature, and I don't think it has anything to do with being fifty or being fifteen. It's human nature to love someone who gives themselves to you.
>
> (p. 182)

In this case, one may question if the coach falls in love with the woman or the athlete he is training and shaping to become a compliant athlete according to his style of coaching. As one's style of coaching is shaped by his life views, philosophies and way of living (Kidman and Lombardo, 2010), oftentimes when working long-term with a female athlete the adult male coach could also be moulding a woman according to his standards: 'It's the idea that I could raise and shape this woman the way I wanted a woman to be' (Chroni, 2012, personal communication with a male coach who was in an intimate relationship with his top female adult athlete for 2.5 years). Analogously, one may also question whether the female athlete falls in love with the man close to her or the coach (in the man) who gives her ample time and attention to make a champion. Is this what true love is about? A number of male coaches went on to marry their female athletes, but does marriage normalise and moralise the intimate relationship between the coach and the athlete? According to the findings of Bringer *et al.* (2002), who interviewed 19 swimming coaches in the UK, any coach–athlete relationship with the athlete being under the age of consent is considered inappropriate. However, when the athlete is above the age of consent, then the relationship was viewed as unprofessional from a moral standpoint, while coaches held a wide spectrum of views over its appropriateness ranging from 'totally inappropriate' to 'it's a question of civil liberties'. It is, then, vital for shaping people's view over sexual exploitation occurrences with female athletes of any age, to highlight that it is the areas where a female athlete lacks control and the coach assume full control (knowledge, expertise and decision making) that pave the way for exploitation to occur, regardless of the athlete's age. It is also essential to note here that sexual exploitation occurrences and perceptions of appropriateness regarding an intimate coach–athlete relationship vary among countries (see, for example, Bringer *et al.*, 2002; Toftegaard, 2001) just as do the definitions of sexual exploitation forms as well as the laws in effect against it (see Fasting, 2005; Lang and Hartill, 2014).

While understanding why and how sexual exploitation occurs is vital for the fight against it, the main focus of this chapter is whether female athletes can respond to exploitation. Do they have another option than to silently consent to the exploitation? Can they speak up and ask for it to end? What comes to light is that in many cases female athletes put up with the exploitation in order to safeguard their dreams for a promising sport career:

And in my personal case, when I started to get to the next level of swimming, when I did start to qualify for larger meets like junior nationals when I was 12 or 13, another thing that he told me in one on one conversations was 'If you were to tell anybody what was going on here between us, you wouldn't be able to ever swim for me again and then you wouldn't make the Olympic Trials and you wouldn't get a scholarship for college.' So there was a real serious threat hanging above my head that, if I did tell anybody, whether it was a teammate, or an adult, then I wouldn't be able to swim and he wouldn't be able to coach and, you know, really, all would be lost in my small world back then. And so there was a real fear, a true fear of that.
(Debra Denithorne-Grodensky, USA Olympic swimmer; Trucks, 2014b)

He [O'Rourke] was God to me, to all the other swimmers, to everybody's parents. What he said went because of my love of swimming and my dream to swim for Ireland in the Olympics. This man was my swimming coach and he was going to help me make my dream come true.
(Karen Leach, Irish swimmer; Torney, 2011)

The competing athlete has something at risk, for example, dreams of being an Olympian, a college scholarship, playing time or financial gain. There is a complex 'hook' keeping the athlete engaged in a relationship even when abusive and unhealthy. The athlete has to make decisions for the family, the team and the coach. When speaking up about the abuse, the athlete could be subject to retaliation from the team, if there is a perceived threat of their dreams being compromised as a result of the coach removal. The parents that sacrificed everything to make sure that the child-athlete's dreams are fulfilled or the coach that convinces the athlete that the only reason for her/his success is because of the 'coach'.

(Starr, 2013b)

These extracts reveal that the choice we often presume the female athlete has is more like a one-way road: not to do or say anything. Chroni (2013a) presented a case study of a south European women's football team, whose club president was sexually touching and fondling young female players when they were between the ages of 12 and 14 (seven of the players confessed to being victims during a player-only team meeting). When he attempted to act on a new, yet older, player (18 years of age), she spoke up and the team's secret got out. At the player-only team meeting, which was called to discuss the team captain's decision not to play any longer for the team once the issue surfaced, one of the players said: 'What do you want us to do now? We are playing at the national team and there is no other local women's football team, and I am not leaving the national team, the national team was my dream.'

Recent works (Brackenridge *et al.*, 2012; Fasting *et al.*, 2010) suggest elite athletes are at greater risk of sexual exploitation as they often perceive that too much is at stake if they disclose their experiences. As there is frequent reference to the need for continuous pathways between grass-roots participation and elite sport, we ought to acknowledge here that in the case of sexual exploitation, whether you are playing for a local football team in south Europe or a national team in the USA, Canada or the UK, silence seems to be the option most commonly chosen. Fasting *et al.* (2007) reported in their findings that passivity was the most frequent behavioural response among the 25 female athletes who had experienced some form of sexual harassment, followed by avoidance, direct confrontation and to a lesser extent humorous confrontation. The elite athletes in their study neither confronted the harasser nor reported the incident(s), but instead chose to talk with their teammates about it, particularly if the harasser behaved in similar ways to more than one athlete. Some athletes shifted their responses from passivity to confrontation over the years as they grew older. This passive response to exploitation parallels the narrative of acceptance that Brackenridge and Fasting (2005) identified earlier in the biographical analysis of two sexually harassed female athletes. As Fasting *et al.* (2007) elaborated regarding their findings, direct confrontation can be difficult for a female athlete as the coach-harasser has physical and organisational power. Furthermore, some of the factors the researchers recognised as applicable among athletes are the fear of not being selected for the team and not wanting to hurt the harasser so his job and/or family will not be negatively affected. Similarly, in the case study of Chroni (2013a), when a parent confronted the club president, he responded: 'What do you want now to happen? Ruin my family life?' Starr (2013a) also pointed out that when a misconduct case breaks the silence, some perpetrators still receive sympathy and support from those who admire and respect their work as coaches.

Considering the abuse of power and the silent treatment discussed above, how does one come to view the Kayla-type relationship as a consensual one when it involves an athlete who is told that she is talented and has hopes to make it to the elite of the elites, and a coach who holds and controls her hopes and dreams through his coaching knowledge and expertise? These dreams and aspirations make the female athlete vulnerable to consenting to any type of relationship with a strong, caring and knowledgeable coach. 'An athlete's hope and dreams is all it takes to be vulnerable to the coach paedophile and the failures in this system' (Starr, 2013a). When one's dreams can only be realised through formal coaching and the coaching is problematic due to the abuse of power, a failure in the system becomes apparent and action is required.

Today, in the elite sport culture, it is the end result, the victory, that is highly valued. These are the ideals of the contemporary Western world and culture (Edensor, 2002). In the case of exploited female athletes there appears to be a price to pay for aiming for victory. As Starr (2013a) wrote: 'No Olympic dream is worth the lifetime of pain and destruction that sexual abuse brings.' Research evidence reveals that the after-effects of a sexual relationship between a coach and an athlete can be detrimental for the athlete, regardless of the athlete's age (Brackenridge and Fasting, 2005; Brackenridge and Kirby, 1997; Fasting *et al.*, 2002; Kirby *et al.*, 2000). The lifetime of 'pain and destruction' was eloquently elaborated by *Debra Denithorne-Grodensky and* Jancy Thompson (US swimmers) in the interviews they gave on their experiences of abuse by their coaches. In the extracts that follow, *Denithorne-Grodensky elaborates on the long time she spent in therapy to re-collect herself, and* Thompson explains how the painful experience led her to quit swimming. Alas, she is not the only athlete to have left her sport following abuse by her coach (Fasting *et al.*, 2002; 2007). Dropping out following sexual exploitation is an issue that should heavily concern us.

> I spent a lot of time in therapy, and it's allowed me to recollect the memories without *reliving* the memories and therefore categorise them for what they are. And separate them, yes, but that took a good 15 to 20 years to be able to do, and a whole lot of therapy to be able to do.
> (Debra Denithorne-Grodensky; Trucks, 2014a).

> It wasn't swimming that was depressing me. It was my swim coach and what was happening to me at the time. Therefore, the only way that I could get my swim coach at the time, Norm Havercroft, out of my life and to stop hurting me was just to quit swimming. Therefore, it was very painful. It's like a death. Because that person, Jancy Thompson the swimmer, pretty much died the day that I quit and was no longer Jancy Thompson the swimmer. And that's a really intense feeling, but that's the only way I can explain it is that it's like a death. Because I am not that person anymore. That person died. And there's just so many different

emotions and feelings and feelings of loss and hatred and pain and stuff like
that behind it that is just gone.

(Jancy Thompson; Trucks, 2014c)

While a number of female ex-athletes have spoken about their sexual exploitation experiences retrospectively, today we still lack in-depth knowledge
about what is happening at the grass-root level of sports. Vertommen *et al.*
(2013) concluded that athletes who are sexually exploited at the local club
level and do not progress to the elite level of their sport typically disappear
from the sport scene and do not report the incident via a sport organisation
(consider here the under-reporting mentioned earlier). Most often, athletes
speak up long after the exploitation is over (see, for example, the stories of
Annabelle Cripps, Deena Deardurff Schmidt, *Debra Denithorne-Grodensky and
Karen Leach*). *Debra Denithorne-Grodensky explains how she and her teammates
were 'brainwashed' by their coach, making it impossible for any one of them to speak up
at the time the abuse was taking place.*

> I don't think I would have had the strength to trigger it during my swim-
> ming career. I mean, obviously I didn't. I didn't say anything the whole
> time that I swam. And interestingly enough, when we were prosecuting
> Andy King ... and I say 'we' because there were nine or ten of us that he
> either attempted sexual abuse or succeeded with, and those were just my
> immediate teammates in the time frame of 1983 to 1986. And so when we
> all came back together and were trying to prosecute him, the one common
> thread, no matter how severe the sexual abuse was, the one common
> thread that we all agreed on, and we didn't have terminology at the time,
> but we were saying, 'Gosh, it was like we were all brainwashed.' And that
> was really part of the grooming process. And that went team wide, both
> the boys and the girls. We all collectively were told over and over again
> how bad all the other club coaches in the area were. And he would cite
> different things that each coach would do that would be viewed as poor
> coaching. So at the end of the day he really had us all believing that there
> really weren't other local coaches that we could go swim for, effectively,
> and do better with.
>
> (Debra Denithorne-Grodensky, US Olympic swimmer; Trucks, 2014b)

Another group that ought to be considered are the parents of exploited
athletes, especially for those under the age of consent. What choice(s) do
they have – to speak up or to become blind, and if they speak up will they be
heard? In Chroni's (2013a) case, when some of the victimised young players
talked to their parents, they were not believed. In Thompson's case (Trucks,
2014c), people knew (among them parents) but still there was not much they
could do for her: 'People complained. Parents complained. Parents wrote letters. And what they have was "Yeah, we have a file on Norm Havercroft, but
there's nothing we really can do"' It appears that parents face analogous risks

and obstacles to those of their abused daughters, both concerning the decision to speak up and spoil their child's sporting dream as well as for changing the situation experienced by their daughter.

Does, after all, a choice exist between enduring exploitation and ending it for the female athlete? Taking into account the stories and the literature presented above, the only fitting answer appears to be: 'In principle yes but in practice no.' The consequences of speaking up appear to be as detrimental (in a different way of course, as the female athlete places a halt to her sport dreams) as those of not speaking up.

Alternative pathways to support sport dreams and experiences

While sexually exploitative behaviours in sport have been allowed to occur unchallenged for many years (Brackenridge, 1995), during the last decade a number of organisations have taken steps against it. For example, the IOC (International Olympic Committee, 2007) issued the 'Consensus Statement: Sexual Harassment and Abuse in Sport', which called for multiple actions against sexual harassment and abuse. The UN-DAW document 'Women 2000 and Beyond' (2007) called for protective attention, particularly for girls and women in sport. The UNICEF (2010) review document 'Protecting Children from Violence in Sport' identified the need for more research on children's sport experiences to further protect them from exploitation. A number of international, continental and national directives call for action, but many countries still do not have laws and policies in place to safeguard the female sport participant from sexual exploitation and to provide her with clear procedures in the case that she is victimised (Chroni et al., 2012). Most importantly, though, athletes appear not to trust the processes in place and feel that any actions will not accomplish anything (Cense and Brackenridge, 2001). Recent findings reveal that in the Netherlands, only 22 per cent of the 323 reports filled at the NOC*NSF Helpline (Netherlands Olympic Committee, Netherlands Sports Confederation) during the years 2001–2010 were filed by the victims (of which the great majority were athletes). Most reports and/or questions came from sport organisation staff members (Vertommen et al., 2013). Vertommen et al. (2013) concluded that since young people are most often the victims, alternative communication channels, like chat support, ought to be developed in conjunction with social media education and awareness-raising campaigns.

Chroni et al. (2012), upon reviewing all existing recommendation documents, identified that all recommendations against sexual exploitation in sport are geared towards two central courses of action: prevention and control. To prevent the phenomenon, the actions of research for supplementing our knowledge, the development of codes of ethical behaviours, education and training of all individuals involved in sport, as well as development of action plans and policies against the phenomenon have been suggested. To control the phenomenon, the actions suggested include the establishment of protective procedures and the monitoring of sexual exploitation incidents. But Chroni (2013b), in a review of sexual harassment in sport, criticised that while

> some progress has been made, seeing that harassers continue to harass makes one question whether the advancements in knowledge and understanding along with the laws, policies, and procedures against SH [sexual harassment] succeed as anticipated in preventing and controlling the social phenomenon.
>
> (p. 183)

Alternatives among the infrastructures and cultures of grass-roots and elite sport are therefore a necessity for the retention and life of the female athlete. These alternatives should allow the female athlete to follow a safer path in her sport experience.

The question is 'What could these alternative pathways be when recommendations around the globe offer similar ideas and some of them have been put to use with some success?'. Considering prevention as the best form of treatment, education on sexual exploitation (forms and accompanying issues) is the central point considered here. Pina *et al.* (2009) pointed out that the existing anti-harassment training programmes may be failing as they focus on the legal protection of the organisation and do not address the essential issues of the phenomenon (e.g. power misuse and abuse, hierarchical issues, gendered environments, etc.). It appears that we are educating people based on what is unethical and illegal to do, aiming to protect them against the legal system, anticipating that athlete welfare will come as a by-product of these teachings. We are teaching ethics and appropriateness by putting forward what is unethical and inappropriate; we are teaching them what not to do instead of what to do and why to do it. As an extension to Pina *et al.*'s (2009) criticism comes Starr (2012) regarding the content of educational videos used for the certification of individuals involved in sports that mainly 'depict young children being cultivated by acquaintance paedophiles':

> Why aren't we seeing videos of a 17-yr-old voicing how a close relationship with his or her coach went from athlete affection as a reward for their hard work on the practice field to molestation or, from the psyche and perspective of the artfully manipulated athlete, 'a loving relationship'. This scenario just doesn't pull at our heartstrings in the same way. Why aren't we seeing a video of a 25-year-old, who we assume is a consenting adult, talking about such a relationship? We react with even less sympathy in this case, if any at all. ... If we truly want to address sexual abuse and harassment in sports we need to call it what it is, an abuse of power between the coach and the athlete that occurs at all ages. We are misled if educational materials imply something else.

The content issue was partially addressed by the International Olympic Committee (n.d.), which developed a series of videos portraying sport-related cases of various sexual exploitation behaviours. Another key educational element for the future and for all involved in sport, pointed out by Starr, is the grooming process and the transition from affection to intimacy; how these occasions are normalised and viewed as appropriate and abstaining from such a relationship may be perceived by the coach as restraining him from his civil right to love anyone he chooses.

A step in the desired direction would be to educate coaches differently. To stop preparing experts who will take over the athletes' lives in order to produce winners and eventually train them on what controlling behaviours not to use. But can controlling coaches and coaching styles change when sport clubs and organisations clearly aim to produce winners and this style has been proven effective in the past? Coaches do not operate alone; they are usually part of a system, part of sport as well as organisation structures and cultures. The existing literature recognises sport and organisation structures and cultures as factors that impact the occurrence of sexual exploitation (Brackenridge, 2001). Local, national and international sport organisations' philosophies towards producing winning athletes should then also be revisited. Does this signify that sport organisations should stop aiming for medals? No, it signifies that their philosophies and missions, along with their staff's approaches to these, ought to change. When it comes to dealing with sexual exploitation, Starr (2013a) upheld the view that 'Sport governing bodies care more about producing winning athletes than their obligation to enforce legal, moral and ethical guidelines established by our society', which directly questions the actions taken to this day and indirectly implies the need for a safer approach towards optimal performance and winning results. Brackenridge (2012) advocated that 'A performance rationale for prevention is our holy grail'; a performance rationale that will focus on the human being and not on the human doing, one that will empower and not disempower the athlete. If we manage to see how an athlete's welfare can enhance instead of inhibit her performance success, a giant step forward will have been made. This will have a direct implication on the coaching style which should care to meet the athlete's needs and wills. Recent research evidence reveals coach authoritarian behaviours as a predictor of experiences of sexual harassment for the female athlete (Sand *et al.*, 2011). Under the authoritarian style the needs and wills of the athlete are overlooked. As Starr (n.d.) pointed out, 'The power dynamic of striving for an Olympic Gold and the coach holding the keys to that kingdom will always produce a "coach is most important" resolution rather than an "athlete first" platform.'

Sand *et al.* (2011) concluded that a holistic approach to coaching ought to be adopted. Kerr and Stirling (2008) also suggested that an athlete-centred philosophy in coaching can provide us with a strong shield against abuse in sport, where the athlete's needs are a priority within the coach–athlete relationship. These research-evidenced conclusions increase the need for a coaching style that will espouse 'the total development of the whole person' (Kidman, 2010, p. 474) and eliminate the power abuse that opens the door to sexual exploitation. The athlete-centred coaching caters to the athlete's needs, considers the athlete first, facilitates learning and development but does not control them, and instead shares the power with the athlete (see Kidman and Lombardo, 2010). Today,. the coach-centred approach prevails, yet without a guarantee for the end result. On the contrary, it can go both ways to either develop the athlete to live her dream of success or to be exploited:

> The same style that develops an athlete to be an Olympic Gold Medallist is often the same coaching style that brings abuse of all kinds. Unless we can understand this issue as a sports/coaching style and interrelated power structure issue, then any investigation by an outside agency will continue to miss the mark.
>
> (Starr, n.d.)

Recent research also suggests that contrary to the most commonly heard elite sport success stories, there is more than a single road to the dream of high sport performance (Carless and Douglas, 2013), but many of these stories are also not heard.

Conclusion

It appears that female athletes who aim to live the elite sport narrative cannot respond to sexual exploitation without paying a price. If they speak up, they risk losing the dream of becoming elite. In some cases the women are groomed to believe that speaking up is not even an option – does this then raise a question over the female athlete's civil rights? If they don't speak up and do endure the exploitation, the experience can be detrimental to the physical, psychological and social self of the female athlete. How is the decision made? We do not know. Further research is required to understand the negotiations of exploited elite athletes. But sexual exploitation can happen to women who play sports even when the elite level is not dreamed of. In this case, they are also groomed not to speak up, but again we lack knowledge specific about what happens to them as their stories are rarely heard. What we know today is that coaches ought to change the way they train and relate with their female athletes; they ought to consider the athlete first, her needs and wants, as well as share with her some decision making; they ought to develop the athlete's skills, but also her autonomy so she can say no, when necessary. But to change the tradition in coaching style we also need sport and organisation cultures to shift their focus from the success of the human doing to the success of the human being that will instil autonomy and empower the female athlete, and will never ask her to sacrifice any part of her self-esteem and dignity.

References

Brackenridge, C. (1995). Sexual harassment in sport. Paper presented at the 41st Annual Meeting of the American College of Sports Medicine, Minneapolis, MN, 31 May–3 June.

Brackenridge, C. (1997). 'He owned me basically…'. Women's experience of sexual abuse in sport. *International Review for the Sociology of Sport*, 32: 115–130.

Brackenridge, C. (2001). *Spoilsports: Understanding and Preventing Sexual Exploitation in Sport*. London: Routledge.

Brackenridge, C. (2012). What we know about sexual harassment and abuse in sports. Keynote presentation at the EU Conference 'Better, Safe and Stronger! Prevention of Sexual Harassment and Abuse in Sport'. Berlin, Germany.

Brackenridge, C. and Fasting, K. (2005). The grooming process in sport. Narratives of sexual harassment and abuse. *Autobiography*, 13: 33–52.

Brackenridge, C. and Kirby, S. (1997). Playing safe? Assessing the risk of sexual abuse to young elite athletes. *International Review for the Sociology of Sport*, 32: 407–418.

Brackenridge, C., Kay, T. and Rhind, D. (2012). *Sport, Children's Rights and Violence Prevention: A Sourcebook on Global Issues and Local Programmes*. London: Brunel University.

Bringer, J.D., Brackenridge, C. and Johnston, L.H. (2002). Defining appropriateness in coach–athlete sexual relationships. The voice of coaches. *Journal of Sexual Aggression. An International, Interdisciplinary Forum for Research, Theory and Practice*, 8: 83–98.

Burton-Nelson, M. (1994). *The Stronger Women Get, the More Men Love Football: Sexism and the American Culture of Sports*. Boston, MA: Houghton Mifflin Harcourt.

Carless, D. and Douglas, K. (2013). Living, resisting, and playing the part of the athlete. Narrative tensions in elite sport. *Psychology of Sport and Exercise*, 14, 701–708.

Cense, M. (1997). *Red Card or Carte Blanche. Risk Factors for Sexual Harassment and Sexual Abuse in sport: Summary, Conclusions and Recommendations*. Arnhem: NOC & NSF.

Cense, M. and Brackenridge, C. (2001). Temporal and developmental risk factors for sexual harassment and abuse in sport. *European Physical Education Review*, 7: 61–79.

Chroni, S. (2013a). Interventions against forms of sexual exploitation in sport from a Greek perspective. Invited Symposium 'Strategies for preventing sexual harassment in sport – in between voluntariness and obligation' at the 18th ECSS Annual Conference, Barcelona, Spain.

Chroni, S. (2013b). Sexual harassment of female athletes. In G. Pfister and M.K. Sisjord (eds), *Gender and Sport: Challenges and Changes*. Berlin: Waxman Publishing Co.

Chroni, S., Fasting, K., Hartill, M.J., Knorre, N., Martin Harcajo, M., Papaefstathiou, M., Rhind, D., Rulofs, B., Toftegaard Støckel, J., Vertommen, T. and Zurc, J. (2012). *Sexual and Gender Harassment and Sexual Abuse. Initiatives for Prevention in Sport*. Frankfurt: Deutsche Sportjugend im Deutschen Olympischen Sportbund e.V. Retrieved from www.dsj.de/fileadmin/user_upload/Bilder/Handlungsfelder/Europa/europ_PSG_Projekt_2012/Catalogue_Initiatives_in_Europe_and_beyond__2012_2.pdf

Csáky, C. (2008). *No One To Turn To. The Under-reporting of Child Sexual Exploitation and Abuse by Aid Workers and Peacekeepers*. London: Save the Children. Retrieved from www.un.org/en/pseataskforce/docs/no_one_to_turn_under_reporting_of_child_sea_by_aid_workers.pdf

Di Martino, V., Hoel, H. and Cooper, C.L. (2003). *Preventing Violence and Harassment in the Workplace*. Dublin: European Foundation for the Improvement of Living and Working Conditions. Retrieved from www.eurofound.eu.int/publications/files/EF02109EN.pdf

Downes, S. (2002, April). Every parent's nightmare. *Observer Sports Monthly*. Retrieved from http://observer.theguardian.com/osm/story/0,,678189,00.html

Edensor, T. (2002). *National Identity, Popular Culture and Everyday Life*. Oxford: Berg.

Fasting, K. (2005). Fight or flight? Experiences of sexual harassment among female athletes. In P. Markula (ed.), *Feminist Sport Studies: Sharing Experiences of Joy and Pain* (pp. 129–149). Albany, NY: State University of New York Press.

Fasting, K., Brackenridge, C. and Walseth, K. (2002). Consequences of sexual harassment in sport for female athletes. *The Journal of Sexual Aggression*, 8(2): 37–48.

Fasting, K., Brackenridge, C. and Walseth, K. (2007). Women athletes' personal responses to sexual harassment in sport. *Journal of Applied Sport Psychology*, 19: 419–433.

Fasting, K., Brackenridge, C. and Knorre, N. (2010). Performance level and sexual harassment prevalence among female athletes in the Czech Republic. *Women in Sport & Physical Activity Journal*, 19: 26–32.

Fasting, K., Chroni, S., Hervik, S.E. and Knorre, N. (2011). Sexual harassment in sport toward females in three European countries. *International Review for the Sociology of Sport*, 46: 76–89.

Fasting, K., Chroni, S. and Knorre, N. (2014). The experiences of sexual harassment in sport and education among European female sports science students. *Sport, Education, & Society*, 19: 115–130.

International Olympic Committee. (n.d). Sexual harassment and abuse in sport. Educational videos. Retrieved from http://sha.olympic.org.

International Olympic Committee. (2007). Consensus statement. Sexual harassment and abuse in sport. IOC Medical Commission Expert Panel. Retrieved from www.olympic.org/Documents/Reports/EN/en_report_1125.pdf

Kellett, P. (2002). Football-as-war, coach-as-general. Analogy, metaphor and management implications. *Football Studies*, 5: 60–76.

Kerr, G.A. and Stirling, A.E. (2008). Child protection in sport. Implications of an athlete-centered philosophy. *Quest*, 60: 307–323.

Kidman, L. (2010). Holism in sports coaching. Beyond humanistic psychology: a commentary. *International Journal of Sports Science & Coaching*, 5: 473–475.

Kidman, L. and Lombardo, B (2010). Athlete-centred coaching. Developing decision makers (2nd edn). Worcester: IPC Print Resources.

Kirby, S., Greaves, L. and Hankivsky, O. (2000). *The Dome of Silence: Sexual Harassment and Abuse in Sport*. Halifax: Fernwood Publishing.

Lang, M. and Hartill, M. (2014). *Safeguarding, Child Protection and Abuse in Sport. International Perspectives in Research, Policy and Practice*. London: Routledge.

Lawton, J. (2012, 3 August). James Lawton: Kayla Harrison's courage sheds light on Judo's darkest corner. *The Independent*. Retrieved from www.independent.co.uk/sport/olympics/comment/james-lawton-kayla-harrisons-courage-sheds-light-on-judos-darkest-corner-8002241.html

Lombardo, B. (2010). Holism in sports coaching. Beyond humanistic psychology: a commentary. *International Journal of Sports Science & Coaching*, 5: 477–478.

Pina, A., Gannon, T.A. and Saunders, B. (2009). An overview of the literature on sexual harassment. Perpetrators, theory, and treatment issues. *Aggression and Violent Behavior*, 14: 126–138.

Sand, T.S., Fasting, K., Chroni, S. and Knorre, N. (2011). Coaching behavior. Any consequences for the prevalence of sexual harassment? *International Journal of Sport Science & Coaching*, 6: 229–242.

Starr, K. (n.d.). The Vieth Report. Did it hit the mark or miss all together? Retrieved from http://safe4athletes.org/blog/item/66-the-vieth-report-by-usa-swimming-did-it-hit-the-mark-or-miss-all-together?

Starr, K. (2012, 12 September). The truth about coach–athlete relationships. Retrieved from http://safe4athletes.org/blog?start=20

Starr, K. (2013a, 24 May). When did the system fail Kelley Davies Currin and the rest of us? Retrieved from www.huffingtonpost.com/katherine-starr/when-did-the-system-fail_b_3328817.html

Starr, K. (2013b, 10 May). Breaking down sexual abuse in sports. Retrieved from http://safe4athletes.org/blog/item/52-breaking-down-sexual-abuse-in-sports

Toftegaard, J.N. (2001). The forbidden zone. Intimacy, sexual relations and misconduct in the relationship between coaches and athletes. *International Review for the Sociology of Sport*, 36: 165–183.

Tomlinson, A. and Yorganci, I. (1997). Male coach/female athlete relations. Gender and power relations in competitive sport. *Journal of Sport and Social Issues*, 21: 134–155.

Torney, K. (2011, 14 March). 'My swimming coach destroyed my life.' Retrieved from www.thedetail.tv/issues/1/nspcc/my-swimming-coach-destroyed-my-life

Trucks, R. (2014a, 13 June). Sexual abuse in women's sports, Part IV. Former swimmer Katie Kelly on USA swimming. Retrieved from https://sports.vice.com/article/former-swimmer-katie-kelly-on-sex-abuse-scandals-in-usa-swimming

Trucks, R. (2014b, 18 June). Sexual abuse in women's sports, Part IV. Former swimmer Debra Denithorne-Grodensky. Retrieved from https://sports.vice.com/article/sexual-abuse-in-womens-sports-part-iv-former-swimmer-debra-denithorne-grodensky

Trucks, R. (2014c, 19 June). Sexual abuse in women's sports, Part V. Ex-swimmer Jancy Thompson. Retrieved from https://sports.vice.com/article/sexual-abuse-in-womens-sports-part-v-ex-swimmer-jancy-thompson

UNICEF (2010). *Protecting Children from Violence in Sport. A Review With a Focus on Industrialized Countries*. Florence: UNICEF Innocenti Research Centre. Retrieved from www.unicef-irc.org/publications/pdf/violence_in_sport.pdf

Vertommen, T., Schipper-van Veldhoven, N., Hartill, M.J. and Van Den Eede, F. (2013). Sexual harassment and abuse in sport: The NOC*NSF helpline. *International Review for the Sociology of Sport*. Retrieved from http://irs.sagepub.com/content/early/2013/07/26/1012690213498079.

Women 2000 and Beyond. (2007). *Women, Gender Equality and Sport*. New York: UN Division for the Advancement of Women of the United Nations Secretariat. Retrieved from www.un.org/womenwatch/daw/public/Women%20and%20Sport.pdf.

11 A sporting utopia

Easing the essential tension in sport policy

Dave Collins and Richard Bailey

Introduction

There is an essential tension at the heart of sport policy. The multidimensional nature of sport, and how policy makers might deal with it within a limited political and economic space, has been a dominant concern for many years (Bergsgard *et al.*, 2007; Green 2004; Houlihan and Green, 2009). Indeed, it appears that attempts to deal with this tension represent the history of sports development around the world.

At one level, sport is often understood by politicians and in policy documentation as a good thing in and of itself. The different aspects of sport, from elite performance to casual recreation, are often presented as parts of a synergistic, unified and worthy whole (Green and Houlihan, 2005). It is implied – and occasionally stated out-right – that the different outcomes of sports participation are mutually supportive, so the different expressions of sport act together to reinforce each other's outcomes. An explicit statement of this view can be found in the UK New Labour government's Playing to Win (DCMS, 2008), in which increased sporting participation, health benefits and elite sporting success are presented as elements of an organic, self-reinforcing and self-perpetuating whole:

> Why should government invest in high performance sport? ... as a driver of the 'feelgood factor' and the image of the UK abroad; as a driver for grass-roots participation, whereby sporting heroes inspire participation.
>
> (DCMS/Strategy Unit, 2002, p. 117)

Playing to Win offers a vision of sport in which the different levels of play are merely expressions of a synergistic whole, through which elite and mass participation in sport create a 'virtuous cycle' (Grix and Bailey, 2009), in which success at the highest levels inspires participation at all lower levels, due to the 'feelgood factor', enhanced national identity, role models and so on. This growth in general engagement in sport, it is posited, is good for the health of the nation, and good for sport, since it provides the next generation of superstars (see Figure 11.1).

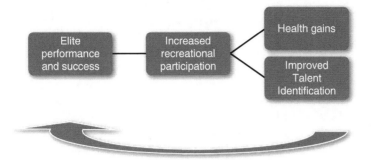

Figure 11.1 The 'virtuous cycle' of sport.

Similar reasoning was employed during the London pitch to host the 2012 Olympic and Paralympic Games:

> We can no longer take it for granted that young people will choose sport. Some may lack the facilities. Or the coaches and role models to teach them. Others, in an age of 24-hour entertainment and instant fame, may simply lack the desire. We are determined that a London Games will address that challenge. So London's vision is to reach young people all around the world. To connect them with the inspirational power of the Games.
>
> (Lord Coe, Singapore, 6 July 2005)

There is, unfortunately, a dissonance between the sometimes evangelical claims and suppositions made and the actual evidence base (Grix and Bailey, 2009), which could lead cynics to conclude that discussions about sport-for-all are little more than post hoc justifications for a decision that has already been made and for entirely different reasons. Green (2006, p. 233) suggests:

> The storyline that elite sporting success motivates the generality of the population to participate and compete is what might be termed a 'usual suspect' in any discussions of the ways in which funding for elite development is allocated.

Despite the bold promises made while bidding for the Games, it became evident that the legacy of mass participation would be rather more limited (e.g. Helm, 2013; Paton, 2013).

The policy pendulum

Policy interests swing like a pendulum over time (Collins, 2008), and attention often becomes focused on one specific agenda at the expense of others. In this political reality, resource and policy investment in the currently prioritised dimension of sport becomes justified by a version of the logic of virtuosity in which non-priority areas take care of themselves. This might explain why the appearance of a defence of sport in all of its aspects in documents like *Playing to Win* ultimately gave way to elite performance and competitive success.

Does this mean that the hope that it is possible to achieve positive outcomes in both elite sport and sport-for-all is necessarily doomed to disappointment? Despite a history of failure, we suspect that it is still an achievable goal, but not by the simplistic and misleading routes outlined in *Playing to Win* and countless other policy documents. Instead, what is required is careful planning, commitment and effort, alongside an honest appraisal of the challenges facing such an ambition. As an essential step to achieving this sporting utopia, therefore, we need to consider what roadblocks exist to prevent this inherent assumption.

A main concern is that, despite the inherent assumption of commonality between performance and participation, this is far from the case in real life. Indeed, a common representation of the relationship between the different aspects of sport is one of mutual exclusivity. In the language of mathematical games theory, sport policy is presumed to have the character of a zero-sum games in which whatever is gained by one side of a contest is lost by the other (Davies, 1997). Many societal processes follow this logic, and it is inevitable in political contexts that are increasingly pluralistic, and in which inter-group differences are likely to be reflected as inter-group rivalries of the zero-sum sort (Rittel and Webber, 1973). In another respect, however, it is not inevitable, especially if it can be demonstrated that progress or achievement in different domains are not inherently mutually exclusive, and that there is a non-zero-sum or even synergistic relationship across domains. In this context, however, even though practical methodologies may exist for inclusive achievement, the zero-sum presumption can be extremely obstructive to the realisation of closely related aims like those of sport development.

Evidence suggests that this predicament is common around the world, and, in most cases, it seems to be taken for granted (Bergsgard *et al.*, 2007). However, it is not the only way to frame the issue. Some sports systems, such as that introduced in India, have been explicitly based on a multiple-track model of elite performance success and broad-based participation (Mangan and Fan Hong, 2003). In the case of India, both sets of outcomes were explicitly presented as equally desirable within the policy, and, to some extent, this was expressed in terms of funding. However, this sort of approach continues to be the exception.

We suggest that another route is possible. Indeed, we propose that adopting the Three Worlds model/framework (e.g. Collins *et al.*, 2012; Bailey *et al.*, 2010) offers a better fit to the research evidence, avoids the 'inevitable' zero-sum presumption and can better meet both individual and social needs.

Three Worlds

The Three Worlds model has the premise that publicly funded sport development systems have an obligation to aspire to support both elite sporting success, *and* individuals who can fulfil themselves through sport achievement *and* a population with an enthusiasm and opportunity for lifelong physical activity. Needless to say, policy makers will claim that this is precisely their ambition. However, as we have argued above, such ambitions have proved difficult to realise in practice. Furthermore, the way in which these different concerns have been managed in practice by different government departments and from separate budgets is not indicative of a holistic and balanced approach (Grix and Carmichael, 2012; Weed *et al.*, 2009).

We call the categories of participant motivation in sport and physical activity the Three Worlds. Our use of this term to describe our framework reflects the philosopher Karl Popper's cosmology in which categorical worlds are ontologically distinct, but necessarily and continually interacting (Popper, 1972). This interaction is vitally important as the model relates not just to the existence of these Three Worlds, but crucially, the necessity for effective and smooth transition between them. Divisions between different worlds are somewhat arbitrary, at least in terms of development, in that a common base underpins all three (Jess and Collins, 2003). Elite players represent a point on a developmental–performance continuum that begins in recreational or participatory settings, and often (but perhaps not often enough) returns to such settings following retirement. Therefore, the Three Worlds are characterised by a relatively fluid interaction, which is represented diagrammatically in Figure 11.2.

Sports participation can be usefully conceptualised in terms of three primary distinct contexts: the realisation of Elite Referenced Excellence (ERE), Personal Referenced Excellence (PRE) and Participation for Personal Wellbeing (PPW). ERE relates to the realisation of excellence in the form of high-level sporting performance where achievement is measured against others with

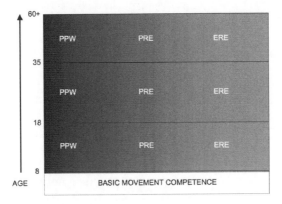

Figure 11.2 The Three Worlds continuum.
Source: Collins *et al.*, 2012; Bailey *et al.*, 2010).

the ultimate goal of winning at the highest level possible, such as medals at international level, national squad membership, etc. PRE refers to the achievement of excellence in the form of participation and personal performance, where achievement is more personally referenced by, for example, completing a marathon or improving one's personal best, whether against high- or low-level competition/challenge. PPW equates to recreational participation in physical activity to satisfy needs other than personal progression within the skill-set of the activity, such as the improvement of one's social life (for example, by making friends and developing new relationships), the enhancement of one's social identity (by becoming a member of an established group or club), personal renewal (through engagement with an activity which is found fulfilling) or the maintenance of aspects of self-concept (by getting and staying in good shape).

Our use of the word 'excellence' is, perhaps, surprising as conventional usage in sports contexts refers to elite performance (Thompson, 1992). However, we contend that the concept applies with equal validity to the realisation of any personally relevant achievements and the development of personal qualities at any point in life. In this respect, our usage has a precedent in the work of Miller and Kerr (2002). Other terms that are all familiar within the literature, such as 'competence' and 'mastery' (Petitpas and Champagne, 2000) might have also been used in this context. Our preference is for 'excellence' since it specifically undermines the association of that word with elite sport, and we wish to acknowledge fully how significant personal achievement beyond adequacy is at *all* levels of performance. In this respect, we are following in the tradition of White (1959; 1963), who argued that individuals are motivated by an independent tendency to explore and influence the environment, and that this allow the ego to go beyond the confines of instinctual drives. White proposes that all living things are motivated by a need to master their environments and to move freely in their worlds. He called this drive 'effectance', which was defined as personal competence to interact successfully with the environment in a way that allows individuals not only to maintain themselves, but also to grow and flourish (White, 1963). Earlier influential statements of this position came from Karl Bühler (1922) and Jean Piaget (1954), and more recently Nakamura and Csikszentimihalyi (2003). Deci and Ryan (1985; see also Ryan *et al.*, 2008) have elaborated on this line of argument by suggesting that competence and autonomy are innate psychological needs that must be satisfied for psychological well-being. This drive towards mastery helps explain learners' bold attempts to acquire new skills and to emulate the complex behaviours of role models. It also provides a plausible mechanism for the extensive investment of time and effort necessary for the development of expertise (Ericsson *et al.*, 1993). Of course, not all sports participation can be explained in these terms, although we suspect that they relate far more to sports participation than is commonly suspected.

There is some resemblance between this Three Worlds model and Siedentop's (2002) conceptualisation of sports participation in terms of three primary goals:

1   the public health goal;
2   the educative goal; and
3   the elite-development goal.

Focusing on youth sport, Siedentop argued that there was an inevitable tension between these goals:

> One can legitimately question the degree to which elite-development goals of a junior sport system can be served as part of a comprehensive system and still direct sufficient resources to achieve the educative and public health goals that are more fundamental to the system as a whole.
>
> (p. 396)

According to Siedentop's analysis, there is an inevitable zero-sum competition for resources between the different goals of sport.

Our framework of objectives of participant development was worked out without reference to Siedentop, but the parallels are quite evident (see Table 11.1).

There is a similarity between the two approaches, which may be because both models have a strong degree of face validity, and broadly reflect the types of interests that people have when they enter a pathway in sport. However, it is worthwhile making a few points at this stage to help articulate and distinguish our own position. First, it is entirely possible, even likely, that individuals will be attracted to different objectives at different stages of their engagement with sport. They may also have different objectives in mind at the same time, when playing different sports (an individual may be a competitive golfer and a recreational swimmer, while also learning Tai Chi for health reasons). Furthermore,

Table 11.1 Parallels between Siedentop goals of sport participation and the Three Worlds model

Siedentop's goals of youth sport		Possible parallel with the Three World model
Elite performance goal	'to allow the most talented and interested young athletes to pursue excellence' (p. 395).	Elite Referenced Excellence (ERE)?
Educative goal	'supported primarily for the educational and developmental benefits. ... If the educative goals was to dominate ... it would be as inclusive as possible ...' (p. 394)	Participation Referenced Excellence (PRE)?
Public health goal	'to contribute to the public health of a nation ... it would emphasise playful activity above all and would specifically target for inclusion those ... who are most at risk' (pp. 394–395)	Participation for Personal Wellbeing (PPW)?

since the predictive power of early talent identification is so weak, it is likely that almost all of those who set out with the aim of ERE performance will eventually have to modify their goals at some point (Abbott *et al.*, 2002; Bailey and Morley, 2006). Second, the objectives are not mutually exclusive unless the system makes them so. Achievement in one area can be accompanied by achievement in the others although, as Siedentop makes clear, in policy terms one often dominates. Finally, and most importantly, we do not accept Siedentop's exclusive equation of elite performance with the pursuit of excellence. It is entirely possible and reasonable for a player to engage in sport with seriousness and a striving for personal excellence for the whole of his or her life without ever achieving, or even seeking, ERE-related elite representation (Kowal and Ross, 1999).

Note also the crucial enabling role played by an effective base of movement competence, both actual and self-perceived. A realistic confidence in one's capacity to make the various transitions necessitated by lifelong physical activity involvement is an essential but often neglected outcome of the generally school-based stages of any system; indeed the generalised self-confidence associated with motor competence can even extend to parallel achievement in other domains, such as academic performance (Collins *et al.*, 2010; Syväoja *et al.*, 2013). These basic skills offer a core vocabulary of movement, without which progress will be delayed or stalled. In this context, the need to facilitate movement between the Three Worlds is self-evident: the proposition is that, built on a common fundamental skills base and the confidence that should be developed with it, all individuals can be empowered to progress back and forth between these three settings of physical activity (Gallahue and Ozmun, 2006).

The Three Worlds model stands in stark contrast to many traditional frameworks of sport development, in which either participation by the masses is presumed to be subservient to elite performance (pyramids), or in which elite performance is claimed to offer sky hooks for hoisting up sport-for-all, or in which the language and concepts make it clear that elite success is the most prized outcomes (Green, 2002; 2006; Grix and Carmichael, 2012; Kirk *et al.*, 2005). In other words, these traditional sports development models are really talent development models, focused differently.

The Three Worlds framework acknowledges a set of statements that seem to us axiomatic, but are apparently overlooked by many sports development models:

1   Most people who participate in sport do not seriously aspire to elite performance (Bailey *et al.*, 2010; Allender *et al.*, 2006).
2   Earlier comments on excellence notwithstanding, almost all of those who do aspire to elite performance will not succeed (Bailey and Morley, 2006).
3   Almost all of those who do succeed begin involvement with sport as children, but not necessarily playing the sport with which they find later success.

4   All of those who do succeed will eventually stop competing at that level
    (Abbott *et al.*, 2002; Vaeyens *et al.*, 2008; Güllich, 2011).

There is no suggestion here that ERE is a less worthwhile goal than PRE
or PPW. Rather, it is simply acknowledged that ERE, by definition, can only
ever relate to a small proportion of the population, while the other settings can,
in principle, relate to all. However, we do question the implicit assumption of
documents like *Playing to Win*; namely, that ERE is a more worthy ambition
than other goals.

The realisation of elite achievement, personal self-actualisation and health-
related activity goals requires sport policy agencies to acknowledge the necessity of a sound base that underpins all these options. These groups also need
to provide mechanisms that facilitate and encourage movement across the
continuum throughout the life course. These conditions are easy to state, but
their obvious absence in practice warns against complacency or the illusion of
misplaced/ill-focused action.

Clues to generating a Three World-focused system

As we stated earlier, the realisation of the different aims of sport is a complex
process, requiring the application of an integrated, interdisciplinary approach.
Such an approach reflects the biopsychosocial nature of the complexity of
human development (Kiesler, 1999), in which there is a dynamic interaction between biological, psychological and social factors, all of which play a
significant role in human functioning (Engel, 1977). Approaches that fail to
acknowledge the multifaceted nature of development, perhaps by focusing
too narrowly on physiological processes or anthropometric characteristics,
are in danger of missing the complex, dynamic and non-linear nature of
development (Abbott *et al.*, 2005), and are, therefore, inherently inadequate
(Bailey *et al.*, 2010; Smoll and Smith, 1996). Unfortunately, interdisciplinary
approaches continue to be rare, within both academic research and policy
documentation.

In order to achieve the difficult but desirable goals suggested by the Three
Worlds approach, three interlinked factors are necessary. First, all must be
equipped with the necessary tools to enable positive choices in sport and
physical activity. Given the captive and more pliable audience available in
formal education, this is usually most conveniently accomplished at primary/
elementary level. The aim is to equip children with both actual and perceived
movement competence, so that they can and are willing to try new activities, viewing them as positive challenges rather than negative threats (Jess and
Collins, 2003; Horn and Harris, 2002; Collins *et al.*, 2010). Second, there is
a need for a capacity to try new things and to persevere; a set of skills that
provide a determination to be better. Recent research has highlighted how a
simple assessment of such capabilities, which are increasingly labelled 'grit', is
associated with adolescents' ability to control their body weight (Duckworth

et al., 2012), as well as more global/usual achievement domains such as sport and academic challenge (Duckworth and Quinn, 2009). Extending these ideas, the inclusion of systematic development of the Psychological Characteristics of Developing Excellence (PCDEs – MacNamara *et al.*, 2010a; 2010b) has been shown to generate a wide range of benefits across multiple domains, including the pursuit of ERE, school–university transition (MacNamara and Collins, 2010) and self-directed musical performance (Kamin *et al.*, 2007). Third, there is a need is to look at physical activity and sport participation as long-term objectives rather than in terms of immediate weight-loss targets or even shorter-term 'daily doses' of physical activity. Thus, initiatives which look to monitor children's pulse rates or which offer a set of activities purely to get them active are missing the point that the aim of physical education must be lifelong physical activity and attainment (Giblin *et al.*, 2014). In short, there is a compelling case for high-quality physical education and sport-for-all, rather than prescriptions of a certain amount of time, as is the policy in many national systems around the world (Hardman, 2009).

Conclusion

A combination of biopsychosocial (motor, attitudinal/behavioural and interactive) skills approach has already been piloted and evaluated in schools to good effect – the DPYPS project (Developing the Potential of Young People in Sport – Collins *et al.*, 2010). As such, there is already an effective working model, designed for a British social context, on which further Three Worlds initiatives could be based. In simple terms, the three-legged stool of actual motor competence, perceived motor competence and developed PCDEs underpins the design and effective pursuit of these desirable aims – the utopia of our title (cf. Giblin *et al.*, 2014). Of course, it is important to acknowledge the pilot nature of these ideas, although the literature base and evidence so far are very promising. Given the lifespan aspirations stressed in the early part of the chapter, it might be asked how well this child-focused initiative can transfer to, or impact on, older participants. This, of course, is one of the key questions running through recent sport and exercise science (e.g. Breuer and Pawlowski, 2011; Fernandes and Zanesco, 2010; WHO, 2008).

Research suggests that the psychological constructs of self-determination and perceived competence are facilitators (and their absence obstacles) of participation in adulthood, as well in childhood and youth (Horn and Harris, 2002). Furthermore, there is a persuasive case for concentrating efforts on the relatively captive and biddable audience of primary school-aged children, albeit supplemented by focused support during the subsequent years (Sallis and McKenzie, 1991; Wheeler, 2012). Since it is not possible to predict with any confidence the directions in which young people's abilities and interests might develop, a framework like the Three Worlds model seems a necessary condition for conceptualising such ongoing engagement.

References

Abbott, A., Collins, D., Martindale, R. and Sowerby, K. (2002). *Talent Identification and Development: An Academic Review.* Edinburgh: sportscotland.

Abbott, A., Button, C., Pepping, G.-J. and Collins, D. (2005) Unnatural selection. Talent identification and development in sport. *Nonlinear Dynamics, Psychology and Life Sciences,* 9: 61–88.

Allender, S., Cowburn, G. and Foster, C. (2006). Understanding participation in sport and physical activity among children and adults. A review of qualitative studies. *Health Education Research,* 21(6): 826–835.

Bailey, R. and Morley, D. (2006). Towards a model of talent development in physical education. *Sport, Education and Society,* 11(3): 211–230.

Bailey, R., Collins, D., Ford, P., MacNamara, A., Toms, M. and Pearce, G. (2010). *Participant Development in Sport. An Academic Review.* Leeds: Sports Coach UK.

Bergsgard, N.A., Houlihan, B., Mangset, P., Nodland, S.I. and Rommetvedt, H. (2007). *Sport Policy. A Comparative Analysis of Stability and Change.* Oxford: Butterworth and Heinemann.

Breuer, C. and Pawlowski, T. (2011). Socioeconomic perspectives on physical activity and aging. *European Review of Aging and Physical Activity,* 8(2): 53–56.

Bühler, K. (1922). *Die geistige Entwicklung des Kindes.* Jena: Gustav Fischer.

Collins, D., Martindale, R.J.J., Button, A. and Sowerby, K. (2010). Building a physically active and talent rich culture. An educationally sound approach. *European Physical Education Review,* 16(1): 7–28.

Collins, D., Bailey, R., Ford, P.A., MacNamara, Á., Toms, M. and Pearce, G. (2012). Three Worlds. New directions in participant development in sport and physical activity. *Sport, Education and Society,* 17(2): 225–243.

Collins, M. (2008). Public policies on sports development. Can mass and elite sport hold together. In V. Girginov (ed.), *Management of Sports Development* (pp. 59–87). London: Butterworth-Heinemann.

Davis, M. (1997). *Game Theory.* Mineola, NY: Dover Publications.

DCMS (2008). *Playing to Win.* London: DCMS.

DCMS/Strategy Unit (2002). *Game Plan: A Strategy for Delivering Government's Sport and Physical Activity Objectives.* London: Cabinet Office.

Deci, E.L. and Ryan, R.M. (1985). *Intrinsic Motivation and Self-determination in Human Behavior.* New York: Plenum Press.

Duckworth, A.L. and Quinn, P.D. (2009). Development and validation of the short Grit scale (Grit-S). *Journal of Personality Assessment,* 91: 166–174

Duckworth, A.L., Tsukayama, E. and Geier, A.B. (2012). Self-controlled children stay leaner in the transition to adolescence. *Appetite,* 54: 304–308.

Engel, G.E. (1977). The need for a new medical model. *Science,* 196: 129–136.

Ericsson, K.A., Krampe, R.T. and Tesch-Römer, C. (1993). The role of deliberate practice in the acquisition of expert performance. *Psychological Review,* 100: 363–406.

Fernandes, R. and Zanesco A. (2010). Early physical activity promotes lower prevalence of chronic diseases in adulthood. *Hypertension Research,* 33: 926–931.

Gallahue, D.L. and Ozmun, J.C. (2006). *Understanding Motor Development. Infants, Children, Adolescents, Adults* (6th edn.). Boston, MA: McGraw-Hill.

Giblin, S., Collins, D., MacNamara, A. and Kiely, J. (2014). Deliberate preparation as an evidence-based focus for primary physical education. *Quest,* 66(4): 385–395.

Green, M. (2004). Changing policy priorities for sport in England. The emergence of elite sport development as a key policy concern. *Leisure Studies*, 23(4): 365–385.

Green, M. (2006). From 'sport-for-all' to not about 'sport' at all?. *European Sport Management Quarterly*, 6: 217–238.

Green, M. and Houlihan, B. (2005). *Elite Sport Development: Policy Learning and Political Priorities*. London: Psychology Press.

Grix, J. and Bailey, R.P. (2009). The UK government's rationale for elite sport investment. Looking for the evidence in 'evidence-based' policy. Unpublished manuscript, University of Birmingham.

Grix, J. and Carmichael, F. (2012). Why do governments invest in elite sport? A polemic. *International Journal of Sport Policy and Politics*, 4(1): 73–90.

Güllich, A. (2011). Training quality in high-performance youth sport. Invited presentation. Science for Success, KIHU, Jyvaskyla, Finland.

Hardman, K. (2009). A review of the global situation of physical education in schools. *International Journal of Physical Education*, 3: 2–20.

Helm, T. (2013). After all the promises, where is the legacy of London 2012? *Observer*, 26 January: www.theguardian.com/education/2013/jan/26/london-olympics-legacy-schools (accessed 23 December 2014).

Horn, T. and Harris, A. (2002). Perceived competence in young athletes. In F. Smoll and R. Smith (eds), *Children and Youth in Sport: A Bio-Psycho-Social Perspective* (pp. 435–464). Dubuque, IW: Kendall-Hunt.

Houlihan, B. and Green, M. (2009). Modernization and sport. The reform of sport England and UK sport. *Public Administration*, 87(3): 678–698.

Jess, M. and Collins, D. (2003). Primary physical education in Scotland. *European Journal of Physical Education*, 8: 103–118.

Kamin, S., Richards, H. and Collins, D. (2007). Influences on the talent development process of non-classical musicians. Psychological, social and environmental influences. *Music Education Research* 9(3): 449–468.

Kiesler, D. (1999). *Beyond the Disease Model of Mental Disorders*. New York: Praeger.

Kirk, D., Brettschneider, W.-D. and Auld, C. (2005). *Junior Sport Models Representing Best Practice Nationally and Internationally*. *Junior Sport Briefing Papers*. Canberra: Australian Sports Commission.

Kowal, J. and Ross, S. (1999). Excellence in sport. Philosophical and performance considerations. *Avante*, 5: 18–30.

MacNamara, Á. and Collins, D. (2010). The role of psychological characteristics in managing the transition to university. *Psychology of Sport and Exercise*, 11, 353–362.

MacNamara, Á., Button, A. and Collins, D. (2010a). The role of psychological characteristics in facilitating the pathway to elite performance. Part 1: identifying mental skills and behaviors. *The Sport Psychologist*, 24: 52–73.

MacNamara, Á., Button, A. and Collins, D. (2010b). The role of psychological characteristics in facilitating the pathway to elite performance. Part 2: examining environmental and stage related differences in skills and behaviours. *The Sport Psychologist*, 24: 74–96.

Mangan, J.H. and Fan Hong (eds) (2003). *Sport in Asian Societies*. Abingdon: Frank Cass.

Miller, P. and Kerr, G. (2002). Conceptualising excellence. Past, present, and future. *Journal of Applied Sport Psychology*, 14: 140–153.

Nakamura, J. and Csikszentimihalyi, M. (2003). The motivational sources of creativity as viewed from the paradigm of positive psychology. In I.G. Aspinwall and U.W. Staudinger (eds), *A Psychology of Human Strengths. Fundamental Questions and Future Directions for a Positive Psychology* (pp. 257–269). Washington, DC: American Psychological Association.

Paton, W. (2013). Peers warn over 'faltering' legacy of London Olympics. *Daily Telegraph*: www.telegraph.co.uk/sport/olympics/news/10455824/Peers-warn-over-faltering-legacy-of-London-Olympics.html (accessed 23 December 2014).

Petitpas, A.J. and Champagne, D.E. (2000). Sport and social competence. In S.J. Danish and T.P. Gullotta (eds), *Developing Competent Youth and Strong Communities Through After-School Programming* (pp. 115–137). Washingtonm DC: CWLA Press.

Piaget, J. (1954). *Intelligence and Affectivity: Their Relationship During Child Development*. Palo Alto, CA: Annual Review

Popper, K.R. (1972). *Objective Knowledge: An Evolutionary Approach*. Oxford: Oxford University Press.

Rittel, H. and Webber, M. (1973). Dilemmas in a general theory of planning. *Policy Sciences*, 4: 155–169.

Ryan, R., Huta, V. and Deci, E. (2008). Living well. A self-determination theory perspective on eudaimonia. *Journal of Happiness Studies*, 9: 139–170.

Sallis, J. and McKenzie, T.L. (1991). Physical education's role in public health. *Research Quarterly for Exercise and Sport*, 62: 124–137.

Siedentop, D. (2002). Junior sport and the evolution of sport cultures. *Journal of Teaching in Physical Education*, 21: 392–401.

Smoll, F. and Smith, R. (eds) (1996). *Children and Youth in Sport. A Bio-psycho-social Perspective*. Dubuque, IW: Kendall-Hunt.

Syväoja, H.J., Kantomaa, M.T., Ahonen, T., Hakonen, H., Kankaanpää, A., Tammelin, T.H. (2013). Physical activity, sedentary behavior, and academic performance in Finnish children. *Medicine and Science in Sports and Exercise*, early online publication.

Thompson, I. (1992). *Giftedness, Excellence and Sport*. Edinburgh: Scottish Sports Council.

Vaeyens, R., Lenoir, M., Williams, A.M. and Philippaerts, R. (2008). Talent identification and development programmes in sport. Current models and future directions. *Sports Medicine*, 38, pp. 703–714.

Weed, M., Coren, E. and Fiore, J. (2009). *A Systematic Review of the Evidence Base for Developing a Physical Activity and Health Legacy from the London 2012 Olympic and Paralympic Games*. London: Department of Health.

Wheeler, S. (2012). The significance of family culture for sports participation. *International Review for the Sociology of Sport*, 47(2): 235–252.

White, R.W. (1959). Motivation reconsidered: The concept of competence. *Psychological Review*, 66(5), 297–333.

White, R.W. (1963). *Ego and Reality in Psychoanalytic Theory*. New York: International Universities Press.

World Health Organisation (WHO) (2008). *Physical Inactivity: A Global Public Health Problem*. www.who.int/dietphysicalactivityfactsheet_inactivity/en/index.html (accessed 10 February 2012).

Index

Page numbers in *italics* denotes a figure/table